Human Rights in India

Human Rights in India

Prospective and Retrospective

Edited by

Sudarshanam Gankidi

RAWAT PUBLICATIONS

Jaipur • New Delhi • Bangalore • Guwahati • Kolkata

ISBN 978-81-316-1060-2

Published by
Prem Rawat for **Rawat Publications**
Satyam Apts., Sector 3, Jawahar Nagar, Jaipur 302 004 (India)
Phone: 0141 265 1748 / 7006 Fax: 0141 265 1748
E-mail: info@rawatbooks.com
Website: www.rawatbooks.com

New Delhi Office
4858/24, Ansari Road, Daryaganj, New Delhi 110 002
Phone: 011-23263290

Also at *Bangalore, Guwahati* and *Kolkata*

Typeset by Rawat Computers, Jaipur
Printed at Nice Printing Press, New Delhi

Dedicated to
Professor G. Haragopal
My teacher and human rights crusader

Contents

Acknowledgement

Publication of a book is always a tiresome process. This book holds no exception. It took more than five years to consolidate and finalise this book. The idea of publishing an edited volume initially came out of a young scholar's colloquium on human rights I conducted in 2012 at the University of Hyderabad when I was heading the Centre for Human Rights. We also happened to organise two more conferences including one on human rights defenders (HRD) in 2011 and the other one on the role of police and human rights mechanisms in criminal justice administration in 2012, which have further enhanced our thrust to work on this book. All the three events were attended by the best of the scholars and practitioners in the field. As a result, we could selectively move with highly useful papers in this edited volume.

A number of people and organisations helped us to complete this mammoth task. University of Hyderabad has offered both administrative and moral support in each aspect. Especially the then Vice-Chancellors of the university, Professor Seyed E. Hasnain and Professor Ramakrishna Ramaswamy and the Pro Vice-Chancellors, Professor Prakash C. Sarangi and Professor V. Kannan were of extreme help. Further, Professor G. Haragopal, my teacher, who was instrumental in bringing human rights education to University of Hyderabad, has been a guide and a philosopher who directed us to make every effort to promote human rights teaching and research in the university. The other esteemed personalities such as Professor V.S. Prasad, the former Director of National Assessment and Accreditation (NAAC); Professor Narasimha Reddy, former Dean, School of Social Sciences, University of Hyderabad and my friend Professor Balaramulu, ICSSR National Fellow, have offered their unconditional support and guidance to run our activities at the centre.

The help and support received from colleagues at the University where I work is commendable. Chandrasekhar B., Ratnam K.Y., Professor Krishna Reddy Gaddam, Professor Sudhakara Rao and Professor Nancharaiah have helped us to conduct the conferences successfully. David Raju, from the central administration of the university; Gupta, Prakash and Suresh from the Department of Political Science, and Raju from the Centre for Human Rights have offered the general administrative support. My own graduate students—Nemalikanti Pradeep Chaitanya, Suresh Digumarti, Jagannatham Begari, Arun Mallik and Rafiq, among others—have tirelessly worked to complete this project. My special thanks are to Dr Rama Krishna Reddy Kummitha without whose help this volume would not have been a reality. I am thankful for his constant help and support in completing the work.

The financial assistance received from the University Grants Commission (UGC) for the Centre for Human Rights enabled us to organise the colloquium and the conference on HRD without which publication of this edited volume would have never been possible. We were also generously supported by the Bureau of Police Research and Development (BPRD) for conducting the other conference on police and human rights. I would also like to especially thank each paper presenter and participant who participated in the deliberations of the events and contributed to the academic, research and intellectual discourse. Without their presence, the rigour required to publish this volume would not have been achieved. In the end, I would like to thank Rawat Publications team for their patience and guidance for enriching the quality of the volume.

Contributors

Santosh Kumar Biswal is an Assistant Professor at the Symbiosis Institute of Media and Communications, Symbiosis International University, Pune.

Sudarshanam Gankidi is a Professor in the Department of Political Sciences, University of Hyderabad, Hyderabad.

Ajay Gudavarthy is an Associate Professor at the Centre for Political Studies, Jawaharlal Nehru University, New Delhi.

Khaikholen Haokip is an Assistant Professor at the Centre for Studies and Research in Society and Development, Gujarat Central University, Ahmedabad.

Jasleen Kaur is a doctoral research student in the Department of Human Development and Childhood Studies, Lady Irwin College, University of Delhi.

Chaitanya Pradeep Nemalikanti is an Assistant Professor in the School of Law, Christ University, Bangalore.

G.B. Reddy is a Professor in the Department of Law, Osmania University, Hyderabad.

Jayaram Singh Samal is a doctoral research student at the Centre for the Study of Law and Governance, Jawaharlal Nehru University, New Delhi.

Astha Saxena is a doctoral research student at the Central Institute of Education, University of Delhi.

Neerja Sharma is an Associate Professor in the Department of Human Development and Childhood Studies, Lady Irwin College, University of Delhi.

Rafiq Ullah Sheikh is a doctoral research student at the Department of Political Science, University of Hyderabad, Hyderabad.

Deepshikha Singh is a consultant with the NCERT, New Delhi.

Moksha Singh is an Assistant Professor in the Department of Humanities and Social Sciences, National Institute of Technology (NIT), Raipur.

Acronyms

ACRWC	African Charter on the Rights and Welfare of the Child
AFSPA	Armed Forces Special Powers Act
AI	Amnesty International
APPA	Andhra Pradesh Police Academy
BPRD	Bureau of Police Research and Development
CBI	Central Bureau of Investigation
CBSE	Central Board of Secondary Education
CCDD	Citizens Concern for Dams and Development
CEDAW	Convention on the Elimination of All Forms of Discrimination against Women
CLAHRO	Civil Liberties and Human Rights Organisation
CORE	Centre for Organisation Research and Education
CPT	Committee on Police Training
CRC	Convention on the Rights of the Child
CrPC	Criminal Procedure Code
CRPD	Convention on the Rights of Persons with Disabilities
DISE	District Information System for Education

FIDH	International Federation for Human Rights
GPI	Gender Parity Index
HGP	Human Genomic Project
HIV	Human Immunodeficiency Virus
HRA	Human Rights Alert
HRD	Human Rights Defenders
HRE	Human Rights Education
HRLN	Human Rights Law Network
HRP	Human Rights Perspective
ICCPR	International Convention on Civil Political Rights
ICESCR	International Covenant on Economic, Social and Cultural Rights
IDCO	The Industrial Infrastructure Development Corporation of Orissa
ILO	International Labour Organisation
INGO	International Non-governmental Organisation
J&K	Jammu & Kashmir
KMHR	Kuki Movement for Human Rights
KNA	Kuki National Assembly
MHRD	The Ministry of Human Resource Development
NGO	Non-governmental Organisation
NHRC	National Human Rights Commission
NIMH	National Institute for the Mentally Handicapped
NNC	Naga National Council
NPC	National Police Commission
NPE	National Policy on Education
NPMHR	Naga Peoples Movement for Human Rights
NSSO	The National Sample Survey Organisation
OMCT	World Organisation against Torture (Organisation Mondiale Contre la Torture)
PAC	Police Accountability Commission
PADC	Police Act Drafting Committee

POTA	Prevention of Terrorism Act
PWD	Persons with Disability
RCI	Rehabilitation Council of India
RD	Right to Development
RTE	Right to Education
SC	Scheduled Caste
SEZ	Special Economic Zone
SI	Sub-inspector
SIPHRO	Sinlung Indigenous Peoples Human Rights Organisation
SPO	State Project Officer
SSA	Sarva Shiksha Abhiyan
SSI	Socio-Scientific Issues
ST	Scheduled Tribe
STS	Science, Technology and Society
TADA	Terrorist and Disruptive Activities (Prevention) Act
UCM	United Committee Manipur
UDHR	Universal Declaration of Human Rights
UGC	University Grants Commission
UNCRC	United Nations Conventions for the Rights of the Child
UNCRPD	United Nations Convention on the Rights of Persons with Disabilities
UNDP	United Nations Development Programme
UNESCO	The United Nations Educational, Scientific and Cultural Organization
UNLF	United National Liberation Front
UNPO	Unrepresented Nations and Peoples Organisation
UT	Union Territory
WCAR	World Conference against Racism
WHO	World Health Organization
ZHRF	Zomi Human Rights Foundation

Introduction

Sudarshanam Gankidi

Human rights are the essential elements that entitle human beings with certain necessities to lead a dignified life. Accordingly, human rights are considered as rights that are granted to all individuals upon their birth. The Indian State has selectively sanctioned certain rights to the citizens, which are guaranteed under the Constitutional provision. In addition, from time to time, the state has ratified several international conventions that were deliberated on promotion of rights of the people. Accordingly, it has initiated various policies and programmes, which aimed at realising the fullest strengths of the citizens. The rights sanctioned for the citizens are termed under two sub-heads: (a) civil and political rights and (b) economic, social and cultural rights. Though these two sets of rights are crucial for human existence and growth, there remains a larger question about their inter-action with each other and which set of rights is most essential in case a clash exists between them. The overall question that remains unaddressed is that whether political and civil rights precede economic, social and cultural rights or vis-à-vis. The United Nations (UN) has adopted both the sets of rights under different convents in 1966 and 1976 respectively. However, this debate has overwhelmed especially due to Western liberal societies, which basically aspire to give priority to individual choices and their freedoms; hence, they projected that the civil and political rights such as right to life, right to freedom, right to speech and right to participate in democratic processes should be given priority as they uphold other basic rights. Whereas the developmental discourse in the developing countries alarm that the economic, social and cultural rights including right to housing, right to food, right to cloth and right to work are pre-conditions to enjoy the civil and political rights. Hence, the introduction chapter analyses current social order in Indian society and presents the need for adopting ways through which the rights of the individuals need to be promoted.

After securing independence in 1947, several efforts were made in India to establish a social system based on socialist ideology, which isolates social problems and creates a strong social base where all sections of the people could potentially live in harmony. Accordingly several policies were enacted and implemented. Given the number of notable freedom fighters involved in the initial policy formulation, significant importance was attributed to social issues and accordingly adequate space was given to the socially deprived sections. For example, the most marginalised in the country such as scheduled castes (SCs) and scheduled tribes (STs) and other backward classes have been provided with affirmative action where a number of posts are reserved for them in legislative, government employment and educational institutions. First a couple of decades after independence, the promising socialist policy discourse worked reasonably well where the aspirations and interests of the marginalised sections were taken into consideration in both policy formulation and implementation. However, starting from the 1970s, with state-imposed arbitrary emergency, there was a dramatic shift in the state policy where the individual interests were left behind. State's aspirations and interests moved further towards aiming to achieve market interests starting from 1990s when neo-liberal policies were introduced (Kummitha 2015).

The state subsequently emerged as a ruffle whose primary interests transformed from promoting the interests of the marginalised and common people to safeguarding the interests of the elite capitalist class that would finally benefit the politically elite groups. As a result, the developmental discourse was significantly neglected except enacting a few social policies, which had in fact altogether failed to negate with the primary interests of the states. This has attributed for the existing social disparities and further altered social functioning. The data show that poverty has become most daunting reality that deprives people of quality of life. The United Nations Commission on Human Rights views that extreme poverty affects social functioning, and it further violates all other human rights (Sengupta 2010). It implies that extreme poverty excludes people from having access to basic human rights. It is estimated that about 77 per cent of Indians live on a consumption expenditure of less than INR 20 (around USD 0.4) a day (Arjun Sengupta Committee 2006). Whereas the overall human development is quite depressing as India remains at 134 rank out of 187 countries listed in the human development index. In detail, 21 per cent of the total population in India remains undernourished and 42 per cent of the children under the age five are malnourished in which the affected are the most excluded (Food and Agriculture Organization of the United Nations 2011). India accounts for more than 20 per cent of the total child births in the world with 1.83 million children dying before their fifth birthday (UNICEF 2011). A majority of the Indian population that represents about a whopping 51 per cent defecate in open (WHO/UNICEF 2011). In spite of 8.2 per cent growth achieved during 2007–2011, poverty declined by only 0.8 per cent. The national poverty rate altogether stands at 37.2 per cent (Tendulkar Committee 2009). In spite of these disturbing figures, the state continues to move further to maximise its economic aspirations, leaving the larger public interest at stake.

The recent growth in the gross domestic product as projected by the economists may have helped India to compete with superpowers in acquiring respectable position in the global arena; however, the internal exclusions and conflicts of different nature result keep india on its low ever. It has become quite persistent in contemporary economies that a significant difference exists among the social groups and classes. However, India being the biggest democracy in the world with its neo-liberal centred approach and crony capitalist policies widened the gap further which is quite difficult to address unless a major policy shift is initiated. This altogether contributed in resulting various social segregations where the areas of exclusion are widened and certain sections such as below middle class which were never part of the exclusion discourse are now being claimed as excluded due to the relative poverty that they encounter (Kummitha 2015). The government and its associates hardly realise that the maximisation of economic growth alone would not be a sufficient condition to maximise social well-being.

The recent developments across the globe have proven that economic development and human growth do not take place simultaneously, especially it is impossible in case of developing countries because of the persistent inequality that deepens the exclusions. Given the nation-states priorities towards solo economic growth, leaving the larger interests at stake, there arises a fundamental question about the possible solutions that could reduce such gaps. There is no doubt that the current social order and policy discourse rules out the aspirations of the poor and the marginalised. The resistance that arise under such circumstances has been violently suppressed by the state in a number of occasions. More often, the criticism against the state policy is tagged as anti-national activity.

Altogether, the economic development gravely negates with the basic welfare and rights of the peoples. On the contrary, when we see the growth and development from the social development perspective, there is a larger agreement that growth should be a by-product of human development. The United Nations Development Programme (UNDP) underscores that the concept of human development is much broader than the conventional theories of economic development (Ahsan 2011). It talks about a range of important issues in society including economic growth, trade, employment, political freedom or protection of cultural values—from people's perspective. It, thus, focusses on enlarging human choices. Further, as Sen (1998) proclaimed in his social choice theory, it should presuppose promoting the interests of the individuals in a society. The modern state must project individual as a basic measurement point and ideally propose policies that fulfil aspirations of all the citizens. If such a shift is not possible with a single policy, then a series of policies may be adopted to make such transformation possible.

However, on the other hand, the nexus between growth and human development widens the gap between and among the communities that result in social unrest. Resources of the state that need to minimise the social disparities are being offered to a marginal proportion of elites where their profits are maximised at the expense of the poor and the deprived. The resources are being explored by the dominant sections of the society and state in most of the cases either acts in support of the exploiter or maintains silence in such issues. Justice Narayana Reddy's judgement in Reliance Natural Resources Ltd. versus Reliance Industries Limited case, May 2010 proclaims:

> By no stretch of imagination are we a resource poor country, yet the greater incidence of unrest is in states and regions that have plenty of natural wealth and paradoxically suffer from low levels of human development. The problem arises because exploitation of those resources occurs without appropriate supervision by the State as to the rates of exploitation, equitable distribution of the wealth it generates, collusions between the extractive industry and some agents of the State and the consequent evisceration of the moral authority of the institution of the State. (Suresh and Nagasaila 2011, p. 29)

Hence, to maximise the utilisation of the resources for maximising the greater choices and realising the rights of the people need to be an act forwarded by the state.

State further opted to commit crimes to encourage the drain of the national wealth by certain dominant pockets. According to Kannabiran (2000), two categories of crimes exist in a social context. While the law dealing with crimes by citizens is relatively addressed with effective policy, the areas of crimes committed by the state agencies are deficient. Further, he puts forward the proposition that the citizens need to have an inherent 'right to insurrect' against the state. When the state abdicates its constitutional obligations, citizens have no option but to assert their 'political right to insurrect'. People, at least those who are in the centre of the society must fight for those who are kept or pushed out of the margins. For this purpose, they will have to use all their rights to keep their choices on top and make sure that the state and its governance do not compromise on the interests of the marginalised. Various civil society initiated movements that have been aggressive to realise the rights at various points of time historically, need to be conceived at their best as the technology has advanced the capability of being aggressive. Civil liberties movement that evolved to protect the interests of the marginalised and excluded, is a turning point in the evolution of human rights in India. The next section briefly discusses about the civil liberties movement and its essence in human rights protection in India.

Historical Evaluation of Civil Liberties Movement in India

It is believed that the civil rights movement in India began during the rule of the British. The movement has had a strong link with the freedom movement that fought against the colonial rule. Though there were many activities that took place with regard to protection and promotion of the rights of the people in the country, it was in 1936 that the first formal organisation namely All India Civil Liberties Union was formed by a group of freedom fighters including Jawaharlal Nehru, Rabindranath Tagore, Sarojini Naidu, Jayaprakash Narayan and Abul Kalam Azad. The major intention of the then civil liberties movement was to strictly oppose the colonial rule that had exploited both human and natural resources of the country (Chakrabarti 2011). Though the immediate aim of the civil liberties movement before independence was to oppose the British rule, later the roles and responsibilities of the movement progressed as the independent India opted to act against the will and aspirations of the people of the country and against the promises made in the Constitution. Under the self-rule regime after independence, the need for such civil liberties movement had further arose to ensure that the rights of the poor and marginalised are protected. However, this need is due because unlike the British rule, now a structured Constitution and promises for the well-being are laid down, which are quite often neglected, hence, there is a strong need where such promises can be fulfilled. In order to realise those promises, some form of social structure from the civil society needs to show a way forward. Hence, the civil liberties movement has spread across the country, rooting in different states in terms of articulating for the poor and excluded. The need for such a move became essential after the emergency period, which was the result of undemocratic aspirations of the political elite.

The human rights movement, on the one hand, highlighted the atrocities caused by the state, and on the other hand, the dominant actors in the society to some extent also believed that the right to development is an essential aspect that needs special emphasis which reinforces to improve the social policy. Hence, there are many human rights companions who emerged as the defenders of human rights and proven to act against social ills that suppress the rights of the people. Accordingly they are often exposed to social realities where they have to fight against the dominant groups. Many of these defenders fight against violation of human rights in general without being prioritised by any set of rights.

State as a Violator

Whenever the state attempts to overpower the rights and suppress the social dialogue, there has been resistance to object such a move. For instances, the aggressive civil liberties movement in India has been a by-product of the national emergency. This resistance is either of non-violent nature such as protests or *dharnas* or forming into a group that fights for the rights of the excluded or violent such as naxalite movement. In most of the cases, the state's stand towards poor and excluded provoke people to be aggressive. As a result, a few sections of the people turn to opt path to fight with the state. Irrespective of such path that the civilians opt, state creates repressing environment to suppress such movement. The issues such as Maoist insurgency have been always seen as a strong ripple to the authority of the state, and always violent approaches have been adopted to reduce the insurgency rather than addressing its basic concerns including the exploitation of tribals and the exploitation of forest resources. Yet, we remind what Thapar (2012) emphasised upon while delivering the keynote address of XIV Convocation of the University of

Hyderabad, that *The space earlier given to dissent and debate is now so narrowed that it almost does not exist*. Criticism is seen as anti-national and as sedition. State has become so restless that it doesn't compromise on its stand and further violates rights of the people. Recent instances show the means for such backward perspective. A man was recently detained illegally by cops for six days and was tortured for asking a question to the Chief Minister of Chhattisgarh. Yet another brutal incident took place when a common person asked a question to the Chief Minister of West Bengal, the latter was offended and forced the cop present at the event to arrest him. These incidents are visible because of the active presence of media, however, there are countless incidents that do not come to the public scrutiny. These incidents deny the citizens to question those who represent them. Political arrogance sometimes clinches its peak that determines the oppression and exclusion.

As the current trajectory projects, states behave as an irresponsible entity, which exists only to cater the interests of the cream of the elite sections namely businessmen, politicians and high level bureaucrats. This elite section operates in such a way where they have mutual agreements that benefit each other leaving others on the crossroads. Laws such as Armed Forces Special Powers Act (AFSPA), Terrorist and Disruptive Activities (Prevention) Act (TADA), Prevention of Terrorism Act (POTA) and sedition laws allow the state to detain those who question the stand of the state as a violator of the rights that it ought to safeguard. State has, however, failed to understand that detaining or killing someone on an illegal ground would give shocking signals to public, who later do not hold any respect for the state and develop anti-state behaviour, which is altogether a dangerous calculation for a harmonious society. The protests are quite often turned into a violent battle, and it is estimated that most of the times it is the state that either provokes the protesters or attacks peaceful protest movements. State in the first phase creates an environment that hurdles the sustenance of these excluded, say, special economic zones (SEZs), developmental projects or any other developmental activity and later the protests that arise out of such catastrophe have been resisted by the state with a weapon, that is, non-violence in the name of law and order. Protests against Posco project in Orissa (2007), Nandigram violence in West Bengal against setting up an SEZ in 2007 and anti-Kudankulam protest against a nuclear plant in Tamil Nadu (2012) are clear indications. These activities from the state would further widen the gap between the state and its citizens. As a result, neither the state understands the ambitions and aspirations of its citizens nor the citizens respect the existence of the state.

We have already discussed that the state enacts a set of social policies that aim at addressing social disparities and promote equilibrium up to some extent, however, the ways in which policies are being implemented and lack of a systematic surveillance liquidate mere attempts put forward. In addition, the way these policies are implemented and the resources distributed for their healthy implementation is a matter of concern. There are incidents in the recent past where the laws enacted are quite ambitious, whereas the resources allocated to achieve such goals are too grim. For example, right to education (RTE) that was included in 21A is a recent fundamental right that is sanctioned to all individuals, however, the law speaks neither for a well-defined implementation mechanism nor for financial commitments that ensure the effective implementation of the act (United Nations 2012). Similarly, the prison statistics 2009 claim that only two out of 28 states of India are able to fully utilise the funds allotted to them (National Crime Records Bureau 2009). On the other hand, the quality of life is alarming in terms of violations that the poor and the downtrodden face due to lack of basic facilities in prisons. It is to believe that negligence and irresponsible attitude continue to act as hurdles for protection and promotion of human rights. These two externalities prove that proper implementation of a law is hit by either (a) lack of proper fund and resource or (b) even if allotment is fairly done, the execution is poor in terms of utilising the allotments that will enhance the quality of life.

Yet, in an another instance, HRD seem to have similar experience as they face significant pressure from both state and various capitalist entities, and there are many incidents being registered in the recent past where the defenders are eliminated. After the implementation of Right to Information Act, the quantum of such violations has outraged, despite the strong legal mechanism (Asian Centre for Human Rights 2011). In spite of the pressures from various agencies, the efforts of the defenders are restless to realise both economic, social and cultural rights and civil and political rights so that attaining one set of rights help the other easier to attain.

A Way Forward

As projected, the state's behaviour towards realisation of economic, social and cultural rights takes a back seat as the marketisation takes a driving seat. As a result, attainment of civil and political rights further seem to have grave consequences. In a democratic country like India in order to promote the latter, initially it has to strengthen its base for the promotion of social equality. While attempts are made to achieve the same, the state needs to take a predominant role to create an environment where individuals are given an opportunity to enjoy their rights. The state in such direction is compelled to frame necessary policies and create a process that works to protect and promote the rights of the people (Sengupta 2010).

If the basic rights such as right to food, health and education are fulfilled, it is hard to find the prevailing conditions of poverty in any given social order. The underlying trajectory is that promoting such a move would help to procure economic, social and cultural rights that contribute to attain civil and political rights up to some extent. Based on this understanding of various issues involved in Indian social order, this volume highlights certain grave human rights issues prevailing in the sub-continent.

The book is divided into four subsections based on the different themes. While the first section of the chapters focusses on 'Human Rights, State, Police and Judiciary', the second section titled 'Human Rights and Civil Society' offers a glimpse of agitations taken up by civil society organisations, human rights protection groups and other enthusiasts. The first and second sections have three and two chapters respectively. The third section is titled 'Human Rights, Children and Education', whereas the final and last section deals with 'Human Rights and Persons with Disabilities'. There are two chapters in the third section and three in the last section. A brief discussion about each chapter is presented.

The first chapter, *Beyond Global Human Rights*, focusses on three prominent debates that are particularly relevant to the emerging discourse and politics of human rights in India. The issues include (a) the debate on the centrality of the legal (concrete) dimension of the human rights, against the moral (abstract) dimension that translates into prominence for civil-political rights since they are the only rights that are justiciable; (b) the debate on universal human rights versus cultural relativism of many of the states in the non-European part of the world; and finally, (c) the debate on the 'third-generation' human rights as articulated in the 'right to development' foregrounds the original idea of indivisibility that is constitutive of human rights. Overall, the chapter attempts to demonstrate the point that the discourse, politics and practices of human rights emerge from a complex and continuous exchange between political movements and institutions at both the national and international levels, by drawing continuities between the discourse around 'right to development' and taking the instance of the anti-liquor movement led by women in Andhra Pradesh.

The second chapter, *Role of Judiciary in Humanising the Criminal Justice System in India*, makes an attempt to analyse the criminal justice system that prevails in the country. The criminal justice system generally consists of criminology, penology and victimology. In spite of the good intention of framers of the laws relevant to the above areas, sometimes inhuman practices came to be witnessed. It may be noted that the higher judiciary in India has evolved a humanitarian jurisprudence in many areas of criminal justice administration, consistently since 1980s. A number of instances have been recorded where the courts in recent times made bold efforts to arrest the trend of inhuman practices committed in case of arrested persons, accused persons, witnesses, convicted persons, juveniles, and their relatives and friends. This list is only illustrative and not exhaustive in nature. In this chapter, an attempt is made to analyse the role of judiciary in humanising the criminal justice system in India in its various aspects.

The third chapter, *Police and Human Rights Observance: Dilemmas and Interventions*, argues that the elemental obligation of the state is to protect the human rights of its citizenry. Accordingly, it is the law enforcement agency of the state, which is primarily entitled to observe and uphold the rights of all citizens equally by adhering to the procedure laid by the law. Paradoxically, in India, there are various situations and instances where police acts are seen contrary to their charted duties. In this regard, sensitisation of the police has become an urgent need of the day and human rights education (HRE) has been observed as an instrument to fulfil that need. In this context, the chapter examines to what extent HRE can sensitise the police. The study compares the attitude of sub-inspector (SI) rank officers on observing human rights and HRE training being received from Andhra Pradesh Police Academy (APPA), India. Though HRE emerged as a potential factor in sensitising the police attitude, the results indicate that experienced police officers express significantly less sensitivity towards observing human rights norms relative to new police recruits. This suggests that there is a dilemma over HRE from the perspective of police officers and the major reasons observed are their 'personal conceptions of justice and belief in the ideal of crime control', which evolved through their experience. Based on the study, the chapter argues that HRE can sensitise the police by insisting on the 'ideal of due process' and offering feasible solutions with realistic approach to avoid human rights violations.

The fourth chapter, *Human Rights NGOs in Manipur: Contexts, Roles and Challenges*, provides a descriptive and analytical context of human rights non-government organisations (NGOs) in Manipur in terms of their origins, roles and challenges. It is based on case studies of eight such organisations in the state. Decades of insurgency and counter-insurgency operations, inter-ethnic conflicts and the imposition of special laws such as the AFSPA, 1958, in Manipur have resulted in democratic governance, rule of law and human rights concerns being relegated to the backburner in the state. Given its poor human rights record, the state has been a breeding ground for a number of NGOs championing the cause of human rights. The organisational basis of human rights movements in Manipur emerged first during the early 1980s, in the backdrop of the Meitei and Naga sub-nationalist armed movements. The movements further expanded in the 1990s with the emergence of similar human rights organisations representing the ethnic Kuki-Chin tribes and sub-tribes, in the backdrop of inter-ethnic conflicts involving the Kuki, Naga and Paite ethnic groups. The study observes that the mandates of these organisations have over the years expanded to include broader human rights concerns such as the economic, social and cultural rights, women's rights and right to self-determination. The chapter, while cognisant of their vital contributions, further contends that the human rights movements in the state is characterised by fragmentation and partisanship along ethnic lines—having implications on their effectiveness and credibility. By confining to human rights issues that concern their ethnic constituencies, these organisations further accentuate ethnic faultiness and precludes the emergence of an all human rights movement in the state.

The fifth chapter, *Displacement and Tribal Resistance to Development in Kalinganagar, Jajpur District of Odisha: A Concern for the Rights of Indigenous People,* argues that in the name of development, globalisation, neo-liberalism and rapid economic growth have resulted in monopolisation and exploitation of natural resources. This process of monopolisation of resources by the state results in narrowing down the natural resource base for survival of economically poor, powerless and marginalised, that is, mostly the tribal and dalit population. It is argued in the literature that the development may be boon for some but they are a curse for the rest. The response of the local and tribal communities to this new threat, which is being unveiled by the very process of development, has often manifested through violent or strife resistance, whose resources and livelihood are under threat. Such conflicts, involving tribals and marginal communities, are on a rise in India. They have emerged as serious challenges to the current practice and developmental discourse. Thus, the central objective of the chapter is to study the process of displacement by acquisition of agricultural land for setting steel industry in Kalinganagar, Jajpur district in Odisha by Tata Company and the role of the state in this context. The focus of the study is to understand the mechanism involved in the process where the government is grabbing the tribal land at a low price for the public purpose use and selling it to the private industry. The study seeks to throw light upon the establishment of private industry and its impact on the livelihood, socio-economic and psychological status of people, who have lost their valuable land. It specifically looks into the violation of rights of the indigenous tribal's community and its impact on their lives in general and on the social and cultural aspects in particular.

The sixth chapter, *Hearing Children's Voices: A Study of Jammu & Kashmir State*, claims that childhood undergoes a series of ideological changes as it has always been historically and culturally conditioned. From not being entitled to hold any right during the medieval ages, the beginning of the 20th century saw a shift in the way how a child was understood. The ideology of protection of the child has given way to advocacy of rights of the children. In a diversity of practices, dealing with children has been a strong discourse on child participation. It challenges traditional roles and encourages the involvement of children in decision-making process. Recent years have witnessed a growing enthusiasm internationally for accepting the role of children as social actors and encouragement of the practice of child voice. Still in different societies children have been underrepresented because of their age and not made part of the decision-making processes that could promote their self-determination. Based on such a discourse, this chapter draws on the experiences of children who have lost their parent(s) in incidents related to armed conflict ensuing in the state of Jammu & Kashmir and put in various orphanages across the region. It is observed that these children are experts in the social construction of their own worlds. They are found to be capable enough to not only actively participate in the decision-making processes that directly concern them but also in offering solutions to larger issues of social and political nature.

The seventh chapter, *A Human Rights Perspective on Education and Research in Science and Technology*, highlights the role of science and technology and its implication for human rights discourse. An in-depth analysis is poised in this direction. In addition, the chapter proposes to highlight issues such as preservation of one's genetic identity, prevention of unethical usage of human genome for research purposes that could be some of the serious issues of concern in the near future given the recent advance in the sphere of gene technology. This would bring to the fore issues that are usually veiled by some of the basic human rights that receive more attention. The major aim of this chapter is to understand the strand of discussion on human rights vis-à-vis development in science and technology and integrate these into science education and research.

The eighth chapter, *Learning Disability and the Indian School: A Study in Delhi*, focusses on the legal and social aspects related to learning disabilities that are specific to Indian context. The chapter, based on empirical data from an ongoing study, discusses how disability is addressed by the stakeholders, especially in the education sector. Students with learning disabilities have remained an under-recognised group in the educational environment. For this group of students, the issue is not of access to educational settings as they are already in regular schools but they remain unidentified and, hence, their access to various provisions by the boards of education is an area of concern. The curriculum, teaching methodologies and evaluation procedures require modifications for supporting students with learning disabilities but schools are seldom taking such initiatives for them. The situation in both private sector and public sector schools is alike. It is proposed through this chapter that, in addition to sensitisation and promoting awareness among people about the disability, the greatest need is for teacher orientation and training to identify and support children with learning disability and other disabilities in their classrooms. Since the child and her/his parents are often at the 'mercy' of the teachers in school, their enlightenment and commitment seem to emerge as a critical variable in the well-being of students with learning disability.

The ninth chapter on *Equal 'Human' Status to Women and Girls with Disabilities: Gender-Disability Dimension of Human Rights*, discusses the human rights abuse in case of women and girls with disabilities with a focus on the unique disadvantages that they face in Indian society. The chapter particularly focusses on the lack of gender-disability perspectives in the equity policies and programmes in India and suggests possible strategies to protect and promote human rights of women and girls with disabilities.

The tenth chapter, *Disability Space in News and Entertainment Media in India: A Case Study*, explores the disability representation in news and entertainment media through content analysis. The media is contributing the least to the area of disability and its related issues have been reduced from 'watchdog' to the 'lapdog'. The current study has made a thorough attempt to explore the disability representation in media, especially in news and entertainment media. The study reveals that coverage of disability in the newspapers and films are scant, derogatory, not newsworthy and event motivated. Most of the time, journalists and film-makers are covering the issue of disability, with little knowledge on the subject, its movements and other developments pertaining to the disability. The actual issues of disability in various media have taken a backseat, leaving the disabled population in sheer deprivations.

References

Ahsan, M. (2011). 'Women and Human Development in the Muslim World: Reflections on Islamic and UNDP's Approach', in T. Lovat (ed.), *Women in Islam: Reflections on Historical and Contemporary Research*. Dordrecht: Springer.

Arjun Sengupta Committee (2006). Report on Conditions of Work and Promotion of Livelihoods in the Unorganized Sector.

Asian Centre for Human Rights (2011). 'RTI Activists: Sitting Ducks of India'. Retrieved on 5 October 2012, from http://www.achrweb.org/ihrrq/issue3-4/India-Sitting-Ducks-2011.pdf

Chakrabarti, D. (2011). 'The Human Rights Movement in India: In Search of a Realistic Approach'. *Economic and Political Weekly*, XLVI(47), 33–40.

Food and Agriculture Organization of the United Nations, India (2011). 'FAO Country Profile'. Retrieved on 14 May 2012, from http://www.fao.org/ countries/55528/en/ind/

Kannabiran, K.G. (2000). 'Foreword', in V. Suresh and D. Nagasaila (eds), *PSA Pillai on Criminal Law*. 9th Edition. New Delhi: Butterworths Tripathi.

Kummitha, R.K.R. (2015). 'Social Exclusion: The European Concept for Indian Social Reality'. *Social Change,* 45(1), 1–23.

National Crime Records Bureau (2009). 'Prison Statistics of India'. Retrieved on 4 February 2012, from http://ncrb.nic.in/PSI2009/Full/PSI-2009.pdf

Sen, A. (1998). 'The Possibilities of Social Choice'. Noble Lecture. Cambridge, Great Britain: Trinity College.

Sengupta, A. (2010). 'Human Rights and Extreme Poverty'. *Economic and Political Weekly,* XLV(17), 85–93.

Suresh, V. and Nagasaila, D. (2011). 'The Colossus of Human Rights Jurisprudence'. *Economic and Political Weekly,* XLVI(4), 26–29.

Tendulkar Committee (2009). 'Report of the Expert Group to Review the Methodology for Estimation of Poverty'. Retrieved on 8 August 2012, from http://planningcommission.nic.in/reports/genrep/rep_pov.pdf

Thapar, R. (2012, October 1). Convocation Address of University of Hyderabad.

UNICEF (2011). 'The Situation of Children in India: A Profile'. Retrieved on 17 October 2012, from http://www.unicef.org/sitan/ files/SitAn_India_May_2011.pdf

United Nations (2012). 'Human Rights in India; Status Report 2012'. Prepared for India's Second Universal Periodic Review at the UN. Working Group on Human Rights in India and the UN, 2012. Retrieved on 14 June 2012, from http://www.wghr.org/pdf/Status%20 report%2023.05%20version.pdf

WHO/UNICEF (2011). 'Joint Monitoring Programme for Water Supply and Sanitation'. Retrieved on 14 October 2012, from www.wssinfo.org/data-estimates/table.

Part I

Human Rights, State, Police and Judiciary

1

Beyond Global Human Rights

Ajay Gudavarthy

At the heart of thinking, practicing and implementing human rights is the dilemma between making them sufficiently general, abstract and universal so as to entitle individuals and collectives across gender, race, colour, class, language, age, sexual preferences and religious distinctions. The imperative of making them context specific, concrete and particular is important for their effective implementation to protect specific individuals and groups experiencing particular modes of marginalisation and denial of socio-economic mobility. Human rights, therefore, essentially refer to those rights that are accrued to us for just being human, and thus 'the subject of human rights are not members of this or that society, but of the community of humankind' (Vincent 1986, p. 9).[1] It is this vision that is enshrined in the Universal Declaration of Human Rights (UDHR) as a 'common standard of achievement for all peoples and all nations'.[2] However, what these rights actually refer to depend on the more specific historical, social and cultural context, both across and within particular societies. For instance, Immanuel Kant argues that 'Freedom (independence from being constrained by another's choice), insofar as it can coexist with the freedom of every other in accordance with a universal law, is the only original right belonging to every man by virtue of his humanity' (1995, p. 238). Such a foregrounding of the idea of freedom could be problematic, in the sense of being Western and Eurocentric, from the point of view of those societies that wish to protect their communities and pose certain limits on free speech, or for certain sections within a society, such as women who might argue that a notion of freedom without constraints or obligations presupposes atomistic individuals hyper-separated from the complex network of social relations.[3] Thus, the question that begs attention is how do we retain the emancipatory, rather than the hegemonic, potential of the universal nature of human rights and transmute them into particular, rather than localised, mechanisms accessible to different social groups in varied political contexts.

It is this 'dilemmatic situation' that translates, more specifically, into a series of debates on human rights. This chapter will focus on three such significant issues that are particularly relevant to the emerging discourse and politics of human rights in India.

(1) The debate on the centrality of the legal (concrete) dimension of the human rights, as against the moral (abstract) dimension that translates into pre-eminence for civil-political rights since they are the only rights that are justiciable. Does dependence on law then make human rights more effective or more susceptible to the imperatives of the state? Is rule of law guaranteeing basic civil-political rights, even at times of crisis, an effective check on state power or can it be overcome by the normalisation of the exception? We shall attempt to explore some of these issues in the context of the growing 'war' against militancy, terrorism and armed struggles in India.

(2) The debate on universal human rights versus cultural relativism of many of the states in the non-European part of the world. While cultural relativism poses challenges to the liberal-universal discourse of human rights, what has it meant to the various marginalised social groups in these societies? It is somewhat akin to the conflict between rights of religious minorities (protesting against Uniform Civil Code) and the gender discourse grappling for certain

common practices based on dignity and equality for women without taking a majoritarian turn. We shall focus on the recent debate on caste and race carried out by the dalit groups in the Durban conference in 2001.

(3) Finally, the debate on the 'third-generation' human rights as articulated in the 'right to development' foregrounds the original idea of indivisibility that is constitutive of human rights. Does this language of development as integration of rights talk a different language from that of the development (growth) based on market-oriented neo-liberal reforms, aided by 'good governance'? How does such a discourse that is essentially part of international and inter-governmental organisations interact with grass-roots political movements that operate at national and local level? We shall attempt to demonstrate the point that the discourse, politics and practices of human rights emerge from a complex and continuous exchange between political movements and institutions at both the national and international levels, by drawing continuities between the discourse around 'right to development' and taking the instance of the anti-liquor movement led by women in Andhra Pradesh.

Civil-Political Rights, Rule of Law and the 'War on Terrorism'

Maurice Cranston in his celebrated essay 'Are There Any Human Rights' argued that human rights need to have a restricted reference to only the 'first-generation rights' such as freedom of speech that are based on the principle of non-interference and therefore are cogent and encompass the 'feasibility of guaranteeing complete and comprehensive fulfilment', which in turn makes it possible to legislate and make these rights justiciable. Without legality being the defining feature of human rights they end up, as Bentham once put it as 'bawling upon paper'. Human rights become effective only as legal rights emanating either from national legislation or international conventions and declarations 'rather than on the basic humanity (or humanness) of the persons involved' (Sen 2006, p. 2). According to Cranston, 'The traditional political and civil rights are not difficult to *institutionalize* for the most part, they require governments, and other people generally to leave a man alone ... . 'The problem posed by claims to economic and social rights, however, are of another order altogether' (1983, p. 13). This centrality of legality seems to be linked to a certain understanding of not just human rights but also law itself. The idea is that law by its very nature holds for everyone and it is a 'sort of thing that demands equality in its application' (Bilgrami 2007, p. 318). Further, it is abstract enough to inform us or enable us to make sense of uncertain situations and institutionalise certain standardised practices, even in conditions of emergency or social crisis of various kinds. It is with this understanding that the International Convention on Civil Political Rights (ICCPR) in Article 6 explicitly states that 'Every human being has the inherent right to life. This right shall be protected by law. No one shall be arbitrarily deprived of his life'.[4] Similarly, it states in Article 9 that 'No one shall be subject to arbitrary arrest or detention. No one shall be deprived of his liberty except on such grounds and in accordance with such procedure established by law'.

In contemporary liberal democracies, it is the principle of rule of law that assures the individuals the 'governments' respect for the sovereign authority of the people', and therefore the guarantee against the violation of 'basic' civil and political rights. It is this promise in rule of law that Marxist historian E.P. Thompson attempted to foreground and extrapolate, contrary to either reducing it to a mere 'juridical illusion' or ideological hypocrisy of liberal democracies and therefore argued that rule of law meant 'the imposing of effective inhibitions upon power and the defence of the citizen from power's all-intrusive claims' (1975, p. 266). With the growing, what has come to be referred to as the 'war on terrorism', which seems to have assumed global proportions, has rule by law been a sufficient condition in dealing with the sense of a social crisis and the accompanying coercion within the parameters set by the due process of law? Has the state continued its balance between, as Gramsci had argued, 'coercion and consent', or has the former subsumed or even consumed the later?[5] Analysing rule of law, in order to comprehend the efficacy of human rights (civil-political rights) as legal rights, would perhaps point towards two dominant forms that it has taken in contemporary times, quite in contrast to its promise of 'inhibiting' the 'all-intrusive powers'. First, the rule of law is 'receiving so much attention now because of its centrality to both democracy and the market economy in the era marked by a wave of transitions to both' (Carothers 1998, p. 97). It is the ongoing process of consolidating market economies by breaking-up 'protectionism' that smaller and weaker economies followed in the first phase of the history of postcolonial countries. Strengthening rule of law refers to institutionalisation of the 'basic elements of a modern market economy such as property rights and contracts' (Carothers 1998, p. 97), making it possible therefore to 'export' rule of law (and democracy), and confirming its inextricable link with market that Friedrich Hayek had proposed in his campaign for the libertarian-right. Second (in many complex ways linked to the first) is the very erosion of law as norms outside of exception, and instead became a mark of 'normalization of the exception'. As Agamben has noted regarding the 'state of exception' that 'it not only appears increasingly as a technique of government rather than an exceptional measure, but it also lets its own nature as the constitutive paradigm of the juridical order come to light' (2005, p. 6). In other words, the 'state of exception' 'is not a special kind of law' meant to deal with conditions like war, but normalised to the extent of becoming 'a paradigm of government', and 'constituting the very basis of modern state power'. It is a situation, as Judith Butler remarks, marking the 'violent hold that law lays upon life'.

The plight of human rights—civil political rights in India—is marked expressly by this shift to the 'normalisation of exception'. The growing war on terror (read human rights) has in effect translated into a situation where on issues of 'national security' and public order, there can be no constraints that law can impose. In fact, in its renewed avatar the raison d'etre of law has to be to protect security and order. Various acts have been promulgated to put this new role of law into action. Among them the TADA, the POTA and AFSPA have gained prominence in terms of their role in gross and extensive violation of the civil and political rights of the citizens of India, as well as the activists struggling on behalf of the citizens as part of a vibrant human rights movement in India (Gudavarthy 2008a). These violations are not aberrations but implicit in the way the acts have been both envisaged and put to use. For instance, under AFSPA Section 4(a) states that any commissioned officer:

> if he is of opinion that it is necessary so to do for the maintenance of public order, after giving such due warning as he may consider necessary fire upon or otherwise use force, even to causing death, against any person who is acting in contravention of any law or order for the time being in force in the disturbed area prohibiting the assembly of five or more persons or the carrying of weapons or of things capable of being used as weapons or of firearms, ammunition or explosive substances.

This can be contrasted with, as A.G. Noorani has argued, the provisions of the Criminal Procedure Code (CrPC), wherein Section 130(3) explicitly states that officer of the armed forces should use 'as little force and do as little injury to person and property' (2009, p. 9). In spite of the contrast with the criminal procedure code and the outrageous powers to kill, the Supreme Court has upheld AFSPA as constitutionally valid in the *Naga People's Movement of Human Rights vs Union of India* (1998) (2 Supreme Court cases 109).[6] The process of 'normalisation of exception' is being further entrenched not only in upholding 'special powers' but also, in fact, making them part of the CrPC itself through the recently constituted *(Malimath) Committee on Reforms of Criminal Justice System*, which has proposed extensive changes to the criminal procedure code carrying in many of the 'special powers' into regular criminal justice system. It suggests for some very fundamental changes in its proposals, which are as follows:

(1) To dilute the provision of 'guilty beyond reasonable doubt' and replace the Evidence Act with the provision that it is sufficient that 'the court is convinced that it is true' (Para 5.13).
(2) Withdrawal of the right to silence to the accused by 'amending the code to provide for appropriate inferences from the silence of the accused' (Para 3.40).
(3) Removal of the distinction between 'cognizable' offences and 'non-cognizable' offences.

(4) 'The confession before a Superintendent of Police or a higher ranking official should be admissible in evidence subject to the condition that the accused is informed of his right to consult a legal practitioner' (7.35.2).
(5) Review of the sunset (time bound expiration) provision in acts such as the POTA.

Universality, Cultural Relativity and the 'Caste Is Race' Debate

Human rights are also unique in their character at another level, as they refer to a 'political culture', wherein they are as much politically constructed as they are historically, socially and culturally located in any given context. In other words, neither can they be taken for granted to be 'available' in any culture nor can they be constructed devoid of the historical 'traditions' of any given society. It is this unique characteristic that allows for imagining human rights to be universal as much as being culturally relativistic to each individual society. It is, therefore, possible to argue that the notion of human rights to be found in the UDHR or the UN can be traced to the historical experience of England, France and the United States. The United Nations in 1945 was undoubtedly dominated by the United States and the Europe. Similarly, when UDHR was adopted, most 'Third World' countries were still under the yoke of colonial rule. However, does this historical fact make human rights essentially Western, in the sense that they originate exclusively from a Western culture or tradition and, therefore, there is nothing universal about human rights and all we have is relativistic languages contesting each other? In fact, such a reading would be guilty of assuming an abstract (a monolithic) Occidental culture that is bereft of antagonistic currents. How do we then explain in the context of the same Western culture philosophers such as Thomas Aquinas vindicating slavery as a consequence of Adam and Eve's original sin? Or St. Paul who emphasised spiritual equality but justified inequalities when he says 'let every man abide in the same calling wherein he was called' (Bielefeldt 2000). These pronouncements resonate the similarity with Hinduism, in the Oriental part of the world, which articulated a strong notion of cosmic unity that all human beings are part of, yet provides justifications for a rigid caste order. In contemporary time, we are all well aware of the role Catholic church has played in its brazen disregard for gender rights through its campaign against abortion, or gay rights in its opposition to having gay priests. It is, therefore, possible to argue that 'human rights do not develop as a natural unfolding' of a pre-existing cultural potential nor does it 'reside in the genes of any particular culture' (Bielefeldt 2000). In many instances, human rights is connected to a tradition, or even history retrospectively, reflecting an hermeneutic standpoint, vindicating the argument that human rights is as much a result of conscious political construction and, therefore, an open-ended exercise as it is grounded in specific social contexts. Bulk of the academic and philosophical exercise is to recover a non-hegemonic version of human rights from this labyrinthine terrain. Reconciling the universalistic postures with that of the relativist pressures presupposes both overcoming essentialised universalism that can advantage powerful nations that exert undue power on weaker nations, as much as the pitfalls of essentialised relativism that can empower authoritarian states and make liberal democratic states non-responsive to the democratic aspirations of grass-roots political movements.

Jack Donnelly, in one of the early intervention to the debate on 'cultural relativism versus universal human rights', argued that there are broadly four ways to approach the interface between them. Through 'radical cultural relativism' culture becomes the sole source of human rights,[7] while a 'radical universalist' approach argues that culture is irrelevant and there are values and rights that are eternal and relevant across space and time. Contrary to the above approaches are two other approaches, namely 'strong cultural relativism' and 'weak cultural relativism'. While the former argues rights are culturally determined but universality of rights serves as a check on 'potential excesses of relativism', the later foregrounds culture as an important source but allows 'relatively rare and strictly limited local variations and exceptions' (Donnelly 1984). According to Donnelly, the weak cultural relativism is possibly the best way to reconcile relativism and universalism. Such an approach, while emphasising the need for universalist categories, allows for variations in 'form'. For instance, right to work needs to be recognised as a universal right in all societies, encompassing issues such as right to seek employment and right to be compensated for unemployment, among others. However, further specification regarding the length and amount of unemployment benefits could vary (Donnelly 1984).[8] In the more contemporary debates, scholars have attempted to foreground principles around which a universal framework of human rights can be sustained. Martha Nussbaum has argued, based on her Aristotelian approach of 'general characteristics of human beings', that it is possible to identify characteristics that are fundamentally human and 'not as a member of a particular group or local community' (Gould 2004, p. 55). She says:

> my proposal is fairly universal and 'essentialist'. That is, it asks us to focus on what is common to all, rather than on differences (although, as we shall see, it does not neglect these), and too see capabilities and functions as were central, more at the core of human life than others. (Nussbaum 1995, p. 63)

She believes that needs such as food, drink, shelter, sex, mobility, relatedness and humour, among others, are common across societies. Amartya Sen has further argued in basic agreement with Nussbaum's approach that there is an impending need to develop common standards in accessing development, such as nutrition and education, as they form the 'capabilities' to function in various ways and are essential to the universal 'freedom to achieve'. Cultural relativism, therefore, cannot be meaningful in contexts where it undermines the 'capabilities' necessary to function. As Susan Okin unequivocally argues, in her commentary on the burgeoning literature on multiculturalism, that 'respect for cultural practices must be subordinate to the requirements of women's equality' (1999, p. 12). Universality in such a framework emerges 'as a potential framework or horizon for interaction', which grows with inter-societal conversations rather than scuttle them. In contrast to abstract universality, we could, following Carol Gould, refer to it as 'concrete universality' that is 'constructed by individuals in concrete and differentiated social relations ... in networks of relationships and networks of engagement, themselves interconnecting' (2004, p. 62). It could be possibly developed around the universal values of care, sympathy and solidarity, which was referred to as 'non-Eurocentric universality' by Bikhu Parekh, premised on a unique dialectic between the particular and the universal where particularity or difference is valued but not particularism, which absolutises it. The universal is valued but not universalism, at least not of the kind that sets itself in opposition to and despises the particular (Parekh 2008).

The above discussion is of particular significance in understanding the politics and discourse of human rights in India. As state increasingly becomes non-responsive and governs through a paradigm of 'state of exception' (as we traced in the first part of this chapter), marginalised social groups access rights moving beyond the nation and talking of a language that is post-Westphalian in nature, playing out the unique dialectic between the universal and the particular. At the World Conference against Racism, Racial Discrimination, Xenophobia and Related Intolerance (World Conference Against Racism), held at Durban in August 2001, dalit organisations led by the National Campaign on Dalit Human Rights spearheaded a campaign to include caste discrimination as part of racial discrimination and discuss the modes of eliminating it by putting international pressure on the Government of India, as its obligation for having ratified the International Convention on Elimination of All Forms of Racial Discriminations in 1969. The UN (universal) framework to understand discrimination based on birth was exclusively West-centric in its recognition of only race and colour, and in ignoring experiences that were specific to Asia and Africa. Article 2 of the convention proclaimed 'No state, institution, group or individual shall make any discrimination whatsoever in matters of human rights and fundamental freedoms in the treatment of persons, on the ground of race, colour or ethnic origin'. Though racial discrimination was defined in terms of exclusion based on descent, the convention did not mention or include 'discrimination arising from non—race-colour-ethnic identities' (Thorat 2008). It was only in 1996 that CERD made a revision to make explicit reference to include caste-based discrimination of SCs and

STs, and the practice of untouchability: 'The committee states that the term 'descent' mentioned in Article 1 of the Convention does not solely refer to race. The Committee affirms that the situation of the Scheduled Castes and Scheduled Tribes falls within the scope of the Convention'. The dalit groups in India, taking a clue from this new mention of SCs and STs, demanded a more elaborate discussion on caste-based practices under para 109 of the agenda of the Durban conference, which referred to 'discrimination on the basis of work and descent'.

However, the Government of India objected to this demand of the dalit groups, displaying Morgenthau's realist approach to international politics, around protecting national pride, 'national interests' and the sovereignty of the nation as caste is strictly an 'internal' matter not to be debated in international fora.

The Government of India in claiming caste as 'unique to Indian society' was, in a sense, claiming a cultural relativism that cannot be easily made sense of by the international organisations that function with a universalist discourse of human rights. Intriguingly, while the dalit groups themselves had to puncture the Western-centric bias to get caste included within the scope of CERD, the Government of India was also critiquing the universalist nature but precisely not to debate caste within the purview of CERD. The debate took interesting twists in India, many of the scholars sensitive to protecting the 'self-determination' of India argued that taking caste to international fora also meant that 'we are looking for foreign help to fight everything, including the caste system' (Gupta 2004, p. 53). Similarly, those alert to the 'imperialism of categories' objected to the forceful reading of caste as race, while the weakening of the caste system is possible only 'if caste is presented as a caste and not forcibly fitted into the category of race, and at the same time, an attempt is made to promulgate an international charter against caste discrimination' (Seth 2004, p. xxvii). This alone would actually make the initial attempts of the dalit groups to recognise the specificity of caste-based discrimination, and it would be pushing the wheel back by asking for caste to be conflated with race. Further, this kind of a conflation might lead to a change in the way caste was understood and provide an opportunity for the state to withdraw some of its social welfare policies such as affirmative action.

Dalit groups and activists working on their behalf were attempting to foreground a 'concrete universality' that is sensitive to the specificities of caste-based discrimination but comprehend universalisation as increasing interconnections and looking for commonalities in discrimination practiced in various social contexts. They, therefore, argued that 'whether it is Australian attacks on Indians or atrocities committed on dalits by Indians or discrimination and oppression of the people of the north-east (which is racial in nature—my addition), they are basically issues that concern humanity and cannot be prevented from being internationalized' (Teltumbde 2009, p. 18). While there is commonality as discrimination against humanity, which is important to recover, there is distinction in the way they are hierarchically privileged in concrete social and historical contexts. Therefore, while caste-based discrimination is neglected, racial discrimination of Indians living elsewhere gets focussed since they belong to specific (privileged) caste backgrounds. In essence, what dalit groups were attempting was a double-edged approach of distinguishing caste—as a system as well as in its operative terms—from race, yet using race, which is globally a more recognised form of discrimination, by reading caste unto race to make use of the political spaces opened by the latter.

Third-Generation Rights, Right to Development and Domestic Violence

Third-generation rights were not merely new, or rights that were not covered under the first two generations of civil-political and social-economic and cultural rights but signified radically new principles beyond the scope of the language of rights in the first two generations. Apart from the end of Cold War, there were various social and political developments that led to a new language of rights among which prominent was the rise of movements for environmental justice, for peace and for nuclear disarmament. Environmental struggles brought into relief the principle of 'intergenerational equity' further problematising the idea of equality. The World Commission on Environment and Development stated that 'needs of future generations will not be compromised while present generation's needs are met'

(Brundtland Report 1987, p. 170). In philosophical terms, John Rawls had conceptualised this responsibility through his 'savings principle' where the contracting parties will agree 'to a savings principle subject to the further condition that they must want all previous generations to have followed it' (1993, p. 274). Movements for peace articulated new ideas about 'collective interests' that have to be fought by humanity as such and there are no natural (social) constituencies that would struggle for peace. Such issues could be fought not solely around interests but common concern about the well-being and the very future survival of humanity. Similarly, the anti-nuclear campaign foregrounded 'a post-Westphalian mode of frame-setting' by foregrounding justice 'for all those affected by a given social structure or institution' (Fraser 2005, p. 82). While national interests prompted nuclear deterrence, it's the post-Westphalian frame that could envisage global peace. It is the spirit and the vision of some of these novel principles that got encapsulated in third-generation rights, such as the right to development.

Right to Development (RD), adopted in 1986 by the UN General Assembly and reaffirmed in the Vienna Declaration of 1993 World Conference on Human Rights, marked a new beginning. It envisaged a new model of development around principles of fair and equitable distribution, political participation, social well-being, cultural recognition and dignity beyond the parameters of development as expansion of gross national product, industrialisation, export growth and capital flows, and marking a break from the top-down process of 'developmentalism'.[9] In order to effectively convert this vision into tangible policies, the Declaration made, among others, four fundamental formulations. First, RD reiterated the principle of indivisibility of rights.[10] Article 6(2) stated that the prime object of the Declaration is to 'eliminate obstacles to development resulting from failure to observe civil and political rights as well as economic, social and cultural rights'. In other words, RD works as a hinge connecting various rights into a 'vector' that 'measures' human well-being. 'The value of the vector improves if at least one right improves and no right deteriorates. If any right is violated, then the vector deteriorates and the Right to Development is violated' (Sen Gupta 2006, p. viii). Second, the emphasis on right to participate replaced human being as an object of development and made him/her an active subject. Article 1 states that 'right to development is an inalienable right by virtue of which every human person and all peoples are entitled to participate in, and enjoy economic, social, cultural, and political development, in which all human rights and fundamental freedoms can be fully realized'. Without the right to participate, human societies are reduced to 'target groups' to be administered state-initiated policies and bureaucratic intervention. For instance, peasants are reduced to 'pure' economic categories such as 'small farmers', undermining as Escobar (1992) argues a 'whole way of life'.[11] The societies are made 'manageable' and the imperatives of 'governmentality' undermines the agency of social groups reducing them to the status of mere 'populations' (Scott 1998). Thus, the right to participation makes both diversity of policies—instead of 'one-size-fit-all' model—a possibility with planning leaving scope for reversing the various models of development. Third, RD recasts development as neither a means nor an end, instead it lays premium on development as a process. In other words, 'the outcomes of the process are human rights, but the process itself would also be claimed as a human right' (Sen Gupta 2006, p. 12). As we understand democracy not only as an end but also as a means to an end, development is also 'not a finite event but a process over time' (Sen Gupta 2006, p. 17). This mode of approaching development makes it open to 'social ethics and public reasoning', as well as make it as much a collective right to be available to specific social groups as much as individuals within those groups (Sen 2006, p. 2). Finally, RD lays emphasis in its realisation on the mutual interdependence within the 'international community of states'. RD argues for the primary responsibility on the individual national states and cooperation from the international community. It expects 'policies at the national level with equitable economic relations and a favourable environment at the international level' (Sen Gupta 2006, p. 18). The responsibility of international community is articulated as an 'imperfect obligation', addressed to all those states which are in a position to help. An instance of such a role by the international community could be found in the recently forged alternative regional organisations such as MERCOSUR and ALBA in Latin America. With the initiative under these regional organisations, there has been, for instance, extensive medical services made available by Cuba to Venezuela, keeping in mind not merely profit but also social benefits to the people of both the countries (Gudavarthy 2009).

Increasingly, there has been the realisation that any effective and meaningful implementation of human rights has to integrate various aspects including the civil-political rights for political participation with social and economic rights for fair distribution, means with ends as an ongoing process and domestic policies with international cooperation. This move towards integrating various rights is visible in some of the prominent judgements by the Supreme Court in the recent past. For instance, in the *Francis Coralie Mullin vs Union Territory of Delhi*, the Supreme Court argued that 'the right to live is not restricted to mere animal existence ... but it also includes the right to live with human dignity, and all that goes along with it, namely the bare necessities of life such as adequate nutrition, clothing and shelter and facilities for reading, writing and expressing ourselves ...' (NHRC, 2014, p. 34). The Right to Education (RTE) was read into the fundamental rights through Right to Life. Article 21A was inserted that recognised the RTE as a fundamental right and imposed a duty on the state to provide free and compulsory to all children from the age of six to fourteen years. It is these judgements that led to the 86th Amendment to the Constitution in 2002 granting legislative recognition to RTE, finally fructifying in the Right to Education Bill, 2008. While state institutions such as the judiciary have to some extent demonstrated an integrationist framework, political movements of various hues have worked for long with such a frame. Women's struggles at the grass-roots, for instance, have been arguing for long that domination and systematic marginalisation of women has been possible due to complex interaction between the political, economic, social and cultural dimensions. Therefore, in dealing with specific forms of domination, such as dowry-related deaths, domestic violence and sexual harassment among others, all these aspects and their manifold interactions have to be taken into account in developing strategies that can effectively undermine the entrenched modes of domination. For instance, it was such an integrationist strategy, which was also at the heart of inaugurating the third-generation rights that was being proposed in a struggle that drew incisive links between the political economy driven by collection of revenues from the sale of liquor, and the masculine culture of controlling the 'private' sphere through physical violence against women. The anti-arrack movement, as it was referred to, began in August 1992, in a remote village of Dubagunta of Nellore district in Andhra Pradesh. Women of the village stopped vending of arrack in their village after three men lost their way and drowned in a tank. Women stopped arrack carts and jeeps from entering the village and demanded complete prohibition of the sale of liquor in the state. Women in this movement in fact went beyond the traditional and conventional divisions between the public and private, in order to comprehend the hidden linkages between family, domestic violence, the state and the liquor lobby. They understood that behind their abusive husbands was the whole support structure led by the arrack contractors, police, goondas, legislators, ministers, officials and bureaucrats. 'The antiliquor movement has not merely raised a women question as being portrayed by the press and a section of the intelligentsia but also targeted its attack on the nexus between the so-called people's representatives, police and arrack contractors' (Reddy and Patnaik 1993, p. 1064). Women consistently articulated the language of including various social (domestic stress, dignity, mental anguish, education and health), economic (constant debt, hunger, falling standard and quality of living) and political (unholy nexus between the politicians-representatives, police and the liquor lobby contractors) issues in the developmental agenda. They further argued that without necessary economic empowerment, social change, political participation and struggle against cultural practices, mere legal (rights) intervention can be formal and counter-productive. Thus, when the Government of Andhra Pradesh refused to prohibit liquor and restricted women's right to forge political movements and instead suggested availing legal options by making use of the Domestic Violence Act (2005), women's groups argued that it has the effect of making law insular to the needs of women. First, they enable to increase state control in new areas of life by making people more accountable, without these legislations being useful or satisfactory at the level of implementation. In other words, actual laws do not work and the victims become more 'vulnerable' by the compulsion of opening up before unsympathetic judiciary and police stations. Second, the provisions of the law are incapable of addressing the larger issues of women.

> A close look at the appeals that women have made in relation to the domestic violence law 498A in the last two decades shows that they are seeking relief which extend beyond those that can be offered by courts and police stations. Women are seeking responsible husbands, a role in decision-making, self-respect and a dignified family life, which in itself often contributes to the violence they experience. (Suneetha 2005, p. 102)

Finally, such legal interventions further add to the logic of the technocratic state in pulling social problems outside the domain of politics and projecting solutions in fine technical interventions. 'Such an "enclosure" in the legal realm individualises the woman into a case and leads to a depoliticisation of the discussion of women's battles in the family. Is it this closure, which is producing the silence that we are noticing?' (Ibid, p. 103). Thus, women's movements at the local level are reiterating the points made at the international level in the Declaration on Right to Development that development needs to be posited around principles of indivisibility, right to political participation by the agents and perceive it as an ongoing process forging complex links rather than a single event.

Notes

1. The idea of what constitutes human can be approached in very many different ways. While it could refer to a basic difference from animals, in terms of our capacity to possess reason and self-reflection, it could as well refer to the ability to recognise and 'feel' pain and, therefore, foreground ability to empathise with the suffering of others, including that of the animals.

2. Adopted by the General Assembly of the United Nations on the 10 December 1948.
3. For communitarian perspective refer Parekh (1993) and for a feminist critique of the liberal idea of freedom refer to an interesting debate between Nancy Hirschmann and Carole Pateman (Hirschmann 1989; Pateman 1992). In the context of India, Gandhi has been a champion of the idea of obligation, which could, notwithstanding its critique of individual-centric rights or freedom discourse, entail politically problematic consequences. Hence, I have attempted to explore this elsewhere (Gudavarthy 2008).
4. ICCPR was adopted and opened for signature, ratification and accession by General Assembly Resolution 2200 A (XXI) of 16 December 1966.
5. Marxists such as Perry Anderson have argued that bourgeoisie-democratic power is simultaneously and indivisibly dominated by culture and determined by coercion (Anderson 1976).
6. Noorani notes that in its judgement, the Supreme Court does not even refer to Article 21 of the Constitution, which recognises the right to life of every person, citizen or foreigner. Refer Noorani (2009).
7. Such an approach can invoke 'mythical cultural past', like the dictators in Africa or right-wing cultural organisations such as the RSS in India, which either no longer exists or is a distortion of history; it can also disregard (as most often it does) those rights, as Donnelly points out, that have no cultural basis such as arbitrary arrests, detention and so on.
8. For instance, while the United Kingdom has social security benefits and monthly allowances for all those unemployed, India has its own version in the recently promulgated NREGA, which allows for 100 days of employment and is geared towards protecting the interests of the rural poor.
9. United States was and continues to oppose the RD, it argued that 'development accrues thanks to economic liberties and private enterprise rather than a claimed Right to Development' (Baxi 2007, p. 129).
10. Indivisibility, in fact, was first emphasised in the UDHR in 1948, but was consistently undermined during the days of the Cold War. It took more than four decades, thanks to the new political and social movements that provided political and discursive context, as

elaborated at the beginning of this section, for indivisibility to be brought back into the human rights discourse.

11. In fact Escobar suggests the use of the term post-development, which according to him refers to 'a discursive anti-colonialist insurrection'.

References

Agamben, Giorgio (2005). *State of Exception*. Chicago: University of Chicago Press.

Amnesty International India (2003). 'The (Malimath) Committee on Reforms of Criminal Justice System: Premises, Politics and Implications for Human Rights', AII, Delhi.

Anderson, Perry (1976). *Considerations on Western Marxism*. London: New Left Books.

Baxi, Upendra (2007). *Human Rights in a Post-Human World*. Oxford: Oxford University Press.

Bielefeldt, Heiner (2000). 'Western versus Islamic Human Rights Conception', in A. Pollis and P. Schwab (eds), *Human Rights: New Perspectives, New Realities*. London: Lynne Rienner Publishers.

Bilgrami, Akeel (2007). 'Secularism and the Very Concept of Law', in Anuradha Dingwaney Needham and Rajeswari Sunder Rajan (eds), *The Crisis of Secularism in India*. Durham: Duke University Press.

Brundtland Commission (1987). *Our Common Future*. Oxford: Oxford University Press.

Carothers, Thomas (1998). 'The Rule of Law Revival'. *Foreign Affairs*, March/April, 77(2).

Cranston, Maurice (1983). 'Are There Any Human Rights?' *Daedalus*, Fall.

Donnelly, Jack (1984). 'Cultural Relativism versus Universal Human Rights'. *Human Rights Quarterly*, 6.

Donnelly, Jack (1985). 'In Search of the Unicorn: The Jurisprudence and Politics of the Right to Development'. *California Internal Law Journal*, Vol. 15, 473–509.

Escobar, Arturo (1992). 'Planning', in W. Sachs (ed.), *The Development Dictionary: A Guide to Knowledge as Power*. Zed Books.

Fraser, Nancy (2005). 'Reforming Justice in a Globalizing World'. *New Left Review*, 36, pp. 1–19.

Gould, Carol (2004). *Globalisation, Democracy and Human Rights*. Cambridge: Cambridge University Press.

Gudavarthy, Ajay (2008a, April). 'Human Rights Movements in India: State, Civil Society, and Beyond'. *Contributions to Indian Sociology*. 42(1), 29–57.

Gudavarthy, Ajay (2008b, May 30). 'Gandhi, Dalits and Feminists: Recovering the Convergence'. *Economic and Political Weekly*. Vol. 43(22), pp. 83–90.

Gudavarthy, Ajay (2009, June 19). 'Globalisation and Regionalisation: Mapping the New Continental Drift'. *Economic and Political Weekly*.

Gupta, Dipankar (2004). 'Caste in Not Race: But, Let's Go to the UN Forum Anyway', in Sukhdeo Thorat and Umakant (eds), *Caste, Race and Discrimination*. Jaipur: Rawat Publications.

Haragopal, G. (2009, July 11). 'Terrorism and Human Rights: Indian Experience with Repressive Laws'. *Economic and Political Weekly*.

Kant, Immanuel (1995). *The Metaphysics of Morals*. Cambridge: Cambridge University Press.

NHRC (2014). 'Retinal Benefits as a Human Rights'. New Delhi: NHRC.

Noorani, A.G. (2009, August 22). 'Armed Forces (Special Powers) Act: Urgency of Review'. *Economic and Political Weekly*.

Nussbaum, Martha and J. Glover (eds) (1995). *Women, Culture and Development*. New York: Oxford University Press.

Parekh, Bikhu (1993). 'Cultural Particularity of Liberal Democracy' in D. Held (ed.), *Prospect for Democracy*. Cambridge: Polity Press.

Parekh, Bikhu (2008). *A New Politics of Identity*. New York: Palgrave Macmillan.

Rawls, John (1993). *Political Liberalism*. New York: Columbia University Press.

Reddy, Narsimha and Arun Patnaik (1993, May 22). 'Anti-Arrack Agitation of Women in Andhra Pradesh'. *Economic and Political Weekly*.

Scott, James (1998). *Seeing Like a State*. London: Yale University Press.

Sen Gupta, Arjun (2001, July). 'Right to Development as a Human Right'. *Economic and Political Weekly*.

Sen Gupta, Arjun (2006). 'The Human Right to Development', in B.A. Andreassen and S.P. Marks (eds), *Development as a Human Right*. Harvard: Harvard University Press.

Sen, Amartya (2006). 'Human Rights and Development', in B.A. Andreassen and S.P. Marks (eds), *Development as a Human Right*. Harvard: Harvard University Press.

Seth, D.L. (2004). 'Caste in the Mirror of Race', in Sukhdeo Thorat and Umakant (eds), *Caste, Race and Discrimination*, Jaipur: Rawat Publications, 85–96.

Suneetha (2005, September 17). 'Adjudicating (Un) "Domestic Battles"'. *Economic and Political Weekly*, No. 38(17), 4101–4103.

Susan, Muller Okin (1999). *Is Multiculturalism Bad for Women?* Princeton: Princeton University Press.

Teltumbde, Anand (2009, August 22). 'Race or Caste, Discrimination Is a Universal Concern'. *Economic and Political Weekly*.

Thompson, E.P. (1975). *Whigs and Hunters*. London: Allen Lane.

Thorat, Sukhadeo (2008). 'Labour Market Discrimination: Concept, Forms and Remedies in the Indian Situation'. *The Indian Journal of Labour Economics*, Vol. 51, No. 1, 31–52.

Vincent, R.J. (1986). *Human Rights and International Relations*. Cambridge: Cambridge University Press.

2

Role of Judiciary in Humanising the Criminal Justice System in India

G.B. Reddy

Lord Denning once observed that the judges could not afford to be timorous souls. They cannot remain impotent, incapable and sterile in the face of injustice. On the same lines, the Supreme Court of India has developed a new jurisprudence of human rights since 1980s and emphasised that the state cannot act arbitrarily failing which its action may be invalidated by judicial intervention. Described as judicial activism, this approach would be justified in view of the fact that the law cannot anticipate the endless permutations of circumstance and situation. The judges in India, particularly those from the higher judiciary, have succeeded in infusing a new life and blood into the dry skeleton provided by the legislature and created a living organism appropriate and adequate to meet the needs of the society. This is more manifested in the field of criminal justice system.

In the case of arrested persons, denial of bails, indiscriminate granting of police remand, torture of person(s) arrested in police custody and denial of legal aid create genuine concerns. In spite of having sufficient safeguards incorporated in the Constitution of India[1] and the CrPC, 1973,[2] the arrested persons in India are often deprived of their rights. Noticing this, courts in India have come out with a number of judgements wherein many guidelines have been laid down for protection of human rights of arrested persons. Some of them are discussed in this chapter.

Right against Handcuffing

The laws in India do not permit handcuffing of a prisoner unless the police suspect the prisoner of attempting an escape. Majority of people do not know that the Supreme Court has criticised handcuffing as inhuman, unreasonable and arbitrary. Despite this clear stand on handcuffing, it is surprising to find that a majority of prisoners in India continue to be handcuffed. The Supreme Court of India has repeatedly condemned the unnecessary use of handcuffs by the police as a violation of the right to personal liberty guaranteed by Article 21 of the Constitution of India. The landmark Supreme Court case on handcuffing is *Prem Shankar Shukla vs Delhi Administration*.[3] In this case, the validity of certain clauses of the Punjab Police Rules, which made handcuffing mandatory during arrest, was challenged. In his opinion, Justice Krishna Iyer stated:

> The guaranty of human dignity which forms a part of our constitutional culture ... spring[s] into action when we realize that to manacle man is more than to mortify him, it is to dehumanise him and, therefore, to violate his very personhood too often using the mask of dangerousness and security.

In this case and other landmark cases, the Supreme Court has laid down strict procedural guidelines specifying both when and how the use of handcuffs is appropriate. According to the court, handcuffing is legal only if the arrestee is (a) involved in serious non-bailable offences and (b) previously convicted of a crime, of desperate character, likely to commit suicide, or likely to attempt to escape. The use of handcuffs and the reasons for their use must be recorded. It is illegal to walk fettered political prisoners through the streets. Furthermore, the police must obtain judicial permission before they use restraints during an arrest or on a detainee. The apex court has summed up its opinion of handcuffs in *Sunil Batra (II) vs Delhi Administration*[4]: 'To fetter prisoners in irons is an inhumanity unjustified save where safe custody is otherwise impossible. The routine resort to handcuffs and irons bespeaks a barbarity hostile to our goal of human dignity and social justice'. Despite these clear, specific and unambiguous judgements from the Supreme Court, the abuse of handcuffs continues.[5] Unfortunately, the Supreme Court's directives appear to be rarely followed.

In the case, *Sunil Gupta vs State of Madhya Pradesh*,[6] handcuffing the petitioners who are educated and not likely to flee from jail was considered unjust and unreasonable by the Supreme Court. In this case, the Supreme Court directed the government to ensure that appropriate action is taken against the 'escorting party', namely the cops, for handcuffing the petitioners. In a landmark case, *Citizens for Democracy vs State of Assam* (1995) 3 SCC 743, it was held that when a person is arrested based on a warrant of arrest that is issued by a Magistrate, the police shall not handcuff the said person unless the Magistrate has ordered handcuffing. It was also held that when the police arrest a person without a warrant, the person maybe handcuffed in consonance with the Supreme Court guidelines. However, once he is produced before the Magistrate, he cannot be chained or handcuffed without the orders of the Magistrate. In the same case, the Supreme Court had observed that handcuffing and chaining in public 'degrades and puts to shame finer sensibilities, and is a slur on our culture'. It was further observed that handcuffing should be shunned as violative of human dignity.

In *Khedat Mazdoor Chetna Sangh vs State of MP*,[7] the Supreme Court observed that 'one should not lose sight of the fact that when a person is remanded by a judicial order by a competent court, that person comes within the judicial custody of the court. Therefore, the taking of a person from a prison to the court or back from court to the prison by the escort party is only under the judicial orders of the court. Therefore, even if extreme circumstances necessitate the escort party to bind the prisoner in fetters, the escort party should record the reasons for doing so in writing and intimate the court so that the court considering the circumstances either approves or disapproves the action of the escort party and issue necessary directions' and that 'if dignity or honour vanishes what remains of life. In these circumstances to uphold human values and to protect the rights guaranteed under the Constitution, we hereby direct the CBI to investigate and register cases and prosecute the officers, however, high or low in the hierarchy of administration for these serious lapses (of handcuffing petitioners)'.

Right against Self-Incrimination

Article 20(3) of the Constitution declares that no person accused of an offence shall be compelled to be a witness against himself. This protection is also known as protection against testimonial compulsion. Recently the Supreme Court has addressed the question to relate to the involuntary administration of certain scientific techniques, namely narcoanalysis, polygraph examination and the Brain Electrical Activation Profile (BEAP) test for the purpose of improving investigation efforts in criminal cases in the case of *Smt Selvi vs State of Karnataka*.[8] The involuntary administration of the impugned techniques prompts questions about the protective scope of the 'right against self-incrimination', which finds place in Article 20(3) of our Constitution. The court in its considered opinion held that the compulsory administration of the impugned techniques violates the 'right against self-incrimination'. This is because the underlying rationale of the said right is to ensure the reliability as well as voluntariness of statements that are admitted as evidence. This court has recognised that the protective scope of Article 20(3) extends to the investigative stage in criminal cases and when read with Section 161(2) of the CrPC, 1973, it protects accused persons, suspects as well as witnesses who are examined during an investigation. The test results cannot be admitted in evidence if they have been obtained through the use of compulsion. Article 20(3) protects an individual's choice between speaking and remaining silent, irrespective of whether the subsequent testimony proves to be inculpatory or exculpatory.

Article 20(3) aims to prevent the forcible 'conveyance of personal knowledge that is relevant to the facts in issue'. The results obtained from each of the impugned tests bear a 'testimonial' character and they cannot be categorised as material evidence.

The court was also of the view that forcing an individual to undergo any of the impugned techniques violates the standard of 'substantive due process' which is required for restraining personal liberty. Such a violation will occur irrespective of whether these techniques are forcibly administered during the course of an investigation or for any other purpose since the test results could also expose a person to adverse consequences of a non-penal nature. In light of these conclusions, we hold that no individual should be forcibly subjected to any of the techniques in question, whether in the context of investigation in criminal cases or otherwise. Doing so would amount to an unwarranted intrusion into personal liberty. However, we do leave room for the voluntary administration of the impugned techniques in the context of criminal justice, provided that certain safeguards are in place. Even when the subject has given consent to undergo any of these tests, the test results by themselves cannot be admitted as evidence because the subject does not exercise conscious control over the responses during the administration of the test. However, any information or material that is subsequently discovered with the help of voluntary administered test results can be admitted, in accordance with Section 27 of the Evidence Act, 1872. The National Human Rights Commission had published 'Guidelines for the Administration of Polygraph Test (Lie Detector Test) on an Accused' in 2000. These guidelines should be strictly adhered to and similar safeguards should be adopted for conducting the 'narcoanalysis technique' and the BEAP test. The text of these guidelines has been reproduced as follows:

(1) No lie detector test should be administered except on the basis of consent of the accused. An option should be given to the accused whether he wishes to avail such test.
(2) If the accused volunteers for a lie detector test, he should be given access to a lawyer and the physical, emotional and legal implication of such a test should be explained to him by the police and his lawyer.

(3) The consent should be recorded before a Judicial Magistrate.
(4) During the hearing before the Magistrate, the person alleged to have agreed should be duly represented by a lawyer.
(5) At the hearing, the person in question should also be told in clear terms that the statement that is made shall not be a 'confessional' statement to the Magistrate but will have the status of a statement made to the police.
(6) The Magistrate shall consider all factors relating to the detention including the length of detention and the nature of the interrogation.
(7) The actual recording of the lie detector test shall be done by an independent agency (such as a hospital) and conducted in the presence of a lawyer.
(8) A full medical and factual narration of the manner of the information received must be taken on record.

This is a welcome judgement which puts at rest the controversy and uncertainty pertaining to narcoanalysis and other forensic tests and their constitutional validity.

Right to Free Legal Aid

Legal aid may be taken to mean free legal assistance to the poor persons in any judicial proceedings before the court, tribunals or any authority. It intends to provide free legal assistance to the poor persons who are not able to enforce the rights given to them by law. Justice P.N. Bhagwati has clearly stated that legal aid means providing an arrangement in the society which makes the machinery of administration of justice easily accessible and in reach of those who have to resort to it for enforcement of rights given to them by law. He has rightly said that the poor and the illiterate should be able to approach the courts and their ignorance and poverty should not be an impediment in the way of obtaining justice from the courts. Right to free legal aid is an implicit fundamental right under Article 21 of the Constitution. The Supreme Court has in several judgements declared that the directive principle contained in Article 39A[9] of the Constitution has ripened into a fundamental right under Article 21.

In *Prabha Dutt vs Union of India & Ors*,[10] the court directed that 'the Superintendent of the Tihar Jail shall allow the aforesaid persons, namely the representatives of *Hindustan Times*, *The Times of India*, *India Today*, the Press Trust of India and *The United News of India* to interview the aforesaid two prisoners, namely, Billa and Ranga' (on a given day). Subsequently in *Francis Coralie Mullin vs Administrator, Union Territory of Delhi & Ors,*[11] the Court pointed out that: 'A prisoner or detenu is not stripped of his fundamental or other legal rights, save those which are inconsistent with his incarceration and if the constitutional validity of any such law is challenged, the court would have to decide whether the procedure laid down by such law for depriving a person of his personal liberty is reasonable, fair and just'.

In *Sheela Barse vs State of Maharashtra,*[12] it was held that legal assistance to a poor accused who is arrested and put in jeopardy of his life or personal liberty is constitutional, imperative and mandated not only by Article 39A but also by Articles 21 and 14 of the Constitution. Article 21 clearly says that every person has an equal right to life and liberty except according to the procedure established by the law. It was said in the case of *Hussainara khatoon vs State of Bihar,*[13] that if any accused is not able to afford legal services then he has a right to free legal aid at the cost of the state. Also in *Sukhdas vs Union Territory of Arunachal Pradesh,*[14] it was held, in case an accused is not told of his right and therefore he remains unprecedented by a lawyer, his trial is vitiated by constitutional infirmity and any conviction as a result of such trial is liable to be set aside. Similarly Article 14 also talks about equality before law. Section 304 of CrPC imposes an obligation on the courts to provide legal aid at the expense of the state to an accused, who has no sufficient means and finances to engage an advocate. There cannot be any real equality in criminal cases unless the accused gets a fair trial of defending himself against the charge and a professional assistance.

Salwa Judum and Special Police Officers in Chhattisgarh—Legal and Constitutional Issues

In a recent judgement in the case of *Nandini Sundar & Others vs State of Chhattisgarh,*[15] the Supreme Court dealt with the ongoing armed insurgency referred to as both Maoist and Naxal or Naxalite activities in the state of Chhattisgarh, and in various other parts of the country. The court dealt with the constitutionality of the state permitting Salwa Judum and appointing Special Police Officers (SPOs) and 'Koya Commandos' to deal with Naxalites. The court observed that creation of a cadre like groups of SPOs, temporarily employed and paid an honorarium, out of uneducated or undereducated tribal youth, many of whom are also informed by feelings of rage, hatred and a desire for revenge, to combat Maoist/Naxalite activities runs counter to democratic and constitutional norms. Consequently, such actions of the state may be an abdication of constitutional responsibilities to provide appropriate security to citizens, by having an appropriately trained professional police force of sufficient numbers and properly equipped on a permanent basis. The court emphatically declared that:

> *these are essential state functions, and cannot be divested or discharged through the creation of temporary cadres with varying degrees of state control*. They necessarily have to be delivered by forces that are and personnel who are completely under the control of the State, permanent in nature, and appropriately trained to discharge their duties within the four corners of constitutional permissibility … . The instant matters, in the case of SPOs in Chhattisgarh, represent an extreme form of transgression of constitutional boundaries.

The court pointed out that the adverse effects on society, both current and prospective, are horrific. Such policies by the state violate both Articles 14 and 21, of those being employed as SPOs in Chhattisgarh and used in counter-insurgency measures against Maoists/Naxalites, as well as of citizenry living in those areas. The effectiveness of the force ought not to be, and cannot be, the sole yardstick to judge constitutional permissibility. The 'force' as claimed by the state, in the instant matters, is inexorably leading to the loss of the force of the Constitution. Constitutional realty does not, cannot and ought not to permit either the use of such a force or its multiplication. Constitutional propriety is not a matter of throwing around arbitrarily selected, and inanely used, phrases such as 'force multipliers'. Constitutional adjudication, and protection of civil liberties, by this court is a far, far more sacred a duty to be swayed by such arguments and justifications.

Consequently, the court ordered that: (a) The state of Chhattisgarh immediately cease and desist from using SPOs in any manner or form in any activities, directly or indirectly, aimed at controlling, countering, mitigating or otherwise eliminating Maoist/Naxalite activities in the state of Chhattisgarh; (b) The Union of India to cease and desist, forthwith, from using any of its funds in supporting, directly or indirectly the recruitment of SPOs for the purposes of engaging in any form of counter-insurgency activities against Maoist/Naxalite groups; (c) The state of Chhattisgarh shall forthwith make every effort to recall all firearms issued to any of the SPOs, whether current or former, along with any and all accoutrements and accessories issued to use such firearms. The word firearm as used shall include any and all forms of guns, rifles, launchers and so on of whatever calibre; (d) The state of Chhattisgarh shall forthwith make arrangements to provide appropriate security and undertake such measures as are necessary, and within bounds of constitutional permissibility, to protect the lives of those who had been employed as SPOs previously, or who had been given any initial orders of selection or appointment, from any and all forces, including but not limited to Maoists/Naxalites; and (e) The state of Chhattisgarh shall take all appropriate measures to prevent the operation of any group, including but not limited to Salwa Judum and Koya Commandos, that in any manner or form seek to take law into private hands, act unconstitutionally or otherwise violate the human rights of any person. The measures to be taken by the state of Chhattisgarh shall include, but not limited to, investigation of all previously inappropriately or incompletely investigated instances of alleged criminal activities of Salwa Judum, or those popularly known as Koya Commandos, filing of appropriate FIRs and diligent prosecution.

This judgement demonstrates the fact that the state power is not unlimited and uncontrolled, and that a socio-economic problem cannot be permitted to be handled by a 'private force'.

Juvenile Justice and Determination of Age

In *Shahnawaz vs State of UP & Another*,[16] the court has treated the date of birth in School Leaving Certificate as valid proof in determining the age of an accused person for the purpose of criminal proceedings. Earlier, in *Rajinder Chandra vs State of Chhattisgarh and Anr*[17] the court considered the entry relating to date of birth in the mark sheet and concluded as under:

> it is true that the age of the accused is just on the border of sixteen years and on the date of the offence and his arrest he was less than 16 years by a few months only. In *Arnit Das vs State of Bihar*[18] this Court has, on a review of judicial opinion, held that while dealing with the question of determination of the age of the accused for the purpose of finding out whether he is a juvenile or not, a hyper-technical approach should not be adopted while appreciating the evidence adduced on behalf of the accused in support of the plea that he was a juvenile and if two views may be possible on the said evidence, the court should lean in favour of holding the accused to be a juvenile in borderline cases.

The applicability of the act and the Juvenile Justice (Care and Protection of Children) Act and the rules with respect to 'juvenile' and 'juvenile in conflict with law' have been elaborately considered by the court in *Hari vs State of Rajasthan & Anr.*[19] The court ultimately held that 'the entry relating to date of birth entered in the mark sheet is one of the valid proof of evidence for determination of age of an accused person. The School Leaving Certificate is also a valid proof in determining the age of the accused person.' This judgement sets at rest a long standing controversy relating to juvenile justice.

Honour Killings and Response of Judiciary

In recent years, several instances are coming to public knowledge regarding harassment, threats and violence against young men and women who marry outside their caste. The nation appears to be passing through a crucial transitional period in our history, and at this juncture the response of the courts in India is worth noticing.

In *Lata Singh vs State of UP & Another*,[20] the Supreme Court observed that the caste system is a curse on the nation and the sooner it is destroyed, the better. In fact, it is dividing the nation at a time when we have to be united to face the challenges before the nation unitedly. Hence, inter-caste marriages are in fact in the national interest as they will result in destroying the caste system. However, disturbing news is coming from several parts of the country that young men and women who undergo inter-caste marriage are threatened with violence or violence is actually committed on them.

Thus, in the opinion of the court, such acts of violence or threats or harassment are wholly illegal and those who commit them must be severely punished. This is a free and democratic country, and once a person becomes a major, he or she can marry whosoever he or she likes. If the parents of the boy or the girl do not approve of such inter-caste or inter-religious marriage, the maximum they can do is that they can cut off social relations with the son or the daughter, but they cannot give threats or commit or instigate acts of violence and cannot harass the person who undergoes such inter-caste or inter-religious marriage. The court, therefore, directed that the administration/police authorities throughout the country will see to it that if any boy or girl who is a major undergoes inter-caste or inter-religious marriage with a woman or man who is a major, the couple are not harassed by any one nor subjected to threats or acts of violence, and anyone who gives such threats or harasses or commits acts of violence either himself or at his instigation is taken to task by instituting criminal proceedings by the police against such persons and further stern action is taken against such persons as provided by law. We sometimes hear of 'honour' killings of such persons who undergo inter-caste or inter-religious marriage of their own free will. There is nothing honourable in such killings, and in fact they are nothing but barbaric and shameful acts of murder committed by brutal, feudal-minded persons who deserve harsh punishment.

In a recent decision of *Arumugam Servai vs State of T. Nadu*,[21] the Supreme Court directed the administrative and police officials to take strong measures to prevent such atrocious acts. The court went on to observe:

> We have in recent years heard of 'Khap Panchayats' (known as katta panchayats in Tamil Nadu) which often decree or

> encourage honour killings or other atrocities in an institutionalized way on boys and girls of different castes and religion, who wish to get married or have been married, or interfere with the personal lives of people. We are of the opinion that this is wholly illegal and has to be ruthlessly stamped out. As already stated in Lata Singh's case (supra), there is nothing honourable in honour killing or other atrocities and, in fact, it is nothing but barbaric and shameful murder. Other atrocities in respect of personal lives of people committed by brutal, feudal minded persons deserve harsh punishment. Only in this way can we stamp out such acts of barbarism and feudal mentality. Moreover, these acts take the law into their own hands and amount to kangaroo courts, which are wholly illegal.[22]

Hence, we direct the administrative and police officials to take strong measures to prevent such atrocious acts. If any such incidents happen, apart from instituting criminal proceedings against those responsible for such atrocities, the state government is directed to immediately suspend the District Magistrate/Collector and SSP/SPs of the district as well as other officials concerned and charge sheet them and proceed against them departmentally if they do not (a) prevent the incident if it has not already occurred but they have knowledge of it in advance or (b) if it has occurred, they do not promptly apprehend the culprits and others involved and institute criminal proceedings against them, as in our opinion they will be deemed to be directly or indirectly accountable in this connection.[23]

In *Bhagwan Dass vs State (NCT) of Delhi*,[24] the Supreme Court advocated death sentence to those responsible for honour killings and observed as under:

> 'honour' killings have become commonplace in many parts of the country, particularly in Haryana, western U.P., and Rajasthan. Often young couples who fall in love have to seek shelter in the police lines or protection homes, to avoid the wrath of kangaroo courts. We have held in Lata Singh's case (supra) that there is nothing 'honourable' in 'honour' killings, and they are nothing but barbaric and brutal murders by bigoted, persons with feudal minds.

In our opinion honour killings, for whatever reason, come within the category of rarest of rare cases deserving death punishment. It is time to stamp out these barbaric, feudal practices which are a slur on our nation. This is necessary as a deterrent for such outrageous, uncivilised behaviour. All persons who are planning to perpetrate 'honour' killings should know that the gallows await them.

Thus, it could be seen that the judiciary has exhibited tremendous concern in ensuring that the inhuman practice of honour killings is seriously dealt with by all the concerned. It is gratifying to note that terming the practice of *khap panchayats* of handing down punishment to couples who go for 'sagotra' or inter-caste marriage as 'flagrant violation' of the law, the Law Commission of India came up with a draft legislation which seeks to make such acts a non-bailable offence. The draft Prohibition of Unlawful Assembly (interference with the freedom of matrimonial alliances) Bill, 2011, envisages that offences under the act will be cognisable, non-bailable and non-compoundable.[25] It is sincerely hoped that the Government of India takes an early decision in this regard in larger public interest.

Police Reforms in India and Judicial Activism

The Supreme Court has also paid attention to the issue of police reforms long overdue in India in a recent judgement. In *Prakash Singh vs Union of India*,[26] it has been averred that the violation of fundamental and human rights of the citizens are generally in the nature of non-enforcement and discriminatory application of the laws so that those having clout are not held accountable even for blatant violations of laws and, in any case, not brought to justice for the direct violations of the rights of citizens in the form of unauthorised detentions, torture, harassment, fabrication of evidence, malicious prosecutions and others. The petition sets out certain glaring examples of police inaction. According to the petitioners, the present distortions and aberrations in the functioning of the police have their roots in the Police Act of 1861, structure and organisation of police having basically remained unchanged all these years.

The petition sets out the historical background giving reasons why the police functioning has caused so much disenchantment and dissatisfaction. It also sets out recommendations of various committees, which were never implemented. The misuse and abuse of police has reduced it to the status of a mere tool in the hands of unscrupulous masters. In the process, it has caused serious violations of the rights of the people. It is contended that there is immediate need to re-define the scope and functions of police and provide for its accountability to the law of the land, and implement the core recommendations of the National Police Commission. The petition refers to a research paper, 'Political and Administrative Manipulation of the Police', published in 1979 by the Bureau of Police Research and Development (BPRD), warning that excessive control of the political executive and its principal advisers over the police has the inherent danger of making the police a tool for subverting the process of law, promoting the growth of authoritarianism, and shaking the very foundations of democracy.

The commitment, devotion and accountability of the police has to be only to the rule of law. The supervision and control has to be such that it ensures that the police serves the people without any regard, whatsoever, to the status and position of any person while investigating a crime or taking preventive measures. Its approach has to be service oriented, its role has to be defined so that in appropriate cases, where on account of acts of omission and commission of police, the rule of law becomes a casualty, the guilty police officers are brought to book and appropriate action taken without any delay.

The petitioners sought that Union of India be directed to re-define the role and functions of the police and frame a new police act on the lines of the model act drafted by the National Police Commission in order to ensure that the police is made accountable essentially and primarily to the law of the land and the people. Directions were also sought against the Union of India and state governments to constitute various commissions and boards laying down the policies and ensuring that police perform their duties and functions free from any pressure and also for separation of investigation work from that of law and order.

In this case, the court referred to the fact that for separation of investigation work from law and order even the Law Commission of India in its 154th Report[27] had recommended such separation to ensure speedier investigation, better expertise and improved rapport with the people without of course any water-tight compartmentalisation in view of both functions being closely inter-related at the ground level. The court laid down the following guidelines to be operative till the new legislation is enacted by the state governments deriving its strength from Article 32 read with Article 142 of the Constitution empowered the court to issue such guidelines:

(1) *State Security Commission*: The state governments are directed to constitute a State Security Commission in every state to ensure that the state government does not exercise unwarranted influence or pressure on the state police and for laying down the broad policy guidelines so that the state police always acts according to the laws of the land and the Constitution of the country.
(2) *Selection and Minimum Tenure of DGP*: The Director General of Police of the state shall be selected by the state government from amongst the three senior-most officers of the department who have been empanelled for promotion to that rank by the Union Public Service Commission on the basis of their length of service, very good record and range of experience for heading the police force. And, once he has been selected for the job, he should have a minimum tenure of at least two years irrespective of his date of superannuation.
(3) *Minimum Tenure of IG of Police and Other Officers*: Police officers on operational duties in the field such as the Inspector General of Police in-charge of Zone, Deputy Inspector General of Police in-charge of Range, Superintendent of Police (SP) in-charge of district and Station House Officer in-charge of a police station shall also have a prescribed minimum tenure of two years unless it is found necessary to remove them prematurely following disciplinary proceedings against them or their conviction in a criminal

offence or in a case of corruption or if the incumbent is otherwise incapacitated from discharging his responsibilities.

(4) *Separation of Investigation*: The investigating police shall be separated from the law and order police to ensure speedier investigation, better expertise and improved rapport with the people. It must, however, be ensured that there is full coordination between the two wings. The separation, to start with, may be affected in towns/urban areas which have a population of 10 lakh or more and gradually extended to smaller towns/urban areas also.

(5) *Police Establishment Board*: There shall be a Police Establishment Board in each state, which shall decide all transfers, postings, promotions and other service-related matters of officers of and below the rank of Deputy Superintendent of Police. The Establishment Board shall be a departmental body comprising the Director General of Police and four other senior police officers.

(6) *Police Complaints Authority*: There shall be a Police Complaints Authority at the district level to look into complaints against police officers of and up to the rank of Deputy Superintendent of Police. Similarly, there should be another Police Complaints Authority at the state level to look into complaints against officers of the rank of SP and higher. The district level authority may be headed by a retired District Judge, while the state level authority may be headed by a retired Judge of the High Court/Supreme Court.

(7) *National Security Commission*: The central government shall also set up a National Security Commission at the union level to prepare a panel for being placed before the appropriate appointing authority, for selection and placement of Chiefs of the Central Police Organisations (CPOs), who should also be given a minimum tenure of two years.

The commission would also review from time to time measures to upgrade the effectiveness of these forces, improve the service conditions of its personnel, ensure that there is proper coordination between them and that the forces are generally utilised for the purposes they were raised and make recommendations in that behalf. The National Security Commission could be headed by the Union Home Minister and comprise heads of the CPOs and a couple of security experts as members with the Union Home Secretary as its Secretary.

The court held that the aforesaid directions shall be complied with by the central government, state governments or union territories (UTs), as the case may be, on or before 31 December 2006 so that the bodies afore-noted became operational on the onset of the new year. The Cabinet Secretary, Government of India, and the Chief Secretaries of state governments/UTs were directed to file affidavits of compliance by 3 January 2007. It is really unfortunate that the central as well as the state governments have not fulfilled the above directions in toto. It can be safely said that the implementation of these guidelines would go a long way in protection of human rights of citizens as well as the police personnel to a great extent.

Compensation to the Victim of Crime and Response of Indian Courts

Criminal law has always discouraged the acts or omissions which in general can affect *right in rem* and violators have always been punished with strict sanctions but the crime rate is not falling and state is in regular quest to preserve social solidarity and peace in society. The initial focus of criminologists were only on the aspect of punishment but the focus started shifting when they were encountered with the fact that the person who is victim of crime is getting nothing out of the whole process of criminal justice system or is getting the so-called satisfaction by seeing the offender punished. Therefore, jurists and penologist in all countries started giving their full attention to the cause of victim in the form of compensation and hence the whole debate started about ways, means and extent of compensation.

There exist plethora of cases where the compensation has been awarded by the Supreme Court to the victims of the crime which not only present the heart full moments but also exposed the sorry state of affairs that has been prevalent in the lower courts even some times High Courts. It is better to examine cases under two heads, that is, (a) under CrPC and POA and (b) under

Indian Constitution in order to appreciate the judicial standpoint on this issue.

Under CrPC

Section 357 of the Criminal Procedure Code, 1973, provides some reliefs to the victims as the court is empowered to direct payment of compensation to any person for any loss or injury caused by the offence. But in practice the said provision has not proved to be of much effectiveness. Thus, the restorative and reparative theories are not translated into real benefits to the victims.[28]

There are a number of cases in which the courts in India directed payment of compensation to the crime victims. In the case of *Prabhu Prasad Sah vs State of Bihar*,[29] the court not only upheld the conviction of 15 years old boy (actually at the time of commission of crime the accused was of 15 years) but also observed that although requirements of social justice demands the imposition of heavy fine but, taking into consideration the condition of the accused awarded a fine of ₹ 3,000 to be paid by him to the children of the deceased. In another case of *Palaniappa Gounder vs State of Tamil Nadu*,[30] Supreme Court following the same view as of earlier not only reduced the amount of fine imposed by the High Court from ₹ 20,000 to ₹ 3,000 but also observed that:

> The Supreme Court has in a number of decisions directed the subordinate courts that 'requirement of social justice demands that heavy fines should be imposed on the accused who has the capacity to pay in lieu of reduction of sentence to compensate to the victims of crimes'.[31]

In the landmark case of *Sarwan Singh vs State of Punjab*[32] where supreme court not only retreated its previous standpoint but also laid down, in exhaustive manner, that what all should be taken into account while imposing fine or compensation. The Hon'ble Court observed that:

> The object of the section, therefore, is to provide compensation payable to the persons who are entitled to recover damage from the person sentenced even though fine does not form part of the sentence ... . If it is found that compensation should be paid,

> then the capacity of the accused to pay compensation has to be determined. In directing compensation, the object is to collect the fine and pay it to the person who has suffered the loss. The purpose will not be served if the accused is not able to pay the fine or compensation for, imposing a default sentence for non-payment of fine would not achieve the object. If the accused is in position to pay the compensation to the injured or his dependents to which they are entitled to, there could be no reason for the court not directing such compensation. When a person, who caused injury due to negligence or is made vicariously liable, is bound to pay compensation it is only appropriate to direct payment by the accused who is guilty of causing an injury with the necessary mens rea to pay compensation for the person who has suffered injury.

It may be noted that the 2008 Amendment Act has inserted a new Section 357A in the Code of Criminal Procedure, 1973, which contemplates a mechanism to provide compensation to the victims of crime. Under this provision, every state government in consultation with the central government shall prepare a scheme for providing compensation to victim or his dependents who have suffered loss as a result of the crime and who require rehabilitation. The District Legal Service Authority or the State Legal Service Authority shall decide the quantum of compensation after the recommendations made by the court.

Under Indian Constitution

The principle of payment of compensation to the victim of crime was evolved by the Supreme Court on the ground that it is the duty of the welfare state to protect the fundamental rights of the citizens not only against the actions of its agencies but is also responsible for compensating the victims. It maybe be noted that compensation by the state for the action of its official was evolved by the courts against the imperial and outdated doctrine of English law: 'King can do no wrong'.

Rudul Sah vs State of Bihar[33] is the most celebrated case where the Hon'ble Supreme Court directed the state to pay compensation of ₹ 35,000 to Rudul Sah who was kept in jail for 14 years even after his acquittal on the ground of insanity and held that it is violation of Article 21 done by the state of Bihar. The case of *Bhim Singh vs State of J&K*[34] is another important case where Bhim Singh, a Member of Legislative Assembly, was arrested by the police only to prevent him to attend the Legislative Assembly, the court not only entertained the writ petition of his wife but also awarded the compensation of ₹ 50,000 to be paid by the state. It has been clearly stated in *Nilabati Behera vs State of Orissa*[35] that doctrine of sovereign immunity is only applicable in the case of tortuous act of government servant and not where there is violation of fundamental rights and hence in a way stated that in criminal matters like causing custodial deaths and torture, this doctrine is not applicable. On the issue of brutal use of force and misuse of authority by the police outside the police station, case of *Saheli vs Commissioner of Police*[36] is landmark where son of Kamlesh Kumari died due to ill treatment by an SI of Delhi Police, the Hon'ble Supreme Court directed the Delhi Administration to pay the compensation of ₹ 75,000. In the case of *Bodhi Satta Gautam vs Subhra Chakraborty*[37] where the Hon'ble Supreme Court invented the concept of interim compensation and enforced the part third right against an individual. One can refer to the guidelines issued in *Delhi Domestic Working Women's Forum*[38] and *Hon'ble High Court of Gujarat*[39] cases also regarding the judicial activism in the case of payment of compensation to crime victims.

Encounter Killings by Police and Judicial Response

In recent years, the issue of fake encounter killings has been attracting the attention of the courts in India. Since most of these killings take place during the absence of any direct witnesses, proving whether they are genuine self-defence killings or fake encounter killings becomes very difficult. However, killing of any outlaw or accused by misusing the power vested in police is a serious human rights violation and needs unconditional condemnation. In *Prakash Kadam vs Ramprasad Vishwanath Gupta*,[40] the Supreme Court has recently held that where a fake encounter is proved against policemen in a trial, they must be given death sentence, treating it as the rarest of rare cases. In the instant case, responding to fake encounter killings by the police, Justice Markandey Katju observed as under:

> The accused/appellants are police personnel and it was their duty to uphold the law, but far from performing their duty, they appear to have operated as criminals. Thus, the protectors have become the predators. As the Bible says 'If the salt has lost its flavour, wherewith shall it be salted?', or as the ancient Romans used to say, 'Who will guard the Praetorian guards?'[41]

Conclusion

The above discussion relating to the role of the courts in laying down new guidelines and giving directives to the executive, though may not be exhaustive, shows that the Indian judiciary more importantly the higher courts have played an active role in humanisation of criminal justice system in India. However, there is an imminent necessity of matching enthusiasm on the part of all the stakeholders who are required to be more sensitive to the cause of human rights.

Notes

1. Under Article 22(1) and (2) of the Constitution, which read: 'Protection Against Arrest and Detention in Certain Cases: No person who is arrested shall be detained in custody without being informed, as soon as may be, of the grounds for such arrest nor shall he be denied the right to consult, and to be defended by, a legal practitioner of his choice. Every person who is arrested and detained in custody shall be produced before the nearest Magistrate within a period of twenty four hours of such arrest excluding the time necessary for the journey from the place of arrest to the court of the Magistrate and no such person shall be detained in custody beyond the said period without the authority of a Magistrate' (p. 1).
2. Chapter V relating to Arrest of Persons in Sections 41 to 60.
3. 1980 (3) SCR 855
4. AIR 1980 SC 1579
5. See http://www.hrdc.net/sahrdc/hrfeatures/HRF63.htm (last visited on 5 April 2012).
6. (1990) 3 SCC 119
7. AIR 1995 SC 31:1994 (6) SCC 260
8. [2010] INSC 340 (5 May 2010).

9. Article 39A of the Constitution of India provides that state shall secure that the operation of the legal system that promotes justice on a basis of equal opportunity and shall, in particular, provide free legal aid.
10. AIR 1982 SC 6: (1982)1 SCC 1
11. [1981] 1 SCC 608
12. AIR 1983 SC 378
13. AIR 1979 SC 1369
14. AIR 1986 SC 991
15. [2011] INSC 574 (dated 5 July 2011)
16. [2011] INSC 679 (5 August 2011)
17. (2002) 2 SCC 287
18. (2000) 5 SCC 488
19. (2009) 13 SCC 211
20. Decided on 7 July 2006, and available at http://www.indiankanoon.org/doc/1364215
21. Decided on 19 April 2011, and available at http://www.indiankanoon.org/doc/1337458
22. Para 16
23. Para 17
24. Decided on 9 May 2011 and available at http://www.indiankanoon.org/doc/1422914/
25. See http://www.indianexpress.com/news/law-commission-for-making-honour-killings-nonbailable-offence/901975/2 (dated 20 January 2012)
26. [2006] INSC 609 (22 September 2006)
27. Available at www.lawcommissionofindia.nic.in
28. It is relevant to note that Section 358 envisages payment of compensation to persons groundlessly arrested; and Section 359 an order to pay costs in non-cognisable cases.
29. AIR 1977 SC 704
30. AIR 1977 SC 1323
31. See *N. B. Panth vs State* (AIR 1977 SC 892), *Sarwan Singh vs State of Punjab* (AIR 1978 SC 1525) and *Guru Swami vs Tamil Nadu* (AIR 1979 SC 1177).
32. AIR 1978 SC 1525
33. AIR 1983 SC 1086
34. (1985) 4 SCC 677

35. AIR 1993 SC 1960
36. AIR 1990 SC 513
37. (1996) 1 SCC 490
38. 1995 (1) SCC 14
39. Decided on 24 September 1998, and available at http://www.indiankanoon.org/doc/1899469/
40. (2011) 6 SCC 189
41. Also see in this connection the judgement of Supreme Court in *CBI vs Kishore Singh*, Criminal Appeal Nos. 2047-2049 decided on 25 October 2010, available at http://indiankanoon.org/doc/1473938/

3

Police and Human Rights Observance

Dilemmas and Interventions

Chaitanya Pradeep Nemalikanti

After the independence, the priorities of the Indian state has changed from maintaining law and order to welfare state. This has resulted the change in rulers and governance, accordingly the functional policy of the state required to ensure change in the policing approach. Organisationally and functionally police administration in India subscribes to an administrative philosophy of negativism (Mishra 1971, p. i). It means administration does not feel accountable to the people for its activities. Notwithstanding to this, the Constitution of India has laid great stress on human rights and dignity and made the state governments accountable for enforcing laws in this connection (Constitution of India 1950: Article 246). The Supreme Court of India, in the case of *D.K. Basu vs State of West Bengal* (1997)[1], stated:

> whenever the human dignity is wounded, civilization takes a step backward. The flag of humanity on each such occasion must fly at half-mast. In such a milieu of enduring colonial structure, diffused democratic control, varied work responsibilities, and lack of professionalism in functional policing have

> increasingly become an object of ridicule and a source of threat to democratic governance and human rights. (Madhava Meenon 1997, p. 24)

As a result, sensitising the police has become an urgent need of the day and in this context, HRE has been observed as an instrument to change the approach of policing.

Approaches of HRE to the Police

From United Nations Commission on Human Rights to National Human Rights Commission (NHRC), police training colleges and academies are taking the assistance of HRE to sensitise the police. The UN has developed HRE materials for the schools, professional organisations, journalists, community groups and local human rights organisations and NGOs. Radio and television broadcasts have taken up some highly inventive and entertaining soap operas or song contests illustrating human rights principles, which also flourish on the airwaves of many countries (William 2004, p. 9). But the concerns of the HRE still remained unfulfilled. According to Haragopal and Sudarshanam (2005), 'human rights education has to grapple with three important concerns; one, clarification of contemporary civilization dilemmas; two, intergenerational transmission of experience; and three, acceleration of the process of transformation' (p. 110). Edwin Delattre (1996) aptly said, what is taught by the academies about ideals should be woven into the realities of the streets. Besides, police officers have to be motivated by a value system with practical examples picked from their own experiences. Otherwise, skills and knowledge gained by the police officers may not be sustained in the long run.

On the other hand, United Nations Human Rights Council has held that 'human rights training programme should have a link with organisational policy of the police system'. Further, the council has mentioned that training is:

> to produce the desired impact on behavioral and professional performance; it must be clearly supported by, and linked to corresponding rules in police training institutions. Institutional policy must reflect the human rights imperatives taught in the

classroom, and management must be trained in and committed to ensuring its application. (Human Rights Training 2000, p. 2)

Thus, it can be understood that human rights training programme is designed for police need to reduce the gap between human rights norms and flexibility in its application.

According to Andhra Pradesh Police Manual (APPM), the law enforcing agency especially the police should be trained in 'human rights' of the citizens, and they should be educated to observe human rights during their day-to-day transaction (APPM 2011, p. 1051). One of the duties of Human Rights Cell (at Director General of Police [DGP, Chief of Police Staff] office, Andhra Pradesh, India) is to coordinate police training colleges/schools with the state academic institutions to ensures that their in-service training curriculum has sufficient elements of human rights jurisprudence for the trainees of all ranks. Such a module would aim at educating and sensitising police personnel. It is expected that 'a growing awareness will reduce these violations and this is possible by educating the law enforcing officers in human rights area'.

One of the important concerns of the HRE is accelerating the process of human transformation towards sensitivity. Any training programme on HRE without targeting the change in the pattern of police behaviour may remain a failed attempt. In academics, it is strongly assumed that the present human rights training offered to the police is not adequately focussed to 'transform' the trainees to deliver sensitive policing. Currently, there is a criticism on the existing human rights curriculum that it would not aim at developing a 'positive approach' towards human rights in the minds of the police. The 'positive approach', which can be called as 'humanistic', emphasises on transformation of the individual, group, society, state and global order. In fact, all these are structurally interconnected. It believes that this transformation can be achieved by providing not only a critical understanding of the past but also the contemporary socio-economic conditions. It focusses on the issues of injustice and inequality. It takes an open position in favour of the disadvantaged and suffering. Here, a transformed police is expected to be concerned towards the disadvantaged and underprivileged sections in the society. This positive approach makes the learner sensitive to the suffering and sees that the human consciousness deepens and gets grounded in concrete reality. Finally, this approach emphasises on values such as equality, freedom, peace and justice. It brings awareness to the learner on noble potentialities of human nature. It covers the subjective and objective factors. The subjective factors include the inner sense of a human being, which is very important to the police, and the objective factors include the form of dominance in social domain in human relations. Further, it is contended that the police are having some sort of superiority complex compared to other sections. This complex can be diluted through this positive approach.

Institutional Mechanisms Observing Human Rights in India

Broadly, there exist two types of mechanisms to observe human rights. These can be categorised into preventive mechanisms and corrective mechanisms. 'Preventive mechanisms' means institutions which aim to restraint the persons/groups from violating the human rights through bringing awareness among different sections of the government as well as society. They include police training colleges, NGOs and academic institutions. Corrective mechanisms are the institutions that mostly respond after the incidents of human rights violations have taken place. They include NHRC, State Human Rights Commissions (SHRCs), National Commission for Scheduled Castes, National Commission for Scheduled Tribes, Human Rights Cell, Women Protection Cell and Child Protection Cell at DGP office. Among them NHRC has the experience of practicing both preventive and corrective activities. As part of its preventive activities NHRC disseminates HRE to all the sections of the society as well as bureaucracy by offering funds to conduct training programmes, seminars and workshops. Besides, it also responds to the complaints registered against police officers with regard to violation of human rights. Table 3.1 specifies the present status of complaints filed and departmental action taken against the police staff.

Table 3.1

Complaints registered against police on human rights violations

Years	*No. of complaints received/alleged during the year*	*Against whom disciplinary action initiated by the department*	*Major punishment awarded by the department*	*Minor punishment awarded by the department*
2011	61,765	26,736	4,482	15,004
2012	57,363	23,720	4,199	11,900
2013	51,120	24,217	3,980	13,729
2014	47,774	29,726	4,637	12,549
2015	54,916	35,240	3,754	14,249

Source: Crime in India Report (2015), National Crime Records Bureau, Ministry of Home Affairs, Government of India.

A total of 54,916 complaints were registered in the country against police personnel during the year 2015. Inquiries were instituted in as many as 16,721 cases. Out of these, departmental inquiries were initiated in 16,308 cases, magisterial inquiries in 94 cases and judicial inquiries in 319 cases. Thus, inquiries were instituted in 30.4 per cent of total such complaints. The total number of cases that either not substantiated or not found true were 20,405, which amounted to 37.2 per cent of the total complaints registered. An increase of 14.9 per cent was noticed in registered complaints against police personnel in comparison to the previous year (from 47,774 in the year 2014 to 54,916 in 2015). Maximum complaints against police personnel were received in Delhi, which accounted for 23.5 per cent (12,913 out of 54,916 complaints) followed by Madhya Pradesh accounting for 18.4 per cent (10,089 complaints), Maharashtra 14.6 per cent (8,004 complaints) and Uttar Pradesh 8.5 per cent (4,659 complaints). The magnitude of departmental action taken by the states/UTs against the erring police personnel indicates effectiveness of supervisory control of the concerned authorities. Disciplinary actions were initiated against 35,240 police personnel. Enquires were conducted against 18,876 police personnel during the year. The cases were either withdrawn or otherwise disposed of regarding 5,523 police officers. After completion of enquiries 447 police personnel were either dismissed or removed from the service. The highest dismissals/removals were reported from Delhi (69) accounting for 15.4 per cent followed by Punjab (63), Uttar Pradesh (49) and Chhattisgarh (35). There were 447 police personnel dismissed or removed from services. Further, minor punishments were given to 14,249 police personnel and major punishments were awarded to 3,754 police personnel as part of departmental action during 2015. In 4,514 departmental enquiries, charges were not proved, and departmental enquiries regarding 8,864 police personnel were pending at the end of 2015. As per the data of Crime in India Report, 2015, from 1999 to 2015, information on details of cases where human rights were violated by police were mostly in the form of excesses such as 'disappearance of persons', 'illegal detentions', 'fake encounters', 'extortion' and 'torture'.

In order to control the damage, central government has constituted Police Act Drafting Committee (PADC) to propose a 'model' police act to replace the outdated act enacted in 1861. The proposed Model Police Bill, 2006, has strongly emphasised on the Constitution of Police Accountability Commission (PAC). Perhaps, BPRD has been modifying the draft police act from time to time and the latest draft bill is called the Model Police Bill, 2015. Following this, state government shall within three months of coming into effect of this bill establish a state-level PAC. The PAC will inquire into public complaints supported by sworn statement against the police personnel for serious misconduct. The commission shall have five members with a credible record of integrity and commitment to human rights (The Model Police Bill, 2006, see Orders 159 and 160). However, any of the aforesaid recommendations made by PADC were never seriously contemplated by the state governments. The establishment of PAC is again subject to commitment levels of state governments to adopt and enact the proposed Model Police Bill. As per the Press Information Bureau (see www.pib.nic.in, press release on 22 July 2015), so far 15 states, namely Assam, Bihar, Chhattisgarh, Haryana, Himachal Pradesh, Kerala, Maharashtra, Meghalaya, Mizoram, Punjab, Rajasthan, Sikkim, Tamil Nadu, Tripura and Uttarakhand have formulated their State Police Act and two states, namely, Gujarat and Karnataka have amended their existing Police Act. Thus, a total 17 state governments have either formulated their state police acts or amended the existing one.

The Ideal of Crime Control versus the Ideal of Due Process

For any democratic state, the over-arching goal of police reforms is to move from a model of policing based on repression and social control to a model based on prevention and investigation (Neild 1998, p. 11). Further initiatives on police reforms need to recognise that change in the existing culture or ethos of an organisation is never easy. Accordingly, police training should be broadened with a view of developing police officers with a better understanding of their role in relation to total organisational goals and better understanding of the means. This important aspect has been widely neglected by the police training institutions in India (Sen 1999). As a result, a serious role conflict existed between their 'role of action-oriented crime fighter' and 'the role of service-oriented public servant' (Delattre 1996). This conflict between being a crime fighter versus being a public servant is what causes a police sub-culture to exist. Packer (1968) has defined the underlying conflict as one between the ideals of crime control versus the ideals of due process. The reason why it is hard to find the middle ground in such a role conflict situation can be described as the problem of 'utilitarian limits'. With the ideal of due process, the means to an end must always be justified, hence limiting the 'any means necessary' mode of thought with the ideal of crime control. Further, during the police training, the point has to be stressed that adherence to human rights norms will enable the police to discharge their legal functions more effectively and competently.

Committees, Commissions and Reforms in the Area of Police Training

Few commissions have been laid down in connection with reforms in the area of police training. They are Committee on Police Training (CPT, 1971), popularly known as the Gore Committee,[2] National Police Commission (1979–1981), Ribeiro Commission (1998) and Padmanabhaiah Commission (2000). Besides, some state governments have also constituted commissions on the issues relating to police training. Among all committees laid by both central and state governments, it is the Gore Committee which has strongly insisted the importance of HRE for the police. One of the major recommendations of the committee was to enlarge the content of police training from law and order maintenance to understanding of human behaviour. Unfortunately, the successive governments have never seriously considered the recommendations of the commission.

However, several commissions have observed 'corruption' as one of the causative factors in policing which directly results into human rights violation. In this regard, the National Police Commission (hereinafter referred to as 'NPC') held that the nexus between financially powerful groups and political power existing in India has a direct link to inequitable policing practices. Mollified exercise of power at different levels in the police is induced by such links. The problem of police corruption cannot, therefore, be satisfactorily tackled unless these links are broken (National Police Commission 1980, Third Report, p. 97). According to the Model Police Bill, 2006, 'the training policy shall aim at achieving the objectives of imparting knowledge in police subjects, developing of professional skills, inculcating the "right attitudes", and promoting constitutional and ethical values among police personnel' (Order No. 138). The bill has insisted on the curricula and persisted for the initial as well as the annual refresher training courses, besides physical skills and fitness, and held that state governments shall lay due emphasis on the knowledge of constitutional and legal rights of the citizens. But, these recommendations are not taken seriously by any state government. In this regard, a study has been conducted to explore to what extent HRE can enhance the level of the police personnel's adherence to the human rights norms.

About the Study

The fundamental problem regarding the police today is how to sensitise officers to work according to the objectives of the system by upholding the constitutional rights and liberty of the people.[3] However, police training colleges/academies at state and national level are offering human rights courses to the police officers of different rank and profile to inculcate the human rights values. In this regard, the present chapter examines to what extent HRE training can sensitise the police. For this purpose, the study has selected APPA in order to examine the impact of HRE on the perception of the police officers. The present study focusses on SI rank officers who have been observed as kingpins at cutting-edge level in the police administration. The study compares the perception of SI rank officers about human rights in general and the HRE training being received from APPA, India. Further, the study also compares the perceptions of the cadet SIs and in-service SIs in order to know the impact of their experience on framing their perception on human rights.

Approach of APPA towards HRE: Overview

APPA was established in 1986 and became functional in 1993. The Quality Audit Team of the Government of India has rated the academy as the 'bench mark institution' for the police training in the country. It is also recognised as the Regional Training Centre by the National Crime Records Bureau and conducts courses on behalf of Narcotic Control Bureau, NHRC, BPRD, Bureau of Civil Aviation and Security and International Committee of Red Cross from time to time. To educate the police in human rights issues, APPA is offering an optional course entitled 'Police Functions and Human Rights' for its trainees. But it is being offered as an optional course not as a compulsory subject. As a result of its 'optional' status, the trainees are not showing interest to opt the course. It is observed that teaching philosophical foundations through theories and concepts help the trainer to inculcate the values and virtues of human rights. This lack of such an approach in teaching may cause a sense of fear in the minds of police trainees. The existing methodology followed by APPA may not be able to clarify the dilemma of police trainees over 'observing the human rights norms'. It is doubtful to say that it can influence the attitude as well as behavioural patterns of the police. In this connection, a field study has been carried out to know to what extent HRE can sensitise the police. The chapter also tries to interrogate the perspective of police officers towards observing human rights.

Data Collection Procedure

In order to find out the impact of service on the perceptions of respondents, a comparative study has been conducted between stipendiary cadet SIs and in-service SI trainees of civil police. For this purpose, APPA has been selected. Study has focussed only on SI rank because they are the officers who come into a continuous contact with the public. Besides, this rank occupies the first level of the supervision and most visible to the public eye (Joshi 1993, p. 106). Data was collected from a total sample of 80 respondents, which include 40 probationary cadet SIs and another 40 in-service SIs. All the respondents of probationers and in-service trainee SIs are selected based on a snowball sampling method and all are coincidentally male. The size of the total sample was fixed according to the total number of officer undergoing training as cadet SIs, that is 300, and in-service SIs, that is 200. Confidentiality and anonymity were guaranteed and all participation was voluntary.

For the purposes of the fieldwork, a questionnaire was designed, which included both open-ended and closed-ended questions. Open-ended questions were used to probe the responses given in the closed-ended questions. The questionnaire used in this study was divided into four sections, which include (a) personal profile, (b) general knowledge on human rights, (c) police training academy approach on human rights training and (d) need for human rights training for police. The questionnaire includes a total of 50 questions. The respondents answered on a five-point Likert-type scale, ranging from one (do not agree with the statement) to five (strongly agree with the statement). The organisational commitment scale included three reverse-scored questions. To further examine the reliability of the instrument, Cronbach coefficient alpha (Cronbach and Suppes 1969) were conducted on the Likert-type questions. Cronbach's alpha reliability coefficient was derived through a statistical programme—SPSS. Out of 40 probationers, 60 per cent of them are in between 20 and 24 years age group and remaining 40 per cent falls in the age group of 25–28 years. Among in-service SIs, 20 per cent are between the age group of 22–30 years with 5–10 years of experience. Another 20 per cent of the respondents are in the age group of 31–40 years. Greater part of the respondents, that is, 60 per cent belong to 40 years and above with more than 20 years of experience.

Police Officers' Knowledge on Human Rights in General

'Human rights means the rights relating to life, liberty, equality and of the individual guaranteed by the Constitution or embodied in the international covenants and enforceable by courts in India' (under Section 2, Protection of Human Rights Act, 1993). These rights are legally protected; they focus on the dignity of the human being; they cannot be waived/taken away; they are equal and independent; they are universal. To experience police officers' knowledge on human rights, general questions such as defining human rights and organisations promoting human rights, such as UDHR, International Covenants and NHRC were put forward. The responses show that majority of both probationary and in-service respondents have good understanding on the basics of human rights. Seventy-three per cent of both groups viewed the right to equality as the most important right compared to other rights. However, both respondents have poor (15%) knowledge on UDHR, international covenants and international organisations working on human rights, and almost all the in-service trainees have poor understanding about international covenants. Their awareness level is less than one-third of its total. No in-service officer is aware of international covenants. Even probationers have only basic knowledge on these agencies. Inference can be drawn that training institution has not given adequate emphasis on international human rights law.

Police Officers' View on NHRC

NHRC is constituted under Section 3 of Protection of Human Rights Act, 1993. The main function of NHRC is to spread awareness on human rights to different sections, including civil servants particularly to the police (Section 12(h) of Protection of Human Rights Act 1993). In addition, the act enables the Constitution of SHRCs and human rights courts for better protection of human rights at state level. Broadly, it monitors, investigates and inquires into the matters of human rights violations, at centre as well as state level. In this regard, questions were asked on the concept of human rights, and their views on human rights monitoring bodies such as NHRC. However, 50 per cent of both respondents are aware of organisations working c. HRE. On the other hand, 80 per cent of in-service police officers referred NHRC as an agency which investigates into the complaints registered against police officers. They do not know that NHRC is meant to conduct awareness programmes on human rights for police.

On Practicing Sensitive Policing

The next question put forth was 'whether police have to be sensitive while dealing with all the cases?' The responses show that more than 80 per cent of the probationers have strongly expressed their willingness to be sensitive and felt that police must be sensitive towards human rights particularly towards marginalised sections. They further said police are not supposed to violate the rights under any circumstances. Contrarily, 60 per cent in-services officers have disagreed this view and felt that sensitivity has to be applied according to the type of the case. Further they felt that it is difficult to adhere to human rights norms while dealing with the hard-core/habitual criminals. However, 'initially, we approach everyone in a polite manner and then if the suspect/accused is not cooperating with the case then we will apply rough and rude methods', one of the respondents mentioned. It can be understood from the responses of in-service officers that adherence to human rights norms are subject to the type of suspect/accused they interact with. It is understood that probationary officers are more sensitive towards human rights than that of their counterparts. Interestingly, majority of the in-service officers have expressed their desire to be sensitive but they said finally it is the circumstance that determines the investigation procedure. It infers that the more police get exposed to the field the more they become insensitive towards human rights.

Views on Affiliation of PTAs with Academic Institutions

CPT (1972) held that Police Training Academies (PTAs) need to affiliate with academic institutions to give more exposure to the officers on sensitive issues from different dimensions. In fact, currently, several academic institutions are now concentrating towards promoting HRE. Numerous studies have expressed that there is a difference between the teaching methods of police training colleges and academic institutions. It is also observed that uncompetitive culture among police trainees and narrow approach in syllabi are major implications in police training college. In this regard, views were invited from the respondents about the existing training curriculum and also their interest to associate with academic institutions for training in human rights. Majority (80%) of both groups have strongly viewed that 'by affiliating with academic institutions like Universities will definitely improve their understanding levels of human rights awareness'. Further, the respondents expressed that academic and value-oriented approach, in terms of the evolution of the concept of human rights training and historical need of human rights awareness, was missing in the existing curriculum. According to them, human rights course at police academy was taught by public prosecutors and their classes were more legal and descriptive oriented. As a result, instead of becoming sensitive towards human rights they are developing apprehensions and dilemmas over the concept of human rights. Thus, it can be inferred that majority of the trainees are not completely satisfied on the existing human rights course being offered by APPA. Therefore, respondents preferred to have affiliation with academic institutions so that the very purpose of undergoing human rights training can be served positively.

On the Lack of HR Awareness

There is an assumption that lack of HRE is a strong reason for majority of human rights violations carried out by police. It is projected that awareness brings positive attitude to practice sensitivity. In this regard, few questions were put forth to know their opinions on the same. The responses show that majority of respondents of both groups (75% probationers; 60% in-service) expressed that 'lack of human rights awareness is the main cause for the violation of human rights by the police'. Contrarily, 40 per cent of in-service officers strongly opposed the assumption and said besides lack of awareness, there are some other factors like manpower shortage, bad working conditions, too much of bossism, pressure from politicians, over expectations of the public (which in turn creates pressure on police performance) forces them to adopt shot-cut methods which lead to human rights violations. From the above, it can be stated that probationers have strong belief in the assumption that says 'human rights awareness will prevent the police from violating the human rights', whereas 40 per cent of in-service officers opined that apart from lack of human rights awareness there are organisational factors that are determining the application of human rights norms.

Another question put forth to know the impact of HRE on police trainees. The responses indicate that both probationers and in-service trainees had a common perception and said HRE will help to avoid violations of human rights by the police. When the researcher probed further, 58 per cent of in-service officers expressed their doubt whether this feel of sensitivity will transform into behaviour or not. However, all in-service trainees have expressed a positive perception and said HRE brought attitudinal change towards human rights.

On Balancing the Ideal of Due Process and Crime Control

Another question was administered to the respondents on the possibility of balancing due process (adherence to human rights norms) and crime control. Here, most of the probationers asserted that crime detention is possible by strictly following human rights norms. Contrarily, majority of in-service officers uttered human rights norms as 'stumbling blocks' in the process of crime detention. Therefore, it is not possible to pursue human rights norms strictly with all types of cases. According to the respondents, police encounter problems especially when they deal with accused persons involved in theft recovery cases and hard-core/habituated criminals. Statistically, only 30 per cent of the respondents expressed their confidence in crime detection and 50 per cent said they cannot deal especially with theft recovery (gold armaments) cases and hard-core criminal by strictly adhering to human rights norms. Further, they said, it is not easy to extract the truthful information from the accused by strictly observing the human rights norms. In a sense, if police concentrate on 'due processes then the task of "crime control" needs to be compromised'. It is also found from the responses that attitude developed from experience is more influential than that of inputs they received during human rights training. It means that human rights training provided to the police is not clarifying the dilemmas raised from the experience. As a result, in-service officers are not so confident on balancing due process and crime control.

On Rights of Accused and Victims

Police are facing frequent allegations on violation of the rights of the accused persons. In this regard, few questions were put forth to know their knowledge levels and perceptions towards the rights of accused and victims. Responses show that the awareness of in-service officers about the rights of the accused and the victims is higher (82.6%) than that of probationary officers (60%). But on the issues of 'right to get speedy investigation and trial' equal percentage (65%) of both categories of respondents have expressed that accused persons have no rights to get speedy investigation and trial. Further respondents argued that the process of investigation depends on availability of evidence, sophisticated scientific tools and public cooperation. It can be inferred that in-service officers are negative about the rights of accused. Surprisingly, 30 per cent of probationers and 40 per cent of in-service officers are not at all aware of the right to do cross-examination by the accused. The question rises here is, how one can expect that a person who is not aware of the rights of accused will protect the same? This will lead to violation of rights of the accused. Further study found that the awareness levels of police in-service officers towards the rights SCs and STs are high (30%) compare with the rights of the accused. It is observed that in-service officers are more sensitive towards the rights of the victims than the rights of the accused.

Observation and Conclusion

One of the objectives behind providing human rights training to the police is to clarify the dilemmas raised out of their experience.

Conversely, human rights training provided to the police at APPA is creating more ambiguity. Majority of in-service officers raised doubts on the viability of observing human rights norms and said 'we are struggling to strike a balance between human rights norms and crime control especially with theft recovery cases', one of the respondent claimed. According to them, human rights norms cannot be made applicable to accused persons with hard-core/habitual criminal background. Otherwise the task of getting reliable information will become tough, which further causes delay in the process of investigation and it increases the caseload, and finally it becomes an issue of police inefficiency. Not only that increased caseload creates stress, which in turn causes human rights violation.

Experienced police officers think that perceiving human rights as 'being "soft" on crime or as "coddling" criminals' need to be changed. Police officers strongly believe that sensitive policing will lead to greater criminality or somehow undermine police effectiveness. This study found four reasons in this regard. First, in-service officers are typically prejudiced towards human rights norms that adherence to human rights will undermine police efficiency; second, inadequate importance to human rights awareness by the police training colleges; third, the methodology on human rights taught as part of the human rights training programmes altogether leaves negative impression among the trainees; fourth, police officers' subjective impression towards the rights of the accused. It is also understood from the responses that human rights awareness of the police is being dominated by their own inhuman work experience. To bring change in police attitude an utmost support should be given to human rights training. Human rights training academic institutions dedicated to HRE, NHRC and SHRC and state police academies need to work together to design the syllabus which clarifies dilemmas raised by the police officers through integrating the human rights perspective (HRP) and crime control perspective by revising code of conduct and sensitising oversight bodies. Most of the police officers knew that they are not supposed to torture, extract bribe and become involved in human rights violation. Therefore, mere increased knowledge of rights will not change the police behaviour unless human rights training inculcate the ideal of due process among police officers which says that the means to an end must always be justified.

For this purpose, the experience of senior police personnel relating to upholding the human rights norm can be tapped for the benefit of the listeners. Otherwise police trainees will see the human rights training centres as spoon-feeding, school teaching approach, military approach or *bhashan*.[4] In this context, it is very important to ensure collegial atmosphere, which offers the exchange of expertise, as acknowledging their professional experience. Besides, a heavy responsibility rests on the shoulders of the senior police management to explicate its officers that 'any-means-necessary' mode of thought with the ideal of crime control will harm the police image. Adherence to the due process will help the police to build better and stronger relationship with the community.

Notes

1. *Basu, D.K. vs State of West Bengal* (1997). [1997(1)SCC416], Supreme Court of India.
2. Professor M.S. Gore, former Director of the Tata Institute of Social Sciences Bombay, was Chairman of CPT and perhaps the first commission laid to study the quality and conditions of Police Training Schools and colleges/academies in India.
3. As noted in the Preamble to the First Report of the National Police Commission (February 1979).
4. *Bhashan* (speech), a word used by police mostly in the context of inapplicability (negative sense).

References

Cronbach, L.J. and Suppes, P. (1969). 'Research for Tomorrow's Schools: Disciplined Inquiry for Education'. Report of the Committee on Educational Research of the National Academy of Education. New York: MacMillan.

Delattre, E. (1996). *Character and Cops: Ethics in Policing.* 3rd Edition. Washington, DC: American Enterprise Institute.

Haragopal, G., and Sudarshanam G. (2005). 'Human Rights Education in India, Concepts and Concerns'. *Journal of National Human Rights Commission*, 4, 110–121.

Human Rights Training (2000). *A Manual on Human Rights Training Methodology*. New York/Geneva: United Nations Publications.

Joshi, R.P. (1993). *Police Training in Community Relations*. Jaipur: Rawat Publications.

Madhava Meenon, N.R. (1997). *A Training Manual for Police on Human Rights*. National Law School of India University, Bangalore: National Printing Press, p. 24.

Neild, Rachel (1998). *Police Training: Themes and Debates in Public Security Reform-A Manual for Civil Society* (Washington Office on Latin America).

Packer, H. (1968). *The Limits of the Criminal Sanction*. Palo Alto, CA: Stanford University Press.

Sen, Sankar (1999). 'Police Training in India', *CBI Bulletin*.

William G. O' Neil (2004). *Police Reform and Human Rights*. New York: A HURIST Document.

Part II

Human Rights and Civil Society

4

Human Rights NGOs in Manipur

Contexts, Roles and Challenges

Khaikholen Haokip

Located at the far north-eastern corner of India, Manipur is a land in which human rights have been under continual threat for more than five decades now. The complexities of ethnic politics, history and prioritisation of national security over human security continue to cast doubt on whether the people's rights can be realised in a practical sense. In particular, the issues connected with the contentious merger of the princely kingdom of Manipur with the union of India in 1948 have proved to be a great challenge to whether human rights can be fully attained. Ethnic-nationalist or self-determination movements and their coercive suppressions by the Indian state, inter-ethnic conflicts and perceived or real inequitable distribution of resources have all contributed to existing tensions that invariably spill over into human rights crisis (Hassan 2008).

Against such a political backdrop and fragile human rights situation in the state, there has been a mushrooming of non-governmental organisations committed to the protection of human rights. The current study provides a descriptive and analytical treatment of this human rights NGO community in terms of their origins, roles and challenges. The importance of studying this domestic human rights NGO community in the state is twofold. First, since the mid-1980s, there has been a gradual shift in the international human rights movement from an era of human rights standard setting to an era of human rights enforcement. Domestic human rights NGOs are crucial to the societal monitoring of human rights enforcement at the local level. Second, the extant literature on human rights movement has overwhelmingly focussed on the vital roles played by international human rights NGOs in the protection and promotion of human rights, with little attention on domestic human rights NGOs.

The current study attempts to fill this gap by focussing on the domestic human rights NGOs in Manipur. This domestic human rights NGO community constitutes the mainstay of the human rights movement in the state, seeking to hold the state and its agencies accountable to their human rights obligations. In order to acquire data, qualitative semi-standardised interviews with the top functionaries and subordinate staffs of the case study organisations have been conducted. In addition, various reports published by the NGOs, containing their mandates, activities and strategies they adopted, have also been examined. The selection of the case study organisations was guided by purposive sampling to ensure that organisations representing different ethnic groups in the state are included in the study.

The chapter is divided into five main sections. The first section provides a contextual socio-political background of the emergence of the human rights movement in Manipur. It provides a background overview of the sub-nationalist movements, the responses of the Indian state and the fragile human rights climate in the state. The second section introduces the concept and practice of human rights NGOs. The third section profiles the case study organisations in terms of the origins and general characteristics. The fourth section deals with the various roles played by these organisations in the protection and promotion of human rights—the issues they focus and the strategies they adopt. The fifth section sheds light on the key issues and challenges faced by the organisations. Then it concludes with a summary discussion on the major findings.

The Contextual Background

Manipur is home to three main groups—the Meiteis, Nagas and Kukis. While the Meiteis live in the Imphal valley, the ethnic Naga and Kuki tribes co-exist in the hill areas of the state. The state is regarded as one of the most-conflict prone and unstable states in the North-East. Each of the state's three main ethnic groups has its own insurgent organisations. There are about 40 insurgent organisations operating in the state—15 active and 25 inactive (Baruah 2007). Seven out of these 40 organisations are declared as terrorist organisations by the Indian government under the Unlawful Activities (Prevention) Act, 1967. The primary causal factor of ethnic insurgencies in the state can be attributed to the resistance offered by the state's indigenous ethnic groups against their integration into the post-colonial Indian state. Another important factor is their disenchantment with the territorial arrangements that placed them and their territories into (a) different political divisions (states) within India and (b) both sides of the two nation-states, India and Burma.

Meitei insurgency is rooted in the controversial integration of Manipur, a princely state during the colonial British rule, into the Indian union in 1949. The various Meitei nationalist groups held that the then King of Manipur, Maharaja Bodhachandra, was made to sign the merger agreement with the post-colonial Indian government under duress. They termed the agreement as unconstitutional and a denial of their right to self-determination (Tarapot 1993). This disenchantment led to the birth of the first Meitei insurgent organisation, United National Liberation Front (UNLF) in 1964, with the objective of liberating Manipur from Indian union. Similarly, the Naga movement for independence began in neighbouring Nagaland way back in 1929 and later spread out to Naga-inhabited hill areas of Manipur. The Naga Club, formed at Kohima in 1918, submitted a memorandum to the Simon Commission in 1929, demanding self-governance for the Nagas (Chaube 1999). The movement further intensified with the formation of the Naga National Council (NNC) in 1946. However, its coercive suppression by the Indian state drove the NNC underground and led to the birth of Naga insurgency in the mid-1950s.

Kuki insurgency in post-independence India is a relatively recent phenomenon, compared to Meitei and Naga insurgencies. However, the Kukis began their struggle for self-governance during the colonial period itself. In the Kuki uprising (1917–1919), the Kukis fought against the intrusion of colonial British into their lands that began in the 1770s (Chisti 2005). Later in 1946, as the departure of the colonial British from India became imminent, the Kukis organised themselves under the banner of Kuki National Assembly (KNA), demanding a separate Kuki statehood under post-colonial Indian state. However, the continued indifference of the Indian state drove a section of the Kuki nationalists to launch armed struggles in the late 1980s for a separate Kuki homeland. The KNA and the Kuki National Front, both formed in the year 1988, are the two oldest Kuki insurgent organisations in Manipur (Haokip 1993).

The Indian state's policy towards the aforementioned ethnic insurgencies in Manipur has largely been informed by that of the law and order approach. This approach has led the Indian state to rely on its various coercive apparatuses to suppress the Naga insurgents (Srikanth 2005), having severe negative consequences for the human rights of the people. The army forces were heavily deployed to quell the Naga insurgency and, later, other ethnic insurgencies in the North-East. Manipur, in fact, also has the highest density of security forces in the country. With a population of a mere 2.5 million, Manipur has approximately 64,000 security personnel being deployed in the state (Sharma 2008). This works out at one security personnel for every 40 civilians indicating the extent of militarisation of the state. Several draconian laws, such as the AFSPA, 1958, which provides legal immunity to the armed forces, were also promulgated to empower the armed forces in the state. A bulk of human rights violations in the state are seen as stemming from the abuses of power under the AFSPA. As Sanjib Baruah (2007) observes, 'Although not every accusation of torture, rape, or extrajudicial killings is true, there can be little doubt that AFSPA creates conditions for abuse'.

However, the violence in Manipur has not simply been between the Indian State and the insurgent groups. There has also been a history of latent or open conflicts along the ethnic cleavages in the state: (a) between the valley dwelling Meiteis and the hill tribes; and (b) between various ethnic tribal groups. The conflict between the Meiteis and the hill tribes centres on the issues of Sixth Schedule, territorial integration and dominance, and land reforms. The Meiteis have consistently opposed the demand of the hill tribes for the extension of the Sixth Schedule in the hill areas of Manipur. Besides the Sixth Schedule, the Meiteis have also regarded the Naga movement for integration of Naga-inhabited areas of Manipur with the neighbouring Nagaland state and the Kukis' demand for a separate Kuki state as threats to the territorial integrity of Manipur. On the other hand, the Meiteis' move to extend the Manipur Land Revenue and Land Reforms Act 1960 in the hill areas of the state is fiercely resisted by the hill tribes as they see the act as a threat to their traditional land ownership systems (McDuie-Ra 2005). The ethnic conflicts between the various hill tribes of the state were also primarily the result of overlapping territorial claims and identity politics. The Kuki-Naga conflict in the early 1990s and the Thadou-Paite conflict in the mid-1990s had led to the death and displacement of thousands of peoples on all sides.

Human Rights NGOs: Conceptual Terrain

Human rights NGOs are a sub-category of a phenomenon of non-governmental organisations or NGOs. Their diversity and the expanding human rights concept constitute a formidable difficulty in arriving at a commonly accepted definition. According to Olz (1997), an NGO is considered to be a human rights NGO as long as it is private in character and being guided by the idea of international human rights as set forth in the international human rights law. In another definition by Bell and Keenan (2004), human rights NGOs are seen as NGOs promoting non-violently a set of rights that are enshrined in international law.

In the two preceding definitions, the private and non-violent nature of human rights NGO is emphasised. To the author, this makes reasonable stance and is adopted in the current work. However, the insistence on international human rights norms being the guiding factor for human rights NGOs is one such issue generating divergent opinions. Whether a human rights NGO is guided by international or domestic human rights norms (or both) is simply a matter of tactical choice for a given organisation and this need not affect its 'designation as a human rights NGO' (Calnan 2008). Many democratic nation-states have accepted the international human rights norms and codified them into their national laws. These national laws are sufficient and powerful enough to be used as standards by NGOs in their human rights work. In such a circumstance, it matters little whether or not a given human rights NGO be guided by international human rights norms.

Injecting the notions of stability and commitment, Tsutsui and Wotipka (2004) define human rights NGOs as 'those non-governmental organizations that are concerned with the promotion and protection of human rights in the long term'. Salient in their definition is the exclusion of NGOs that do not aim for long-term promotion of human rights from the purview of human rights NGOs. The apolitical nature of human rights work is also considered to be an essential trait of human rights NGOs. As Wiseberg (1991) observed:

> A human rights NGO is a private association which devotes significant resources to the promotion and protection of human rights, which is independent of both governmental political groups that seek political power, and which does not itself seek such power. (Quoted in Vajic 2005, p. 93)

She further observed that political non-partisanship constitutes the cornerstone of human rights monitoring, and that a group that subordinates human rights concern over political objectives does not come under the purview of human rights work.

To the author, this 'political non-partisanship', when interpreted in terms of being freed from political objectives such as eying political power or office for its own, is an important trait expected of a human rights NGOs. However, it would make little sense if political non-partisanship is to be seen as not taking sides between political parties or ideologies. This is because human rights NGOs normally have a political agenda in one way or another depending upon the context and circumstances in which they operate. They often turn political in their attempt to influence a country's policy (Calnan 2008). And that their political stance has often more to do with their idea of what human rights are and what stance a country should take on, say, a given human rights/humanitarian situation. Human rights are political in nature and can be enjoyed to the fullest under certain political order only. This, at times, necessitates human rights NGOs to take political position claiming for certain political order wherein these rights can be realised. For instance, the struggle for democratisation, which itself constitutes a political agenda, has become a prominent activity of human rights NGO community, and democracy as a political ideology is often preferred over authoritarianism (Mercer 2002). There have also been observations that maintenance of neutrality in the name of political non-partisanship between different political ideologies often amounts to tolerating gross human rights violations.

For the purpose of this study, a human rights NGO is conceptualised as a private, not-for-profit, non-governmental organisation having human rights protection and promotion as its core mandate. The organisation may be guided by domestic or international human rights norms (or both). The private is used in the sense that the organisation is formed by private initiatives and not as a result of governmental initiatives. They are considered independent as they are primarily funded and supported by private donations and resources generated from the memberships. The not-for-profit indicates that they are guided by public interests and that the earnings and assets of the organisation are used for the furtherance of the organisation's mission and objectives and not for private individual interests of the members of the organisation. And that their human rights work should be based on non-violent, peaceful activity.

Origin and Emergence of Human Rights NGOs in Manipur

The modern international human rights movement based on the exclusive and strictly non-partisan defence of human rights began with the formation of Amnesty International (AI) in London in 1961. However, the historical roots of the human rights movement can be traced to the struggle against slavery in the early 19th century and in the efforts to protect minorities in Eastern Europe after the First World War. The birth of the civil rights movement in the United States in the mid-1950s, which was directed particularly against centuries of racial discrimination, also contributed significantly to the birth of the international human rights movement.

In India, the root of the human rights movement can be traced to the formation of Indian Civil Liberties Union in 1936 as a part of the freedom struggle against the colonial British rule (Jha 2009). After independence, the movement for human rights further expanded in the backdrop of the Naxal Uprisings in the early 1960s and the imposition of National Emergency of 1975–1977. These two political events had led to the violent suppression of the civil and political rights of the people. Several civil liberty and democratic rights groups emerged protesting the actions of the Indian state (Rubin 1987). In the context of Manipur, the struggle for human rights began during the British colonial period. However, the modern notions of human rights activism in the state took roots during the post-independence period, in the backdrop of coercive suppression of the sub-nationalist ethnic struggles in the early 1980s.

Manipur has a large and diverse human rights NGO community which has made its presence felt throughout the state. The community can be divided into two major groups. The first group consists of those human rights NGOs that are primarily based in the Imphal valley and have a Meitei-centric focus. It includes, among others, the Civil Liberties and Human Rights Organisation (CLAHRO), Centre for Organisation Research and Education (CORE), Human Rights Alert (HRA) and Human Rights Law Network (HRLN). The second group consists of the self-declared ethnic-based organisations based in the hill areas of the state. It includes the Manipur unit of the Naga Peoples Movement for Human Rights (NPMHR), Kuki Movement for Human Rights (KMHR), Zomi Human Rights Foundation (ZHRF) and the Sinlung Indigenous Peoples Human Rights Organisation (SIPHRO). They represent their own ethnic or sub-ethnic groups as evident in their names—proclaiming the names of the ethnic groups they seek to defend. While NPMHR represents the Nagas, the KMHR, ZHRF and SIPHRO represent the various cognate Kuki tribes.

There have been two major phases in the evolution of human rights NGO community in Manipur. The 1980s witnessed the first phase, a period that saw the ascendancy of Meitei and Naga insurgencies in the valley and hill areas of the state respectively. The subsequent counter-militarisation and the invocation of AFSPA in 1980 in the whole of Manipur triggered widespread human rights abuses (prior to that, the AFSPA was invoked only in the hill areas of the state affected by Naga insurgency). Several massive public rallies were held, particularly in the Meitei-dominated valley areas of the state, to protest against the invocation of the AFSPA and the concomitant human rights abuses. Such protest movements were led mainly by the student community under the banner of All Manipur Students' Union and the women's groups such as the *Meira Paibis* (torch bearers). This, broadly, was the context for the evolution of the human rights NGO community in the first phase.

The first human rights NGO in the state, CLAHRO, was constituted in Imphal in 1983 by a group of left-leaning Meitei human rights activists. As most of the founding members were legal practitioners, CLAHRO concentrated initially on the mobilisation of law for human rights. It had also coordinated and mobilised the people for the pursuit of justice and human rights. Its primary mandate is to protect the civil liberties of the people of Manipur. Predictably, it has predominantly focussed on the issues of torture, extrajudicial killings, rape, and illegal and arbitrary detention of citizens. This narrow focus could be attributed, for the most part, to the fact that the organisation took birth in the context of the heightened public resentment against the invocation and misuse of AFSPA in the state. It is also the only human rights NGO in the state, which does not restrict its members from having affiliations with political parties. It has close relationship with the Manipur Unit of the Communist Party of India (CPI) and the All India Students Federation, a CPI-backed student organisation (CLAHRO 2006).

The birth of CLAHRO was followed by the formation of NPMHR (South) in 1984, as an autonomous constituent unit of NPMHR based at Kohima in Nagaland. A major impetus for the birth of NPMHR (South) was the perceived need for an autonomous platform to monitor the human rights of the Nagas in Manipur, who are usually referred to as the 'Southern Nagas' within the wider Naga community (NPMHR-South 2007). It is noteworthy to mention that human rights abuses against the Nagas in Manipur were on the rise in the early 1980s as by then the Naga insurgency had expanded to Naga-inhabited hill areas of Manipur. Before NPMHR (South) was formed, human rights abuses against the Nagas in Manipur were monitored by the parent organisation NPMHR. The latter was formed way back in Delhi in 1977 by a group of Naga students and other non-Naga intellectuals sympathetic to the Naga cause. As contained in its 'draft declaration', the main aims and objectives of NPMHR are to ensure and safeguard the right to life and the right of the Nagas together as a people and the unification of all Naga lands (Luithui and Haksar 1984).

The most well-known human rights group in Manipur, CORE, was formed on 4 March 1987 in Imphal. It was founded by a small group of eleven friends, led by an activist intellectual couple, Roy Laifungbam and Anastasia Pinto (CORE 2009). Apart from the disenchantment with poor human rights climate, CORE's roots are also traceable to two major lacunae, which, the founding members felt, characterised the human rights movement in Manipur. First, they felt that the state's pioneer human rights NGO, CLAHRO, was having a narrow focus on human rights by concerning itself alone with the abuses of civil and political rights, and that wider human rights issues such as women's rights, child rights and environmental rights also needed equal attention. Second, they felt that civil society organisations made no efforts to expose cases of human rights abuses to the wider international human rights community, whose attentions are crucial to improving the human rights situation in the state (Laifungbam, personal communication, 25 June 2009). The organisation has a wide mandate focussing on civil and political rights; economic, social and cultural rights; women's rights, human rights and health; and environmental issues. Over the years, CORE has evolved into one of the most visible and influential human rights NGO in North-East India, and was finally conferred a special consultative status with the United Nations Economic and Social Council in 2005.

The second phase in the evolution of the human rights NGO community in Manipur began in the 1990s. The period had witnessed violent inter-ethnic conflicts, apart from the usual human rights excesses of the security forces. The KMHR was founded on 2 October 1995 at the initiative of the Kuki Inpi, the apex traditional administrative body of the Kukis (KMHR 2009). The impetus for the formation of the KMHR was the alleged failure of the Indian government (both the central and provincial Manipur government) to protect the Kuki community from the Naga insurgent organisation NSCN (IM). As a statement of KMHR (2003) reads: 'The failure of the Government of India to protect the innocent Kukis from the Naga rebels, has compelled the Kukis to constitute the Kuki Movement for Human Rights to defend their kith and kin, hearths, homes, and territories'. Similar inter-ethnic conflicts between the Thadous and Paites within the Kuki community in the mid-1990s also saw the formation of ZHRF in 1998. SIPHRO, which represents the Hmar tribe in Manipur, took birth in 2003 in response to the threats posed to the identity and lands by the proposed Tipaimukh Dam and the subjugation of various Hmar tribal villages by the dominant Meitei insurgent organisations.

The second phase also saw the formation of two other human rights NGOs, HRA and the Manipur Unit of HRLN, in the valley areas of Manipur, specifically representing the ethnic Meiteis. HRA was formed in July 1999 and the Manipur Unit of HRLN has been in formal existence since 2004. However, HRLN's engagement with the human rights situation in Manipur began much before its formal inauguration of its unit in the state. Prior to the formation of Manipur Unit, HRLN collaborated with HRA and many other local human rights NGOs based in Manipur in instituting a three-member Independent People's Enquiry Committee, headed by Justice H. Suresh, in 2000 for investigating cases of rape, violence, killings and disappearances under AFSPA, 1958, in the state (Socio-Legal Information Centre 2009). HRLN (Manipur) has today evolved into an effective organisation providing legal assistance to victims of human rights abuses.

Roles and Activities of Human Rights NGOs in Manipur

Human Rights NGOs in Manipur have made remarkable achievements and contributions towards the protection and promotion of human rights in the state. They have made major impact on the conditions of human rights and in making the state more accountable to its actions. They have made effective use of domestic and international human rights standards and mechanisms in their human rights work. Although the roles and activities of these organisations vary in nature and scope, they can however be categorised under the following main roles and activities: human rights campaign, education and documentation; civil and political rights advocacy; advocacy for economic, social and cultural rights; international advocacy; women's rights and children's rights and rehabilitation; and networking and alliances.

Human Rights Campaign, Education and Documentation

Human rights NGOs in Manipur have made significant impact in the domain of human rights campaign. Since the early 1980s, they have provided the organisational basis of the campaigns against human rights abuses and for governmental accountability. A particular instance of this is the campaign against and for the repeal of the AFSPA in Manipur. AFSPA has been seen as a major tool that provided the army the impetus to indulge in human rights excesses. CORE frames its opposition to the act in terms of portraying it as a larger game plan of the Indian government to crush the self-determination movement of the indigenous peoples, which it views as a legitimate aspiration under international human rights. It views the imposition of the act in Manipur as smacking of double standards, as the same has not been imposed in other strife torn areas of the country, such as in Maoist-affected areas of Bihar and Andhra Pradesh (CORE 2002). It also looks upon the act as inextricably linked to a host of human rights abuses, not only in the realm of civil and political rights but also to the larger issues of women rights, child rights, and land and environmental rights.

The case study organisations have also mobilised public opinion by adopting a number of strategies: seminars, workshops, public debates and essay writing competition to promote human rights awareness. Organisations such as HRA and CORE run resource centres in Imphal for supporting local human rights initiative with information and varied forms of assistance. It documents and maintains newspaper clippings reporting violations of human rights and records of their own investigations. The resource centre acts as a storehouse of information for research students, academics and human rights activists having interest with regard to the human rights situation in Manipur (CORE 2006). HRA has also framed traditional human rights curriculum and brought up in a booklet form entitled 'Chainarol' in vernacular Manipuri language in 2006 (HRA 2006). The aim is to equip members of the traditional social organisations and institutions such as the village headman and women groups to best defend themselves against any onslaught on their rights (Loitongbam, personal communication, 17 June 2009). The curriculum maintains a mixture of traditional Meitei practices and principles that were observed in combat situations (such as rules related to combat, treatment accorded to enemy even after slain, and to women and children) and also the modern human rights principles and humanitarian laws.

Civil and Political Rights Advocacy

All the case study organisations are involved in the campaign against the violations of civil and political rights. Prime focus has been given to exposure of fake encounter deaths, torture, arbitrary detention, enforced disappearances and restriction of movements, among others. For any reported case or allegations of human rights abuse, which it sees as meriting detail investigation, the organisations generally begin by constituting a fact-finding team of its own or in partnership with fraternal human rights NGOs. The findings of such investigations are then subsequently transmitted to the international human rights community such as

World Organisation against Torture (OMCT) and International Federation for Human Rights (FIDH), AI, among others, and these organisations in turn issue their condemnations and appeals (FIDH 2006; OMCT 2008). HRA had also extended support to the formation of the 'Fact Finding Team of Independent Citizens' in 2009. The fact finding team investigated and indicted the state of indulging in the fake encounter killings of Chungkham Sanjit Singh and Rabina Devi on 23 July 2009.

In 1987, in one of its earliest and most notable interventions, NPMHR exposed to the national and international community the case of the human rights excesses committed by the army during the 'Operation Bluebird' at Oinam village in Manipur. The operation was a counter-attack launched in response to a raid by the NSCN militants on an Assam Rifles camp at Oinam village in Senapati district. During the counter-operation against the NSCN, the Assam Rifles wreaked their vengeance upon the Naga civilians in the vicinity of the incident. NPMHR (South) played a prime role in investigating the case and in reporting to the international community (Talwalker 1991).

There are also several other notable instances of successful interventions by the human rights NGOs in terms of getting justice and in internationalising the human rights excesses of the security forces. CLAHRO also played a prime role in the protest movement against the custodial killing of Thangjam Manorama Devi by personnel of the 17 Assam Rifles on 11 July 2004. The Assam Rifles abducted Manorama Devi, a former militant of the proscribed Meitei militant outfit UNLF, from her residence on 11 July 2004, and her bullet-ridden body was found in a field about three hours after her arrest (Gonsalves 2005). CLAHRO criticised the failure of the Assam Rifles to adhere to the Section 5 of the AFSPA, 1958, which mandated the army authority to hand over any arrested person to the nearest police station 'together with a report of the circumstances occasioning the arrest'.

CORE's intervention in 2006 had also led to the release of two notable human rights activists in Manipur—namely Leitanthem Umakanta Meitei and Yengkokpam Langamba Meitei—who were arrested and tortured by a team of Assam

Rifles. The duo were arrested, detained and tortured on charges of having links with terrorist organisations (FIDH 2006). CORE took up their case with OMCT and FIDH urging their intervention. In response to the CORE's appeal, the Observatory to the Protection of Human Rights Defenders, a joint programme of OMCT and FIDH which supports and protects HRD around the world, issued an 'urgent appeal' to the international community to urge upon the government of India to secure their release. The two arrested HRD were subsequently released by a local court in Imphal on 6 October 2006 and all charges against them were dropped citing lack of evidence (OMCT 2006).

Advocacy for Economic, Social, Cultural and Environmental Rights

As indicated previously, the initial focus of human rights NGOs in Manipur centred on civil and political rights. However, over the years, this narrow mandate has expanded to include the other wider human rights concerns. With regard to land, environmental protection and biodiversity conservation, one of the most foremost issues which CORE has engaged itself is on the issue of Government of India's plan to construct a mega-dam, Tipaimukh Hydroelectric Multipurpose Project (locally know a Tipaimukh Dam) across the Barak River in the ecologically sensitive, interior Churachandpur district of Manipur. CORE has been serving as the secretariat of the Citizens Concern for Dams and Development (CCDD)—a coalition of 40 NGOs, academics and individuals formed in 1999 to campaign against the proposed construction of Tipaimukh Dam (CORE 2002). NPMHR and SIPHRO too have been campaigning against the proposed dam as the dam is expected to displace thousands of peoples belonging to the ethnic Naga and Hmar tribes.

HRLN Manipur is particularly concerned with the government's apathy towards the poor. For instance, it has exposed how certain government social security schemes bypassed certain interior tribal villages in the state. In October 2008, HRLN Manipur collaborated with an Imphal-based NGO, Don Bosco Social Welfare (DBWS), and launched the Right to Food Campaign for over a period of six days covering interior areas of

Tamenglong, the most backward district in the state. The campaign team, which also included a local TV news reporter, exposed how several interior villages in the district have been deprived of basic public distribution system items such as rice, sugar, and oil and other social security schemes over the last 10 years. They also exposed how basic government's social security measures such as old-age pensions, mid-day meal schemes and Integrated Child Development Services schemes have not even been heard of in such villages (HRLN Manipur 2008).

International Advocacy

Almost all the case study organisations have some form of international advocacy for human rights. However, CORE, HRA and NPMHR (South) have the most visible presence in human rights advocacy at the international level. They have undertaken advocacy efforts at various UN organs. In March 2002, CORE had presented a detailed report, 'Manipur: A Report on the Impunity of Human Rights Violations Under the Armed Forces (Special Powers) Act, 1958' to the UN Special Rapporteur on the situation of Human Rights and Fundamental Freedoms of Indigenous People (CORE 2002). The report, apart from highlighting the rampant misuse of the provisions of the act, urged the Special Rapporteur to recommend to India to immediately repeal the AFSPA, 1958, and ensure its laws to be in conformity with the international human rights law.

NPMHR (South) has also played a major role in taking up the cause of the Nagas at the international level, specifically with the various organs of the UN. It met the UN Human Rights Committee in 1991 at New York to expose the human rights excesses of the security forces in Naga areas. The UN committee in turn expressed concern about the violations of the rights of the Nagas under the cover of AFSPA. This was the first time a UN body took cognisance of the human rights plight of the Nagas (Shimray 2005). It had also participated in the United Nations Conference on Indigenous Peoples at Geneva from 25–29 July 1994 and highlighted the human rights plight of the Nagas. It also lobbied with Hague-based Unrepresented Nations and Peoples Organisation (UNPO) to admit NSCN as its member organisation. NSCN finally became a member of UNPO on 23 January 1993 (Vashum 2005). In 1995, UNPO's Fourth General Assembly resolved to recognise the right to self-determination of the Naga peoples and condemn what it sees as the illegal and continued occupation of Naga territories.

NPMHR (South) has also been actively contributing to the 'Indigenous World', an annual report of International Work Group on Indigenous Affairs (IWGIA), to highlight the plight of the Naga peoples. The IWGIA had also brought out a report on the human rights plight of the Nagas in 1986 (IWGIA 1986). Through its advocacy efforts at global fora, NPMHR (South) has been able to generate international attention on the human rights issues of the Nagas.

Partnerships and Linkages

Human rights NGOs in Manipur also networks with the human rights groups at both the domestic and international domain to address particular human rights issues. It has formed broad coalitions with other organisations for a more effective human rights advocacy. One such coalition is that of the CCDD—a coalition of 40 NGOs, academics and individuals formed in 1999 to campaign against the proposed construction of Tipaimukh Dam (CORE 2003). Similar NGO partnerships include Indian Confederation of Indigenous and Tribal Peoples North-East Zone (ICITP-NEZ), which seek to protect the rights of the indigenous peoples of the North-East of India. At the international levels, NPMHR and ZHRF are constituent members of the Asian Indigenous Peoples Pact), a Thailand-based regional organisation comprising various indigenous peoples organisations in Asia. HRA is also working as a founding member of the 'Working Group on Human Rights in India and United Nations', which also works as an informal advisory group to the UN High Commissioner for Human Rights. HRA, in collaboration with the International Community of the Red Cross, South Asia Regional Officer in New Delhi, was instrumental in the translation of a handbook on International Humanitarian Law in Manipuri vernacular language (HRA 2008). This, HRA believes, will go a long way in observing certain humanitarian law by both the state and non-state actors in conflict.

Since 1994, CORE has been a member of the NGO Group for the Convention on the Rights of the Child (NGO Group for the CRC), a network of NGOs from across the globe 'with the mission to facilitate the promotion, implementation and monitoring of the CRC' (Child Rights Information Network 2008).

Problems and Challenges

Coming to the limitations and challenges that human rights NGOs in Manipur face in the course of its works, issues revolving around the scarcity of funding, government indifference, structural constraints such as poverty and illiteracy figure prominently. Neild (2003) considers that reframing of public discourse that supports surrendering guaranteed rights in the name of security or public order is a major challenge for the human rights NGOs. A major hardship comes in the form of structural constraints such as public indifference, lack of awareness of their rights and poverty. The organisations have to do a lot of persuasion to the victims to file case in law courts or stand as witnesses to acts of human rights violations. Structural poverty and lack of awareness of their own rights also push people to ignore even the most blatant cases of human rights violations. The propensity to think even by the educated community leaders about the need to surrender even certain inalienable rights in the name of security too is a major challenge that human rights NGOs faced (Loitongbam, personal communication, 28 June 2009).

Government intolerance towards any kind of dissenting voices constitutes another obstacle to NGOs effectiveness. Regime repression can force many human rights NGOs to engage in low profile or non-provocative activities—such as organising workshops and conferences aimed at HRE—so as not to provoke the regime's wrath by indulging in politically sensitive issues (Dicklitch and Lwanga 2003). Under such a circumstance, NGOs tend to raise issues that are of no relevance to the issues confronting the national or local societies. In a politically volatile state of Manipur, state's indifference to the works of human rights activists becomes a major challenge to human rights activism. Attempts by civil society organisations for more transparent and accountable functioning on the part of the state have not been appreciated. NGOs, particularly those raising politically sensitive human rights issues, are rather seen by the state as adversaries, anti-nationals or subversive. Human rights activists and functionaries of the human rights NGOs are subjected to frequent police investigation. Mention here may be made of how HRA's monthly publication 'Manipur Update' has been banned by the state. This state's indifference creates a fear of psychosis in the minds of young volunteers who work for the cause that the human rights NGOs espoused. The pressures coming from different directions—including the state and the non-state actors—in the form of do's and don'ts dictated by them frequently interferes in the effective execution of programmes and activities.

Yet another challenge faced by the human rights community in the state is the apparent lack of inter-ethnic integration and an initiative towards a common objective. The coalitions and networking are largely limited to one's own respective ethnic group in the state. For instance, the human rights NGOs based in the valley, representing the Meiteis, network amongst themselves to the exclusion of organisations representing the tribes. A specific example is given by the United Committee Manipur (UCM), a coalition of NGOs, which represent those that are based in Imphal. While all the valley-based human rights NGOs are part of the UCM, none of the organisations from the hills is part of it. Similarly, KMHR and NPMHR too networks mostly with civil society organisations representing the Kuki and Naga ethnic groups respectively. The divisions along ethnic lines are amply manifested in the accusations and counter-accusations of selective approach on the issue of the infamous 'Parbung mass rape' incident, wherein cadres of Meitei insurgent outfit UNLF gangraped 21 ethnic Hmar tribal women on 16 January 2006 at Parbung, a remote village in Churachandpur district of Manipur (National Commission for Women 2007). Human Rights NGOs in the state formed a joint coalition to investigate the incident, which was soon aborted following disagreements between the hill-based organisations and the valley-based organisations (SIPHRO 2008).

Conclusion

Over the years, human rights NGOs in Manipur have played immense role in the protection and promotion of human rights. A basic characteristic of human rights NGOs in Manipur is that they were formed largely in response to the human rights crisis engendered by various ethnic insurgencies and counter-security operations. The more specific impetuses were, however, provided by inter-ethnic conflicts and the human rights excesses of the dominant insurgencies against the ethnic minorities. The prime objectives of human rights NGOs in the state are to expose and highlight the human rights excesses of the Indian security forces and for the repeal of the AFSPA, 1958. This means that the organisations in their initial years tended to focus on the civil and political rights advocacy. This could well be attributed to state's prevailing environment in which militarisation and the imposition of AFSPA predominates. However, this primary mandate of the organisations have expanded over the years to include a wider range of human rights issues that fall largely in the realm of the economic, social and cultural rights. For instance, NPMHR in its formative years primarily focus on army atrocities but have now expanded its mandate to include the threats posed to the identity and lands of the Nagas by mega-development projects such as Tipaimukh Dam.

The fact that an NGO is largely the product of the environment in which it operation also holds true for human rights NGOs in Manipur. Largely, these organisations are primarily concerned with issues and challenges related to their own ethnic groups. It reflects the ethnic basis in which they were formed. It means that the human rights programme of the case study organisations are implemented in a compartmentalised manner with an ethnic basis. There exists a need for greater inter-ethnic coordination and networking among these organisations to usher a more effective and encompassing human rights movement. The cause of human rights can be furthered not by operating in isolation but by concerted efforts. Also this further accentuate the ethnic divide in the state and prevents the emergence of an all-encompassing civil society or human rights movement that are being looked upon as mutually shared and representing common interests. An ideal type human rights monitoring by human rights NGOs should be based largely on political non-partisanship, and the credibility and legitimacy of human rights NGOs rest in large part on the objectivity and of its fact-finding and impartial applications of human rights standards. Human rights NGOs in Manipur should, therefore, strive towards this direction.

On the other hand, the linkage with national and international human rights NGOs has enhanced the image, visibility and effectiveness of the local human rights NGOs in Manipur. This has worked to their advantage by providing security from the state's arbitrary actions for fearing of immediate public exposure. The fact that human rights NGOs in the state send out regular routine reports to international and national organisations, file many cases with Asian Centre for Human Rights, Human Rights Watch and International Human Rights Watch, also keeps the state's actions under constant check.

References

Baruah, Sanjib (2007). *Post-frontier Blues: Toward a New Policy Framework for Northeast India*. Washington: East West Centre.

Bell, Christine and Keenan, Johanna (2004). 'Human Rights Nongovernmental Organizations and the Problems of Transition'. *Human Rights Quarterly,* 26, 330–373.

Calnan, Scott (2008). *The Effectiveness of Domestic Human Rights NGOs: A Comparative Study*. Boston: Martinus Nijhoff Publishers.

Centre for Organisation Research and Education (CORE, 2002). Annual Report, 2001–2002. Imphal.

Centre for Organisation Research and Education (CORE, 2003). Annual Report, 2001–2002.

Centre for Organisation Research and Education (CORE, 2006). Annual Report, 2005–2006.

Centre for Organisation Research and Education (CORE, 2009). Information Mannual, Imphal.

Chaube, Shibani Kinkar (1999). *Hill Politics in Northeast India*. New Delhi: Orient Longman.

Child Rights Information Network (2008). 'About the NGO Group for the CRC'. Retrieved from http://www.crin.org/NGOGroupforCRC/about.asp

Chisti, S.M.A.W. (2005). *Political Development in Manipur 1919–1949*, New Delhi: Gyan Books.

Civil Liberties and Human Rights Organisation (CLAHRO, 2005). Annual Activity Report, 2004–2005, Imphal.

Civil Liberties and Human Rights Organisation (CLAHRO, 2006). Annual Activity Report, 2005–2006, Imphal.

Dicklitch, Susan and Lwanga, Doreen (2003). 'The Politics of Being On-Political: Human Rights Organisations and the Creation of a Positive Human Rights Culture in Uganda'. *Human Rights Quarterly*, 25, 456.

Gonsalves, Colin (2005). 'The Murder of Manorama'. *Combat Law,* 4(3), 6–11.

Haokip, Thangkholun (1993). 'The Kuki National Assembly: The Party's Role in the State Politics of Manipur' (Unpublished MPhil Dissertation). Shillong: North-Eastern Hill University.

Hassan, Sajjad M. (2008). *Building Legitimacy: Exploring State-Society Relations in Northeast India*. New Delhi: Oxford University Press.

Human Rights Alert (HRA, 2006). Malem Chainarol Ekaikhumnaba, Imphal.

Human Rights Alert (HRA, 2008). Chainarol. HRA: Imphal.

Human Rights Law Network (Manipur) (2008). Annual Report, 2007–2008.

International Federation for Human Rights (2006). 'Arbitrary Detention in Manipur'. Retrieved from http://www.fidh.org/Arbitrary-detentions-Torture.

International Federation for Human Rights (2006). 'Manipur: Appeal for Release of Human Right Defenders', Parish.

IWGIA (1986). 'The Naga Nation and Its Struggle against Genocide. A Report'. Copenhagen: IWGIA.

Jha, Munmun (2003). 'Nehru and Civil Liberties in India'. *The International Journal of Human Rights,* 7(3), 103–115.

Jha, M. (2009). *India from Indira Gandhi's Emergency: In Encyclopaedia of Human Rights,* edited by David P. Fobsythe. New York: Oxford University Press.

Kuki Movement for Human Rights (2003). 'Kuki Movement for Human Rights'. Imphal: KMHR.

Kuki Movement for Human Rights (2009). 'Kuki Movement for Human Rights in Manipur'. Imphal: KMHR.

Lamkhianpiang, L. (2008). 'The Process of Ethnification of the Zo People'. 60th Zomi Namni Celebration Committee; Lamka.

Luithui, Luingam, and Haksar, Nandita (1984). *Nagaland File: A Question of Human Rights*. New Delhi: Lancer International.

McDuie-Ra, Duncan (2005). 'Searching for Human Security in 'Disturbed' Areas: Women as Agents for Change in Manipur, India'. *Australasian Journal of Human Security,* 1(2), 49–63.

Mercer, Claire (2002). 'NGOs, Civil Society and Democratisation: A Critical Review of Literature'. *Progress in Development Studies,* 2 (1), 7–19.

National Commission for Women (2007). Annual Report, 2006–2007.

Neild, R. (2003). 'Human Rights NGOs, Police and Citizen Security in Transitional Democracies', *Journal of Human Rights*, 2(3), 277–296.

NPMHR-South (2007). 'Know Our Rights'. Tahamzam: NPMHR.

Olz, M.A. (1997). 'Non-Governmental Organisations in Regional Human Rights Systems'. *Columbia Human Rights Law Review,* 28, 308–319.

Rubin, Barnett R. (1987). 'The Civil Liberties Movement in India: New Approaches to the State and Social Change'. *Asian Survey,* 27(3): 371–392.

Sharma, Hanjabam Sukhdeva (2008). 'The Meitei Upsurge in Manipur'. *Asia Europe Journal,* 157–169.

Shimroy, A.S.A. (2005). *Let Freedom Ring: Story of Naga Nationalism*, New Delhi: Promilla and Co.

Sinlung Indigenous Peoples Human Rights Organisation (2008). 'Parbung Rape Incident: A Report'. Lamka: SIPHRO.

Socio-Legal Information Centre (2009). 'HRLN: A Movement for Justice'. New Delhi: Socio Legal Information Centre.

Srikanth, H. (2005). 'Insurgency and Counter-Insurgency: Agenda for Peace in India's Northeast', in C.J. Thomas (ed.), *Polity and Economy: Agenda for Contemporary Northeast India.* New Delhi: Regency Publication.

Talwalker, Clare (1991). 'Security Forces Abuse Human Rights: AI Report on Oinam'. *Economic and Political Weekly*, 26(3), 89–90.

Tarapot, Phanjoubam (1993). *Insurgency Movement in Northeast India.* New Delhi: Vikas Publication House.

Tsutsui, Kiyoteru and Wotipka, Christine (2004). 'Global Civil Society and the International Human Rights Movement: Citizen Participation in Human Rights International Nongovernmental Organisations'. *Social Forces,* 83(2), 580–593.

Vajic, N. (2005). 'Some Concluding Remarks on NGOs and the European Court of Human Rights', in T. Treves et al. (eds), *Civil Society, International Courts and Compliance Bodies.* The Hague: TMC Asser Press.

Vashum, R. (2005). *Nagas Right to Self-Determination: An Anthropological-Historical Perspective*. New Delhi: Mittal Publication.

Wiseberg, Laurie (1991). 'Protecting Human Rights Activists and NGOs: What More Can Be Done'. *Human Rights Quarterly*, 13(4), 525–544.

World Organisation Against Torture (OMCT, 2006). 'India: Arbitary Detention', Geneva.

World Organisation Against Torture (OMCT, 2008). 'India: Extra Judicial Killing of Mr Longjam Uttam Kumar in Manipur', Geneva.

5

Displacement and Tribal Resistance to Development in Kalinganagar, Jajpur District of Odisha

A Concern for the Rights of Indigenous People

Rafiq Ullah Sheikh and Jayaram Singh Samal

In the recent past, one social issue that has caused intense debate among academics, social activist and planners is the involuntary displacement of people from their productive assets (particularly land) and homes, due to industrial or infrastructure projects. Though the process of acquisition of land for setting up mining, irrigation, transportation or mega projects (mostly in the public sector) is not new, the intensity of adverse effects was never comprehended in the past as it is today.[1]

The liberalisation of economy, growing needs of infrastructure in the fast growing cities and new partnership in industrial/economic sectors have threatened traditional source of sustenance of the people. More and more agricultural lands are being acquired for setting up of industrial/infrastructure projects. The situation is aggravated due to major conversion of agricultural lands voluntary or involuntarily into urbanised lands. All this has unleashed a situation where more and more people are being displaced from their communities and traditional ways of life. How many of them are co-opted into the new economic order and how many remain victims of the new model of development remains unknown. However, there is growing awareness of the sweeping powers of government, under the Land Acquisition Act of 1894, which empowers it to acquire private lands and properties in 'public interest'. Growing social activism against such 'sovereign domain' of government is not only in response to untold hardships and miseries caused to the affected people but also a protest against the very model of development that alienates people from their traditional sources of sustenance. With the growing pace of development under liberalisation, the intensity of displacement has also increased. Unaccustomed to new ways of life, the affected people face a hostile situation where they have to compete as individuals, different from their community-based settings. Many lose out in this race for development.[2]

According to one estimate, the country's development programmes have caused the displacement of approximately 20 million people over roughly four decades, but as many as 75 per cent of these people have not been rehabilitated.[3] Their incomes and livelihoods have not been restored. That means the vast majority of development-induced displaced people in the country have been impoverished. According to Kothari (1996),[4] since independence of the country, development projects of the Five-Year Plans have displaced 0.5 million persons each year primarily as a direct consequences of administrative land acquisition which does not include displacement by non-plan projects, changes in land use, acquisition for urban growth and loss of livelihood caused by environmental degradation and pollution.

Development

Development as a concept first emerged, becoming a major theme in economic and political discourse, in the post Second World War era. Development in effect becomes a model for achieving progress through ever expanding growth and consumption fuelled by public and private investment in infrastructure, production capability and expanding market. Development continues to be defined by those with the power to implement their ideas for whom it is the process through which the productive forces of economies and supporting infrastructure are improved through public and private investment.[5]

The modern approach to development is chiefly characterised by capital intensive, high technology, large-scale development projects that convert farm lands, fishing grounds, forest and home into dam-created reservoirs, irrigation schemes, mining operation, colonisation projects, highways, industrial complexes, tourist resorts and other large-scale forms of uses favouring national or global interests over those people at the local level. Putatively designed to spur economic growth and speared general welfare, many of these projects have left people displaced, disempowered and destitute. People around the world from many different societies and cultures, urban, rural, proximate and remote, are raising their voices and taking action against development forced displacement and resettlement. The central problem with development is essentially the uprooting of people and the destruction of homes and communities in the name of progress.[6]

Displacement

Displacement is seen as the result of a model of development that enforces certain technical and economic choices without giving any serious consideration to those options that would involve the least social and environmental costs. Most displacement has been involuntary. There has been very little meaningful participation of affected people in the planning and implementation of the dam project, including the resettlement and rehabilitation aspects. The [illegible] last to [illegible] the dam project. What information they have received has typically been limited and provided very late in the planning and implementation of mitigation measures.[7]

The development projects are usually located in remote villages, hills and forests means that those displaced tend to be indigenous people, who have been the traditional agents of conservation. Here displacement has meant a loss of livelihood, habitat and assets, social disruption and disorder and severance from an ecosystem, which sustain them. Displacement does not constitute a monolithic category in terms of livelihood strategies or socio-economic locations and have borne the brunt of dislocation in varied way. Most critically, these displacements threaten the poor and the weak with even greater impoverishment. Displacement caused widespread traumatic psychological and sociocultural consequences. These include the dismantling of production system, desecration of ancestral sacred zones or graves and temples, scattering of kinship groups and family systems, disorganisation of informal social networks that provide mutual support, weakening of self-management and social control and disruption of trade and market links. The neglected dimension of displacement is its adverse impact on women. Their trauma is compounded by the loss of access to fuel, fodder and food collection, which inevitably requires greater time and effort. Similarly children are adversely affected since not only is schooling less accessible, in most cases there is also disruption in the traditional socialisation process.[8]

L.K. Mahapatra highlights that in the process of any economic development projects (i.e. dam irrigation, power generation or industries and so on), the legitimate rights and interest of the people cannot be taken away just because they are not organised, articulate or violent. Displacement invariably involves uprooting and dismemberment of social, economic webs of life built over generations. In most projects, tribals constitute the majority among the displaced, and second largest number is from the SC, that is, communities that are asset-less according to the existing law. They are basically dependent on common property resources for their livelihoods.[9]

The estimates of displacement vary vastly. According to one estimate, some 35 to 55 million people have been displaced in the independent India. It needs to be underlined here that only 8 per cent of India's population is tribal. And 60 per cent of displaced are tribes, as the huge projects, be it dams or industries, are located in their ancestral habitats.[10]

These projects destroy cultural identity, value and traditions, which invariably accompanies their separation from the land. The livelihood system of Indian tribal societies is sustainable in true sense. Tribal culture tend to be looked down still as 'primitive', yet their systems of cultivation and social cohesion are actually extremely sophisticated. These systems have sustained themselves for centuries without overusing their resources, unlike most mainstream paths of development.[11] So to destroy their culture and lifestyle in the name of displacement is antithesis to development. In the word of Neera Chandoke, it is systematic violation of their right to livelihood, right to culture and community.

In Odisha one can see despite substantial protest from the civil society and opposition political parties, the government seems to be inflexible and is forging forward with its agenda of massive industrialisation. In this chapter, through the study of Kalinganagar project, an attempt has been made to analyse how development projects are affecting life of tribal community and what is their response and how government is reacting.

Human Rights

The end of the 20th century has given a momentum to human rights movement in the new millennium.[12] Human rights are inherent to man as being human person. Variously known as 'Fundamental Rights' or a natural right, everybody everywhere is entitled to enjoy the privilege of Human Rights.[13] Human rights are those minimal rights, which every individual must have by virtue of his being a member of human family, irrespective of any other consideration. 'Human Rights like fundamental rights are "Paramount", sacrosanct and eternal and transcendental in nature and ought to be treated as inalienable and inviolable for preserving the dignity of the people'. They are based on mankind's demand for a life in which the inherent dignity of human being will receive respect and consideration.[14]

The UN centre for human rights defines human right as 'those rights that are inherent in our nature and without which we cannot live as human beings'. These rights relate to life, equality, liberty and security of person, equal protection under law and are free from all forms of discrimination.[15] It may also be useful to refer to the definition of human rights in the Protection of Human Rights Act, 1993. The act defines the term 'human rights' as the rights relating to life, liberty, equality and dignity of the individual guaranteed by the Constitution or embodied in the international covenants and enforceable by courts in India.[16]

Human rights give various freedoms and security to the individual so as to develop his or her personality along with the identity in the society. The human rights are those rights, which every individual must have against as a member of human family irrespective of any other considerations. The term 'human rights' might be comparatively recent in origin, but its idea is as old the history of human civilisation. Human rights are essential for all individuals as they are consonant with freedom and dignity and are conducive to physical, moral, social and spiritual welfare. They are inalienable, sacrosanct and transcendental.[17]

Odisha: A Brief Introduction

Odisha,[18] also known as Orissa, is a state of India, located on the east coast of India, by the Bay of Bengal. Odisha is the ninth largest state by area in India, and the 11th largest by population. Odia is the official and most widely spoken language. There are total 30 districts in the state. The capital and largest city of the state is Bhubaneswar and its other name is temple city.

Odisha is rich in natural resources. About 98.39 per cent of India's chrome ore, 95.11 per cent of nickel ore, 70.39 per cent of bauxite, 26.50 per cent of iron ore and 24.37 per cent of the coal, 29.94 per cent of manganese and 43.38 per cent of graphite deposits of the country are found in this mineral-rich state. The state also has abundant water resources constituting 11 per cent of the country, which will be equivalent to eleven river basins. The total ground water resource assessed during 2000–2001 was 21.01 lakh hectare metres, of which 14.79 per cent has been harnessed.[19] The forest cover (including tree cover) was estimated at 34.2 per cent of the total geographical area of the state in 2001 according to the State Forest Report of the Forest Survey of India. This rich mineral of Odisha has attracted many investors to invest in the state.

Jajpur District

Jajpur is a city and a municipality in Jajpur district in the Indian state of Orissa. It is freely connected by road and rail (Jajpur Road) from the state capital, Bhubaneswar, and it is about 120 km away from it.[20]

Kalinganagar: The Study Area

Kalinganagar is a small town under Sukinda and Danagadi blocks of Jajpur district of coastal Orissa. It is the new industrial hub of the state. It is about 100 km from the state capital, Bhubaneswar, and about 30–40 km from the district headquarter. It is rich in mineral deposits such as iron ore resources. It is rich in iron ores and because of high global demand of steel, Kalinganagar has been in the process of becoming a major global hub in steel and ancillary products. A large number of steel plants, including projects by Tata Steel, are in various stages of implementation. The NH-200, connecting the iron ore/chromite belt of Jajpur and Keonjhar districts with the Paradeep Port, runs through the area.

The topography of the area is marked by undulating landmasses interspersed with hillocks and jungles. Nallas and rivulets form one of the water sources for the area and also provide fish and crab. Brahmani, one of the major rivers of Orissa, runs nearby around 5–6 km away from the Kalinganagar Industrial Complex. Agriculture, mostly rice cultivation, is the main source of living for majority of local populace, predominantly STs. As there is no irrigation facility, it is largely rain-fed. In some villages, people grow pulses after harvesting rice, which do not need much watering. The area has a significant tribal and dalit population. The two blocks—Sukinda and Danagadi—under which the area falls, has a ST population of 36.06 per cent and 28.19 per cent and SC population of 11.89 per cent and 22.31 per cent respectively. The ST population in the acquired area is much higher than the block average. The tribes used to gather food from the forest, practice agriculture and used to drink *Handia*. Of the tribes, people belonging to Ho community constitute nearly 80 per cent and rest of them belongs to Munda and Santal communities.[21]

The oral history suggests that these communities have come from Mayurbhanj, Keonjhar, Ranchi and Singhbhum districts in different phases in later decades of 19th century and early decades of 20th century and have settled here at the invitation of the then Sukinda King. The Madox Settlement Report 1897 also indicates about their settlement. It is also pertinent to mention that Orissa became a province only in 1936.[22]

Idea of Industrial Complex at Kalinganagar

The idea of the Kalinganagar Industrial Complex was conceived in the early 1990s with the advent of the process of liberalisation and economic reforms. And the government of Orissa has signed more than 40 MoUs with various private companies to set up steel plants in the state. The Industrial Infrastructure Development Corporation of Orissa (IDCO) was entrusted with the task of developing infrastructure facilities for the proposed industrial complex in Kalinganagar so that the investors could be attracted to set up industries in the area.

As a first step, IDCO started acquiring land in the year 1992–1994. Although IDCO had acquired the land in the early 1990s, only a portion of it had been actually transferred to different industries. The remaining land was still in actual possession of people, who have been cultivating it as before. The reason for this is that, although the government of Orissa had signed MoUs with many industrial houses, only a few actually came forward to set up their industries.

Plausibly, this lack of interest on the part of investors was due to the slump in the international steel market. And when the prospect for the steel market became favourable again, investors are hurrying up their activities. Tatas are one of the investors who had signed the MoU in 2004 to set up a 6 million metric tons per annum steel plant in Kalinganagar, in two phases, with an investment of ₹ 1,54,000 million. The other companies who have plans to set up their plants in Kalinganagar Industrial Complex include Tatas, Maharashtra Seamless, Uttam Galva, Orion, Mithal, Rohit, Dinabandhu and others. The total capacity of all these plants is estimated to be 12 million tonnes per annum.

Land Acquisition and Compensation

The acquisition of land by IDCO for Kalinganagar Industrial Complex began in early 1990s in different phases. However, in reality, people cultivated most of these 'government land', for generations, over which they do not have *patta*. The land survey and settlement in the area was not done since 1928. After passing the Orissa Estate Abolition Act in 1951, the Estate of Sukinda King was vested with the government. But tenancy rights were not conferred upon the local people who possessed these land. Even after the passing of the Orissa Survey and Settlement Act of 1958 (rules framed in the year 1962), no settlement has been done in the area. The commitments and promises made by successive governments at different times on land reforms, promising land to the landless, have never been implemented in the area.

The IDCO has purchased land from people at the rate of ₹ 15,000 to ₹ 30,000 per acre in the initial phase of acquisition. Over the years, as a 'measure of benevolence', an ex-gratia amount of ₹ 25,000 per acre has been awarded, in different phases, probably in response to people's demand for increased compensation from time to time. The compensation for land was given to only those who had *patta* on the land. This left a huge section of people uncompensated, as they had no *patta* over the land they possessed. After acquiring land from people, IDCO has been selling the land to different industries at a much higher price. And IDCO has sold land to the Tatas at the rate of ₹ 3.5 lakh per acre.

Displacement and Rehabilitation

There is a long and tragic history of displacement in the state, beginning in the 1950s. It is an important point to be noted that during the incident the government of Orissa did not had a resettlement and rehabilitation policy. And during that time in the absence of a policy, rehabilitation of the displaced people was guided by mere administrative circulars, which was project specific. For Kalinganagar Industrial Complex, the government had issued a series of guidelines (the latest being on 18 November 2005) to regulate rehabilitation and resettlement of families affected by acquisition of land. In these guidelines, three areas have been considered for the resettlement and rehabilitation of the displaced families. These are: (a) financial compensation for the loss of land; (b) provision of homestead land and assistance for house building and (c) compensation for the loss of livelihood. Though the price for the acquired land, provision of homestead land and assistance for housing building has been fixed by the government, the provision of jobs to the displaced families is not made obligatory for the companies, in the guidelines. But, people have been promised of jobs by the government and politicians at different times before displacement.

One more very important point to be noted is that on 2 January 2006, just four days after the deadly clash in Kalinganagar, the state government constituted a ministerial committee to finalise the resettlement and rehabilitation policy through democratic opinion building, seeking to address the special needs of the affected communities. The base remains the Orissa State Policy on resettlement and rehabilitation of Project Affected People Draft 2005 in consultation with the UNDP and DFID. However, all these were like rituals and false promises. Nothing worked for the affected people. As a result more than 814 families have been displaced in Kalinganagar. The number of families likely to be displaced and affected in the near future is said to be about 5,000.

The Early Years

By all account, initially the local people welcomed the idea of the industrial complex, believing that the new industries would usher in development of the area, give employment to the local people and improve their standard of living. So when land acquisition took place between 1992 and 1994, undertaken by IDCO, people accepted the compensation at the extant rate without a murmur. They believed the verbal assurance given by government officials that jobs would be provided to them when the industries would start. They continued cultivating the acquired land as before, till around 1997 when the first group of people were displaced. When the land was physically acquired in 1997, to be handed over to the companies, provision was made to shift the displaced people at two resettlement colonies: Trijanga and Gobarghati colonies. Homestead land of 10 decimal (1/10 acre) per family was allotted to each displaced family. When nothing of the sort was forthcoming, the villagers sat on *dharna*, refusing to leave. Matter took a cruel and ugly turn when, late in the evening, police was used to forcefully evict the people. Reportedly, bulldozers were used and 60 people were arrested. The trust of the people in general was shaken.

Post-2004 Phase

In 2004, an organisation to protect the interest of the people affected by the industrial complex was formed. And it called itself Sukinda Upatyaka Adivasi-Harijan Ekata O Surakshya Parishad, which was later renamed as *Visthapan Virodhi Jana Mancha,* Sukinda. In October 2004, they had issued an open letter to the Chief Minister, expressing their concerns and grievances about the hardships faced by them due to the emerging complex and gave several demands: five demands meant for the people to be displaced and six demands concerning the people already displaced. The salient features of the demands included (a) stopping further construction on agricultural land; (b) giving *patta* to the people settled before 1980; (c) returning the acquired land, which was left unused, to the original owners; (d) stopping deliberate targeting of tribal and dalit villages for land acquisition; (e) raising the homestead land to one acre per displaced family; (f) having the parishad a say in rehabilitation matters and (g) providing one job per displaced family.

During 2005, the *Visthapan Virodhi Jana Mancha* resisted all kinds of activities—such as land survey, *bhumi puja*, levelling and boundary wall construction—relating to setting up of industries in the Kalinganagar Complex. They organised protest meetings and sit-in demonstrations in front of construction sites. In April 2005, government had issued notice to do a family survey. But the *Mancha* decided not to cooperate with the government to do this survey as their demand for *patta* of their land was not met.

One of the incidents of 9 May 2005 assumes greater significance, in terms of signifying a culmination of simmering discontent against the administration and the companies under their protection. On 9 May, hearing that the *bhumi puja* for Maharashtra Seamless was going to be performed; people had assembled at the site to protest and obstruct the proceedings. And the people were not carrying any arms was corroborated by one of the officials present at the site. The Additional District Magistrate (ADM) of Kalinganagar came to the site to negotiate with the people. The local police was already present, though not in very large numbers, to provide security to the officials of Maharashtra Seamless. The people reiterated their demands to the ADM and did not move from the place. It is also alleged that the ADM, Shri Santanagopalan, ordered lathi charge and rushed towards the protestors, pushing some of the obstructing women to the ground. This provocated the people and clashes ensued. People resorted to stone-pelting and the vehicle of the ADM was damaged.

The ADM was beaten up, and when the IIC of Kalinganagar PS tried to save the ADM he too was beaten up. Both of them sustained injuries. Seeing the people's rage, the police retreated from the scene that afternoon, to return later with more reinforcements. They entered the villages and went on a rampage. Fearing retaliation, most of the men folk had fled the villages and taken shelter in the surrounding hillocks. Therefore, the brunt of the police fell on the women folk and children. They were roughed up and at least 25 women were arrested. Hearing of the police terror, people from nearby villages also fled their villages and took shelter in the nearby forest. It is alleged that the privations caused the death of two children. Also, an old man, who was severely beaten up by the police, died later.

After the incident of 9 May, the process of mutual distrust was completed. The tribals, led by the *Jana Mancha*, felt betrayed by the government and perceived the administration as friend of the companies and enemies of the tribal people. Further they were planning ways of snuffing out the resistance.

A notice was served to the people for Public Hearing on Tata Steel plant to be held at Jajpur Road on 27 July 2005. On the other hand, on 23 July 2005, Tatas came to perform their *bhumi puja* in the presence of District Collector and the SP. About 3,000 people protested and held demonstrations at the site. The administration responded by lodging cases against some people and their leaders. Again on 7 October 2005, Tatas came, accompanied by police and district administration, for *bhumi puja* and people protested.

On 25 October, Shri Rabindra Jarika, one of the leaders of the *Jana Mancha,* was arrested by the Jajpur police from Bhubaneswar. He had come to Bhubaneswar to attend a conference of some tribal organisations. The manner in which Shri Jarika was arrested, had raised serious questions at that time and many organisations had protested against police highhandedness in this case and the policy of the government to repress all democratic struggles by use of police force.

On 27 October, people gheraoed the Kalinganagar police station protesting against the arrest of Rabindra Jarika. After this incident, police have been trying to arrest the other leaders of the Visthapan Virodhi Jan Manch. On 17 November, people stopped the construction work begun by the Maharashtra Seamless Steel. Since then no further construction work took place till the date of firing. The movement was gaining momentum, and the mood of the people was upbeat.[23]

2 January 2006

On 2 January 2006, with the help of the administration, the Tatas undertook the programme of levelling the land where their plant was to come up. Top district officials, including SP and DM, were present. People of the area had assembled to protest. Coming sporadically from several villages, their numbers had gradually swelled to 300–400, including women and children, some of them carrying bows and arrows, *tangias* (a kind of pick axe) and other traditional weapons, which are customarily carried by tribal people. They were assembled on the adjacent fields to the site, close to Champa Koila village. By all accounts, the mobilisation of the police was massive, around 10 platoons, that is around 300 policemen, requisitioned by the SP for overseeing the levelling of a piece of land. They had taken positions, according to unofficial police sources, divided into three contingents on three sides of the Tata site, which was temporarily fenced by long ropes. When the levelling machine was doing its work, the protestors wanted to enter the rope cordon and stop the machine. The police tried to stop them. So, there arose a situation where there was pushing and pulling from both sides. In an attempt to scare the people, the police used 'stun shells', along with teargas shells and rubber bullets. This resulted in a great confusion when people ran helter-shelter in fright and outrage.

Some of the policemen, while chasing the demonstrators, had tripped on the uneven land around the site. This in turn encouraged some of the fleeing crowd to return back. The police had started firing, ostensibly to give cover to its fallen colleagues. But, inexplicably, they fired to kill, and some of the agitators fell victim. And in between one of the policemen, an unarmed havildar, Gopabandhu Mohanty, slipped and fell in the hands of the fleeing tribals. He was killed by the disoriented crowd. After this, the men in uniform and gears ran amok, the officials present did nothing to restrain them. They were baying for blood, seeking revenge, using the death of a colleague as an alibi. The people, frightened out of their wits, ran, as the police shot unrestrainedly from behind. Bodies, dead and injured, including women and children, lay strewn on the ground. The villagers carried some of their injured and dead people to the villages and admitted the injured into the hospital. The others, dead and injured, were taken to the hospital by the police. The final count, that emerged by, were shocking: one policeman dead and four injured; 12 tribals dead and 38 injured—the dead, as well as the injured, included women and children.[24]

Table 5.1 shows the name, village, age and sex of the people who died in police firing.

Table 5.1

List of people killed in police firing

Name	*Village*	*Age*	*Male/Female*
Landu Jarika	Bamiagotha	29	M
Ramachandra Jamuda	Bamiagotha	35	M
Junga Jarika	Bamiagotha	25	M
Gobinda Laguri	Bamiagotha	14	M
Rama Gagarai	Gadapur	35	M
Bana Badra	Gadapur	35	M
Mukta Bankira	Chandia	40	F
Rangalal Mundei	Baligotha	40	M
Ati Jamuda	Chandia	32	M
Deogi Tiria	Champa Koila	35	F
Sudam Barla	Belhudi	25	M
Bhagaban Say	Gobarghati	25	M

A Concern for the Rights of the Tribal People

India has the largest concentration of tribal people in world, next to Africa.[25] The human rights of the tribal are guaranteed and enforced in one or the other way by the *Constitution of India* and the Scheduled Castes and Scheduled Tribes (Prevention of Atrocities) Act, 1989. The enactment of Scheduled Castes and Scheduled Tribes (Prevention of Atrocities) Act, in the year 1989, after about 40 years of independence exhibits that the social, political, cultural or customary rights of these groups are being violated and overlooked.[26]

Article 10 of United Nations Declaration states:

> *Indigenous people shall not be forcibly removed from their lands or territories. No relocation shall take place without the free and informed consent of the indigenous people concerned and after agreement on just and fair compensation and, where possible, with the option of return.*

It is also the violation of the provision of fifth schedule of the Constitution as it deprives them of control and ownership of natural resources and land essential for *their way of life*.[27]

There is need of concerted effort on the part of the government, human rights monitoring bodies as well as non-governmental organisations to identify and rectify violations of the rights of tribal people. And at the same time, it is important to empower them by providing them with opportunities of *education, employment and community development* to inject a new life to their dying or disappearing *diverse and traditional rights.*

Conclusion

The narration of the entire history of the Kalinganagar agitation above gives a very clear and detailed picture of the state of affairs. It is to be noted that killing unarmed people without warning, shooting them with the intention of killing them and then removing organs and chopping the private parts of the dead after post-mortem not only sound macabre and barbaric but also reflect the brutal and inhuman behaviour of the police towards the tribals.[28] It shows the failure of the entire administration of the local as well as the state government.

The reason for the protest was called because tribals felt that they were not being compensated enough for construction projects by large industrial houses on lands traditionally occupied by them. The brutal and inhumane approach of the police in dealing with the tribals with force and violence resulted in massive violations of their rights and specially their right to life and freedom of expression. Their basic right to live a decent life was taken away by the protectors of the state—the police who are supposed to maintain law and order actually take law in their hands. The people's land was snatched away. They became *homeless and jobless*. Their *culture and traditions are fragmented*. Their social life was destroyed. They were reduced to abject poverty and were helpless.

Notes

1. R.N. Sharma, 'Involuntary Displacement: A Few Encounters', *Economic and Political Weekly,* 38(9), 907, 2003.
2. Ibid.
3. Ibid.
4. Ibid, p. 2.
5. Oliver-Smith, Anthony, *Defying Displacement: Grassroots Resistance and the Critique of Development,* University of Texas Press, Texas, pp. 2–22, 2010.
6. See. Economics and Development, http://www.economics-4development.com/sitemap.xml (accessed on 18 March 2011).
7. World Commission on Dams, 'Displacement Resettlement, Rehabilitation, Reparation and Development', *Thematic Review,* Social Issues I.3, 3, November 2000.
8. Smitu Kothari, 'Whose Nation? The Displaced as Victims of Development', *Economic and Political Weekly,* 31(24), 1476–1484, June 1996.
9. L.K. Mahapatra, *Tribal Development in India: Myth and Reality,* Vikash Publishing House, New Delhi, pp. 37–72, 1994.
10. T.K. Oommen 'Protest against Displacement by Development Projects: The Indian Case', *Indian Social Development Report 2008*, 76, 2008.

11. Felix Padel and Samrendra Das, 'Cultural Genocide: Impact of Development-induce Displacement', *Indian Social Development Report 2008*, 103, 2008.
12. Radha Kalyani (2003). *Police, Crime and Human Rights*, Pointers Publishers, Jaipur.
13. S.C. Joshi (2006), *Human Rights: Concepts, Issues and Laws*, Akansha Publishing House, New Delhi.
14. Radha Kalyani (2003). *Police, Crime and Human Rights*, Pointers Publishers, Jaipur.
15. Sukhpal Kaur, 'Women's Rights: A Historical Perspective', *The Indian Journal of Political Science*, LXX(1), January/March, 2009.
16. Joshi (2006).
17. Dhananjay Vasudeo Dwivedi, 'Thoughts for Human Rights in Vedic Tradition', *The Indian Journal of Political Science*, LXX(4), 1021–1034, October/December, 2009.
18. 'Orissa's New Name Is Odisha', *The Times of India*, 24 March 2011.
19. Orissa Government Portal (http://www.orissa.govt.in)
20. http://www.jajpur.nic.in
21. http://www.isidelhi.org.in/hrnews/isidownload/Tribals/tribals-2006.pdf(TRIBALS-2006)
22. http://www.wikipedia.org/wiki/kalinganagar
23. PUCL (People's Union for Civil Liberties) Bulletin, April 2006.
24. Ibid.
25. Uma K. Devi and Neera Bharihoke (2006), *Tribal Rights in India*, Serial Publications, New Delhi.
26. Ibid. p. 203.
27. Aman Gupta (2005), *Human Rights of Indigenous People*, Isha Books, Delhi.
28. Janardhan Pati, 'A Report on the Bloodbath in Kalinganagar', *Social Scientist*, 34(7/8), 86–90, July/August 2006.

References

Das, Achyut and Das, Vidya (2006). *Chronicle of a Struggle and Other Writings*. Kashipur, Rayagada, Orissa: Agragamee Publication.

Goodland, Robert (2007). 'India, Orissa, Kashipur – "Utkal Bauxite & Alumina Project: Human Rights and Environmental Impacts"'. Library of Congress Cataloguing-in-Publication Data, Washington DC.

Kothari, S. (1996). 'Whose Nation? The Displaced as Victims of Development', *Economic and Political Weekly*, 31(24), 1476–1485.

Manipadma, Jena (2006, February 4). 'Draft Resettlement and Rehabilitation Policy, 2006'. *Economic and Political Weekly*, 41(5), 384–387.

Mishra, Banikanta (2006, February 18). 'People's Movement at Kalinga Nagar: An Epitaph or an Epitome?'. *Economic and Political Weekly*.

Mishra, Ish (2007, March 10). 'Heat and Dust of Highway at Kalinganagar'. *Economic and Political Weekly*.

Orissa Resettlement and Rehabilitation Policy, 2006. Retrieved from www.isidelhi.org.in/hrnews/isidownload/Tribals/tribals-2006.pdf (TRIBALS-2006)

Padhi, Ranjana and Adve, Nagraj (2006, January 21). 'Endemic to Development: Police Killings in Kalinga Nagar'. *Economic and Political Weekly*.

Pati, Biswamoy (2006, March/April). 'Tatas and the Orissa "Model" of Capitalist "Development"'. *Social Scientist*, 34(3/4), 37–42.

Pati, Janardhan (2006, July/August). 'A Report on the Bloodbath in Kalinga Nagar,' *Social Scientist*, 34(7/8), 86–90.

Sahoo, Sarbeswar (2005, April/June). 'Tribal Displacement and Human Rights Violations in Orissa'. *Social Action: A Quarterly Review of Social Trends*, 55(2).

Part III

Human Rights, Children and Education

6

Hearing Children's Voices

A Study of Jammu & Kashmir State

Moksha Singh

The social fabric of Jammu & Kashmir (J&K) has succumbed to the ever growing terrorist violence and proxy war between India and Pakistan. The particular nature of the conflict has resulted in high levels of material destruction, a huge loss of life and phenomenal displacement. Caught up in the turmoil of the conflict, children in the state have especially been vulnerable. Further, in case of the death of the parent(s), it has resulted in different kinds of vulnerabilities for different categories of children. Displacement from homeland, separation, interruption in social interaction, loss of service access (education, health care), impoverishment, security threats to social and physical integrity of the child, transformations in children's roles and responsibilities are the few common consequences of the parental loss.

Based on such an understanding, this chapter is pertinent to the lives of orphans in J&K, India, who have experienced a similar situation of violence and a subsequent material, social, psychological and physical loss. The only viable rehabilitative alternative available for these children is in the form of child care institutions that include orphanages. The chapter first discusses about various concepts used in it before describing the objectives and the methodology adopted to study those objectives. The next section is based on the findings of the study that would follow discussion. The last section proposes certain policy suggestions that could help in the better rehabilitation of the orphans. It is followed by the conclusion.

Concepts

Child: In international documents such as the United Nations Conventions for the Rights of the Child (UNCRC) and the African Charter on the Rights and Welfare of the Child (ACRWC) (ACRWC 1990; UNCRC 1989; United Nations 2000), children are defined as boys and girls up to the age of 18 years. This 'relates primarily to the generally accepted age of majority, though in all countries there are legal exceptions, for example, the age at which a child may be married, make a will, or consent to medical treatment etc.' (Smart 2003, p. 3). For the purpose of this study, a person below the age of 18 years was considered a child. Apparently, it is the age at which a child achieves majority in India.

Orphan: Based on the physical loss incurred, orphans from all causes were categorised into four types in the study. These included the single orphan (a child who has lost one parent), double orphan (a child who has lost both the parents), maternal orphan (a child whose mother has died and includes double orphans) and paternal orphan (a child whose father has died and includes double orphans). This classification was analogous to the framework for the protection, care and support of orphans and vulnerable children living in a world with Human Immunodeficiency Virus (HIV) and Acquired Immune Deficiency Syndrome (AIDS), which defines an orphan as a child under 18 years of age whose mother, father or both parents have died from any cause (UNICEF 2004).

Institution: An institution is a generic name for a variety of residential care facilities (Sloutsky 1997). Residential/institutional care can be defined as 'a group of living arrangement for children in which care is remunerated by adults who would not be regarded as traditional carers within the wider society' (Tolfree 1995, p. 12). In the current work, it specifically relates to orphanages.

Justification of the Study

In J&K, the case of children who have lost their parent(s) to conflict has been largely subdued owing to the wider political attention that the conflict has got from the national and international community. The entire focus of the central and state governments has, therefore, been on devising ways to resolve the crisis. In the process, many areas that are of serious concern for the general public affected by the turmoil have been ignored. Children affected by violence have received the least of attention. There is also a serious gap in the knowledge regarding the impact of conflict on the children and the various types of interventions that could prove effective. Their appropriate rehabilitation and reintegration into the society remains dubious as the government-run policies have not been much effective and the participation of experts in the concerned field is missing. Institutional care, therefore, has so far emerged as the only rehabilitative alternative. However, the voices of the children in these institutions remain missing in matters that directly concern them, an important factor in the socio-psychological recovery of the children affected by trauma (Morantz and Heymann 2010).

Studies (Institute of Jammu & Kashmir Affairs 2002; Dabla 1999; Madhosh 2004; Médecins Sans Frontières 2006) that have been conducted on children affected by conflict in J&K mostly deal with the psychological perspective, focussing on issues that range from psychological well-being of the children, school dropout rates, impact of institutionalisation on the mental health of the children and impact on their academic performances. But not a single study has tried to look at the situation from children's point of view. All these reasons have enthused to carry out the study so that the gaps that exist in the concerned area could be reduced as much as possible.

Social Construction of Childhood

Childhood has always existed as a concept in all the societies (Archard 1993). The only difference being that the children are distinguished from the adults in varying ways (Heywood 2001). In the literary circles, 'childhood' refers to a particular stage of life, whereas a 'child' represents a group of persons. Childhood is a social construction and, therefore, it is determined by the time and the place where the individual is born (Coster 2007). Accordingly, various social and ethnic groups existing within a society assign a different meaning to it, and, therefore, think and act differently while dealing with their children (Heywood 2001). It is regarded that the understanding of the concept of childhood has taken place in ways that has often resulted in the non-recognition of their requirements and capabilities. For example in the medieval thought childhood was not considered an important stage of life and children were simply seen as 'little adults' (The Philosophy of Childhood 2002). Aries suggests that it did not accept that childhood was a period with a character distinct from adulthood, and, therefore, require a different set of rights so that their special needs do not go unnoticed and are met. The children were simply put in the 'great community of men' as early as 5–7 years of age (Heywood 2001).

The construction of childhood, according to Aries (as cited in Eekelaar 1986), is rather recent and started with the beginning of the modern ages (as cited in Jans 2004). The concept of child as a 'non-status' person, however, continued in Europe and the United States until the 17th century (Goonesekere 1998). The child-first perspective, in most parts of the world, emerged with women's activism. In this process, both women and children were benefitted. It helped in promoting the cause of women and, in turn, the 'best interests of the children principle' gained impetus in the political and academic circles (Gordon 2008). By the 1930s, the focus had shifted from improving the standards of living for children to providing them with rights. Thus, where earlier it was the dependent children or children in difficult circumstances that attracted attention now the focal point had been all children (Marshall 1950).

By the early 20th century, moves began to promote the idea of children's rights as distinct from those of adults and as requiring explicit recognition. The UNCRC gave a formal recognition to it. The move promised the effective redressal of the needs of the children as they have both less need and less capacity to exert 'pressure from below', and less potential for using the rhetoric of rights as a political instrument and which can address the relevant audience more directly (O'Neill 1988). This has, in recent years, led to a growing enthusiasm internationally for accepting the role of children as social actors and encouraging the practice of child voice. Article 12 of the UNCRC that lays stress on the participation of children in issues that directly concern them (United Nations Committee on the Rights of the Child 2003) reads:

(1) States parties shall assure the child who is capable of forming his or her own views the right to express those views freely in all matters affecting the child, the views of the child being given due weight in accordance with the age and maturity of the child.

(2) For this purpose, the child shall in particular be provided the opportunity to be heard in any judicial and administrative proceedings affecting the child, the views of the child being given due weight in accordance with the age and maturity of the child.

Article 12 is, therefore, significant as it recognises the child as a full human being who has the ability to participate freely in society. But it is observed that its implementation depends on the cooperation of adults who may because of vested interests do not recognise this (Lundy 2007). Children are used according to the functional requirements of social systems and no consideration is given to the personal characteristics, wants or interests of the child. They are seen by the adults as objects of concern rather than as persons who can speak for themselves (Lewis 2010). Children, therefore, 'continue to find their voices silenced, suppressed, or ignored in their everyday lives. Children may not be asked their views and opinions, and even if they are consulted, their ideas may be dismissed' (James 2007, p. 261).

The Debate and Ideological Shift

In a diversity of practices dealing with children, one can observe a strong discourse on child participation, thereby challenging those traditional roles that have always kept them away from decision-making process. Although there are certain scholars who question the credibility of children participating in matters that have remained the domain of the adults and oppose self-determination for children, preferring adult control of children's lives (Margolin 1978), many supporters of the children's rights movement strive for a full membership of children in society.

Childhood and the living conditions of children are fundamentally influenced by the same economic, political and social powers that constitute the context of adult lives. They determine the living conditions of children and the social construction of childhood (Jans 2004). Hence, participation of children in matters that concern them does become important and meaningful. Qvortrup, for example, would argue that the goal of a free society is to permit each individual to act according to his or her self-interests (as cited in Jans 2004).

Denying children the right to self-determination could pose a number of challenges. It is important to understand a child's viewpoint on issues that concern him so that their special needs do not go unnoticed. There have been number of instances where children have come out with much reasonable solutions to their long standing problems. But the problem still persists as they rely on notions of agency that cannot even account for the actions of powerful, generally adult male. It is, thus, necessary to see childhood as a dimension of agency, experience, and motivation throughout the life course. Maynes (2008) recommends that there is a need to 'reconceptualise and broaden the notion of children's agency' and that the 'life stories, particularly retrospective accounts of childhood, can offer new insights into both the agency of the young and the historical significance of childhood' (p. 114).

In many instances children have themselves started regarding their experiences as important while they agree with the decisions that prioritise their future. For example in a study on children it was found that the children accepted control and protection in respect of physical risk but did not accept constraint in respect of psychosocial risk, especially because it prioritises the future over the present, and denied children's competence and knowledge (Kelly, Mayall and Hood 1997). It is found that the children value and enjoy if they are given the opportunity to express their views. Policy-making in certain parts of the world is now based on new principles such as listening carefully to children and using multi-method techniques to help children express themselves that seek children's voices. Such developments have 'contributed to a strongly "pro voice" climate to the extent that the promotion of "child voice" has become a moral crusade' (Lewis 2010, p. 16).

Objectives

The main purpose of the study was to obtain a detailed description of the lives of the children affected by armed conflict in J&K and who were put in various orphanages across the state under rehabilitative purposes, with special emphasis on the way they understand their situations. Based on the findings of the study, this chapter tries to explore the ways in which these children have come to terms with the reality and comprehend their understanding, needs, relationships and future aspirations. Second, the chapter also attempts to trace the relevance of incorporating voices of these children in programmes that are meant for their rehabilitation. Third, it would propose certain policy suggestions that could help in their better rehabilitation and reintegration into the society.

Methodology

In order to examine, understand and interpret the magnitude and nature of the problem of orphans in the state, potential support systems, rehabilitation, as well as social conditions of these children, this study draws on qualitative research approach. It helped in an interpretative (Denzin and Lincoln 1998) and naturalistic approach to understand the phenomenon in context-specific settings. It was important, as each case required an exploration of their understanding of the situation, conditions they were in, emotions, physical loss, contradictory behaviours, beliefs, opinions and relationships among themselves.

Subjects/Sample

The study was conducted over a period of six months. It was carried out in two phases of three months each. The first phase was carried out in September 2009 and the second after a gap of two months in 2010. The orphanages of Kashmir and Jammu regions made part of the study as these regions have been affected by the conflict and account for the majority of children victims of conflict.

Theoretical sampling was used in selecting the orphanages and the respondents. As Glaser describes, it is a process of data collection 'whereby the analyst jointly collects, codes and analyses the data and decides what data to collect next and where to find it, in order to develop the theory as it emerges' (as cited in Goulding 1999). The samples were determined to begin with, by going to the most obvious places. These included orphanages and the concerned government offices and non-government organisations. It emerged that the orphanages could be categorised into four main types. These are: (a) state-run orphanages, (b) local non-governmental organisations (NGOs/foundations), (c) SOS children's villages, an international non-governmental organisation (INGO) and (d) Indian Army-operated orphanages. The state-run orphanages do not admit conflict-affected children and thus are excluded from the study. The remaining three types are considered for the study. From both Jammu region and the Kashmir region, orphanage of each type was selected.

The growing understanding of the data, concepts and their properties guided further sampling in relation to which participants to select and areas to sample. The sampling technique helped to 'maximize opportunities to compare events, incidents, or happenings to determine how a category varies in terms of its properties and dimensions' (Strauss and Corbin 1998, p. 202) and consequently helped in selecting further respondents. For example, it was found that the type of orphan (single or double) adopted different coping strategies (a major category that emerged during the study) in order to overcome the social, emotional and physical loss. The collection of data continued until theoretical saturation (Auerbach and Silverstein 2003; Pandit 1996) was reached. It was attained with the completion of the 31st interview as new themes stopped emerging (Bryant and Charmaz 2007).

Data Collection

Both primary and secondary sources were used in the research. The primary sources were field based that included interviews, observations and case studies involving introspective accounts of experiences of the orphans. After deciding on the respondents, the place, the time and the types of data to be gathered, separate lists of interview questions was made for both the management and the children victims of conflict and institutionalised. Child's participation was voluntary and was given equal opportunities to participate without any prejudice or stereotyping in approaches adopted. Also, undue intrusion was avoided and confidentiality and anonymity (National Children's Bureau London 2003) of the child was maintained.

Interviews were of qualitative nature. The collection of the data was done with the help of interview schedules in order to learn the participants' perspectives, experiences and meanings for various kinds of actions under particular circumstances. These interviews were in-depth and open-ended. It helped in collecting data on the personal histories, perspectives and experiences of the subjects particularly when sensitive topics were being explored (Family Health International 2005). The questions were so phrased that the researcher's own ideas, interests or theoretical understandings were not imposed on the participants (Giske and Artinian 2007). It allowed for more flexibility, with an iterative style (Wicks and Whiteford 2006) of eliciting and categorising responses to questions, describing variations and explaining relationships and individual experiences. The response of the participants directed which questions to be asked next, aiding in collecting relevant information. They were free to respond in their own words the experiences and perceptions (Yuksel 2010) they had of the situation. Secondary sources were based on archived sources. These included public or private documents/records such as news reports, surveys, government or organisational documents; studies; as well as books and journals.

Analysis

For all the open-ended questions, patterns and trends in the responses were noted by identifying the main themes. The transcribed interviews were carefully read to get the essence of the data. Some common themes emerged in the process through which categories emerged. The process did not stop at this. The relationship among the categories was established which helped in identifying the major trends and patterns. The available literature helped to compare and contrast the findings with existing research.

Findings

Orphans of Conflict: A Case of Jammu & Kashmir

This section focusses on the personal experiences of 31 children who were the direct or indirect victims of militancy and are residing in six different orphanages in the state of J&K. Their experiences have been shared in the form of narratives that offer insight into ways in which they understand and respond to a given situation by deriving relevant meanings. On many accounts children were universal in their responses. However, certain variations were reported in every child who was interviewed. It was important to understand these differences as it made clearer how these young children in varied ways made sense of the violent experiences and the events that followed.

Six themes have been discussed in the chapter that help in explaining these lived experiences of the orphans. These are children's understanding of their situation, participation, coping strategies, rehabilitation and the role of orphanages, self-image/conception of identities as orphans and future needs.

Children's Understanding of their Situation

Despite strong reservations against the 'in care' facility and a move towards the 'reunified' (Weisman 1994), which includes adoption and foster care as a rehabilitative mechanism, institutionalisation emerges out to be the most viable alternative for the orphans in J&K because of the socio-economic reasons.

Article 12 applies to all levels of decision-making and requires consistent and ongoing arrangements to ensure that it is implemented effectively. But in none of the cases, except for one subject, a child was ever consulted about him being moved to the orphanage. The parent(s), relatives or the management of the orphanages did not consider them mature enough to have taken the decision. Laura Lundy explains this by stating that:

> adult concerns tend to fall into one of the three groups: scepticism about children's capacity (or belief that they lack capacity) to have a meaningful input into decision-making; a worry that giving children more control will undermine authority and destabilise the school environment; and finally, concern that compliance will require too much effort. (2007, p. 929)

Interviews with the children, however, revealed that they were well aware of the reasons that had led to their placement into the orphanages and the ways in which it helped them to come out of their distress. For example, one of the children reported that:

> It was my father's disability that forced me to come to the orphanage. My mother had to take care of everything. Our financial condition was not good that time and it pushed her to put me into the orphanage. I would have never been at this place ... if I could. But I am happy that my father is alive otherwise we would have been in more trouble.

In another case, girl child moving to the orphanage was the only solution to her problems as both her parents are dead. She expressed herself by saying that:

> I have forgotten everything of the past and I do not want to remember anything. I do not want to recollect what had happened that day. I will get nothing out of it. As for now I am concentrating on my studies so that I get a good job. I am the eldest. It is my responsibility to take care of my other two sisters who too are at the orphanage. They would stay back for few years after I am out of here. They would join me and I will take care of my siblings.

Participation

Sumaiya Khair (2001) suggests 'children's participation and decision-making not only enables them to grow up as responsible adults but also make them aware of their rights, duties and privileges at the social, economic and political levels'. It helps in the overall development of the child by giving the child the opportunities to develop skills, knowledge and abilities that can be beneficial to them in the future (p. 57). A child interviewed said:

> We do raise our issues to the administration sometimes but these are not always entertained. We recommend that this habit of involving us in various orphanage activities must be encouraged as we feel that getting these recognized helps in raising our self-confidence and we feel that we are ready to face the outside world.

The children were found to be with minimal participation rights and less control over the matters that concerned their future aspirations such as educational and professional interests and so on. They were, however, involved in other institutional activities such as deciding the food menu and participating in school events that the children considered as secondary. It was found that the children appreciated the efforts that the institutions had been making for them but they continuously expressed their desire to be a part of the decision-making process.

Coping Strategies

Children are often viewed as individuals that have little or no comprehension of the sudden changes occurring around them, especially involving the death of a near one. However, this view has been challenged by many scholars who regard 'children as a social group' and that they are experts in the social construction of their own worlds and in distinguishing between their happier and bad times. They offer accounts of good childhood derived from their own experimental knowledge and perception (Kelley et al. 1997).

Similar accounts were obtained from the older respondents who reported that the initial months after that change had been difficult. They were unable to come to terms with what had happened to their families. But as time passed they understood the situations they were in. In order to normalise their lives, they started performing activities that helped them come out of the distress. These included play, creativity, forming associations or disassociating themselves from their surroundings. The respondents, therefore, were found to be strategically coping with their stresses. The efforts varied according to the personal capabilities and interests of the child. For example, many expressed their fears, joys, grief and pain by engaging themselves in activities such as drawings and writings instead of speaking about those. One of the respondents told that they had other ways of coping with the stress. She said:

> I engage myself in active competition, in studies, sports, debates, and other institutional activities which keep me pre-occupied. It also enhances my skills, gives me self-confidence and a spirit to fight back.

Sternberg and Rosenbloom (2000) in their study found that indulging in such exercises helps the children to cope with extreme deprivation and a constant sense of fear. The other exercises included establishing associations with their peer groups, sharing their similar experiences of life and comforting each other by discussing the kind of pain they have gone through. One's membership in any group with similar background is of great emotional benefit. In such aggregations, the children have the opportunity to delve deeper into the 'collective memory and focus on issues relevant to their histories. They experience freedom to share a deeper understanding of their earlier trauma, and a sense of an extended family' (Sternberg and Rosenbloom 2000, p. 15). It helps children in coming out of the grief and in regaining their self-confidence. A child spoke:

> I have noticed a lot of change in myself. When I was placed in the orphanage the only thing that used to come to my mind was to run away from here and take revenge from the killers of my father. I was only ten years old then but was so aggressive, restless and in a state of utter dilemma. The only purpose for me in life was to either kill them or kill myself. Now four years have passed since then and now I laugh at myself. I was small then and did not realise what was happening. A lot has changed since then. I am much more stable now and have adjusted well to the

> orphanage environment. The people are good here. The only thing I want to do now is to work hard, get a good job and take care of my mother and siblings.

Interviews with the children, whether young or older, gave descriptions of the ideal life spent at home, towns or villages. They spoke about the despair that the incident had brought in their lives, the resulting displacement and their loss of contact with every person they knew. All these events had left them shattered. However, after analysing their situation most of them think that coming to the orphanages was a good thing. With time they have learnt to adjust to the changed environment. Most of them had regained contacts with their earlier friends, relatives and village people. They have made new friends and established relationships with the staff and classmates that have further helped them to overcome their grief. They have now created their own 'social world' and are comfortable with their present status. Thus, it can be said that 'contextual variations influence a child's choice of strategies in handling disputes' (Emihovich 1986).

Rehabilitation and the Role of Orphanages

The respondents had a very clear understanding of the role that the orphanages have played in their lives. Where the younger children often expressed that they should not have been brought to the orphanages as they missed the fun they used to have at their villages, staying with their families; the older children presented a much objectivised view of the changes in their lives. According to them, it was an indispensable situation. The family members, who survived, did not have any option but to shift them to the child care institutions. Orphanages, thus, in such case become the most prevalent and easiest response to the problems of poverty and social exclusion. A respondent said:

> My mother was incapable of looking after me and my sister. So, we were sent here. I know she is helpless. We have no source of income. The only place where we got refuge was this orphanage. I will be indebted to them always.

The initial days at the orphanages, however, were tough for all of them. It took time for them to adjust to the strict daily regimens of the institutions while the emotional and psychological suffering was still underway. However, the orphans denied the view that the institutional environment is completely restrictive, with a lack of permanency, and lack of familiness and something which is least desirable (Davidson-Arad, Dekel and Wozner 2004). For one of the respondents:

> The orphanage is quite far away from my native place and so I cannot pay many visits. I sometimes feel bad about it but in a way it has helped me. I utilize the time in undergoing coaching classes. The institution pays for it. They help children who are good in studies. The staff too has been very cooperative. Some problems do arise for example individual attention is lacking ... but not always. I know that this is the only best place for me right now. If I would have been at the village I would not have been able to continue my studies.

The respondents felt secure inside the orphanage compound. But on certain occasions the idea of joblessness, homelessness or discrimination—once they step outside—disturbed them. Therefore, even when the orphanages were trying to facilitate children's activities and prepare them for an independent life as adults, they prefer spending as much time as possible at the institutions until they are completely settled.

Self-Image/Conception of Identities as Orphans

The respondents gave a mixed reaction when asked about what they felt about themselves. Some among them told that coming to the orphanages had been beneficial for them. Orphanage assistance to orphans has contributed to perceptions of these children as 'lucky' (Thurman et al. 2008) among the community members and the children themselves. As all the children were from rural areas they knew that they were getting the best of facilities. Some orphans, however, were not confident of the residential care as they reported the fear of getting stigmatised for being raised in the orphanage environment. For example one girl respondent said:

> I have been tagged as an orphan, with no parents. I have been raised in the orphanage since I was five ... twelve years have

> passed. I am worried about the life ahead. It will be very difficult to find a match for me. Who would like to marry his son with a girl from the orphanage?

The orphans too feel that they are different from the children in any normal family. Most of them do not socialise with other kids who have parents because they think that they do not have the same problems. Among such children it is the collective identity which is important. They identify themselves more with the rest of the residents in the orphanage having similar experiences and problems. These children who have lost their near ones to conflict try to find meaning in their cultural and historical pasts. They identify with the adults primarily within the community (Povrzanovic 1997) and the children who had been a part of it.

Future Needs

During the interviews with the children it was perceived that the vulnerabilities associated with orphanhood needs immediate attention. But not all require the same level of assistance. Some orphans were the neediest amongst their group and needed special attention. For example, age of the orphan is a major criterion that determines his overall well-being. Younger orphans showed social and emotional withdrawal after the parental loss and they were in need of the care of a woman they had no emotional ties with (Oleke et al. 2006). When needs like this and others are not met in time, the child develops certain fears that are further associated with the emergence of various other kinds of uncertainties. One respondent expressed:

> I want to stay at the orphanage until I finish graduation. But I would not be allowed. All financial aid will stop if I do not score well. The very thought of it scares me and it is quite frustrating. The uncertainty about the future constantly worries me and because of which I fail to concentrate on my studies.

As displacement disturbs the coherence of familiar networks, of community, friends and family, there is disconnect in the consistency and security for the young. This was visible among the children at the orphanage and who in their interviews often spoke about it. They feel that these institutions were able to fulfil their physical needs to a greater extent but their social and emotional needs largely remained unmet. The respondents reported that they were satisfied with the infrastructural facilities but they would have been happier if they could stay with their parents, amongst the natural environment of the villages. For the children, this would have helped in getting rid of many other types of uncertainties such as what one is, one's social being and one's identity, and as Bourdieu (2000) states, 'legitimacy of an existence, an individual's right to feel justified in existing as he or she exists'.

Discussion

All the narratives are thorough and compelling. These show that children have 'diversity in what interests them and holds their attention, but their knowledge, understanding of stories and real-life values has deepened' (Karniol and Koren 1987). The point that can be made here is that children not only know what is important to them but they also have a clear idea of what they want others to know about their lives. It, therefore, becomes important to ask children about their quality of life and what they think would be appropriate for them. Studies have shown that children as young as 9–11 years are found reliable enough for serving as the direct source of information (Ben-Arieh 2005; Kelly, Mayall and Hood 1997). Letting a child speak for himself, therefore, gives a chance to explore the unique ways in which he understands the situation and offers insights into the problems and possible solutions.

Children, therefore, are capable of social action and, therefore, should be allowed to enter into dialogical relationships with other people (Uprichard 2010) so that needs and desires could be explored. For example, during the period from 1890 and 1930, young readers in American libraries were given a chance to actively engage with the institution of public library and document what their reading choices were (McDowell 2011). The children were considered capable and important for the system to function effectively.

Such an approach is desperately needed in the case of children who have lost their parent(s). The respondents have no control over their lives when they know what they want. The dialogical relationship is missing, and the voices of the young people in most of the cases is muted (Edmond 2003). In such cases, it is the adult choice that has superseded that of the child. Given a chance to speak for them, there is every possibility that it would offer much better and result-oriented ways for their rehabilitation.

Despite strong traditional pattern of extended family obligations towards parentless children which exists in J&K, large-scale institutional care continues to be the norm for organisations providing care facilities in most parts of the state, with programmes of substitute family care remaining at a relatively embryonic stage of development. The state's policies have not been successful in providing relief to the affected children at their doorsteps and in preventing their families from breaking. The near ones of children are left with no other option but to send them to orphanages across the state. The region has witnessed a high growth of child care institutions but without any proper training of the staff. Lack of understanding among the staff creates hindrance in distinguishing the special needs of the different categories of orphans as they are not affected in a similar way or to the same extent by armed conflict. The problem is further aggravated as the children's voices are undermined in these institutions. Their understanding of the situation and specific needs arising out of it do not get relevant attention. These organisations, therefore, many a times put these children under immense socio-psychological developmental risks.

Policy Suggestions

Keeping in view the above discussion, the chapter makes the following suggestions, which if executed, might help in the successful rehabilitation of the children affected by conflict in J&K. First, measures must be taken by various central and state government organisations dealing with children such as the National Commission for Protection of Child Rights to include children's view in policies that are framed specifically for them.

Furthermore, their involvement should be on a sustained and genuinely dialogic basis that goes beyond the current vogue for one-off and tokenistic participation. Second, it should be made mandatory to consult the target population before framing any policy. The involvement of the child, therefore, should be a legal imperative giving the child the chance to air his views.

Third, for successful implementation of Article 12 of the UNCRC, the implications of four separate factors needs to be done: space (opportunity to express a view), voice (facilitated to express their views), audience (the view must be listened to) and influence (the view must be acted upon, as appropriate) (Lundy 2007). In addition to it, Article 12 should be considered in the light of other relevant UNCRC provisions; in particular: Article 2 (non-discrimination); Article 3 (best interests); Article 5 (right to guidance); Article 13 (right to seek, receive and impart information) and Article 19 (protection from abuse). Fourth, there should not be an undue pressure on them to participate. It should be an absolute decision of the child whether he wants to be a part of the process or not.

Conclusion

Through the above discussion, it can be said that children as a group have little authority in shaping their own lives but are subjected to the organisational and ideological framework created by the adults. It is seen that it is not the children's issues that would set the agenda in the adult world but the interests of the latter, budgetary constraints, priorities of the state. Absence or non-recognition of children in the dialogical process fails to address their issues effectively. In order to gain a meaningful insight into the children's world, their subjective perceptions on issues that concern them deserves attention. Children's well-being can only be addressed if we get answers to questions such as what do children want? What are their needs? How do they feel and act in certain situations? What they want to say about themselves? What they want to contribute? The relevance of the point is that the right of the children to express their views needs to be promoted.

The children who participated in the research willingly and successfully reflected on their situation and matters that concerned them. They articulated issues and concepts that were relevant for their well-being and were found capable enough in dealing with complex situations and then arriving at workable solutions. The retrospective accounts of children offered new insights into both the agency of the young and the significance of what they had to experience and share.

However, any rush in listening to the voices of the children must be carefully scrutinised (Lewis 2010). This should not demean the relevance of the views that children have to offer instead could contribute to policy development. Children, therefore, should be given the chance to express their views. Any action to help the children in need is deemed appropriate only if they themselves are involved into the process.

References

ACRWC (1990). Retrieved from http://www.africa-union.org/official_documents/Treaties_%20Conventions_%20Protocols/a.%20C.%20ON%20THE%20RIGHT%20AND%20WELF%20OF%20CHILD.pdf

Archard, D. (1993). 'Children: Rights and Childhood'. Retrieved from http://books.google.co.in/books?id=5VYvfHwAlx4C&printsec=frontcover#v=onepage&q&f=false

Auerbach, C.F. and Silverstein, L.B. (2003). 'Qualitative Data: An Introduction to Coding and Analysis'. Retrieved from http://books.google.co.in/books?Id=6uFPbXSmBQC&pg=PA102&lpg=A102&dq=theoretical+saturation&source=bl&ots=BPMcPVLgCq&sig=aPNMr69lb8yOuLIFm2ExLnesFWE&hl=en&ei=RF2oTcCnOoaAvgP506CHCg&sa=X&oi=book_result&ct=result&resnum=4&ved=0CDIQ6AEwAw#v=onepage&q=theoretical%20saturation&f=false;

Ben-Arieh, A. (2005). 'Where Are the Children? Children's Role in Measuring and Monitoring Their Well-being'. *Social Indicators Research*, 74(3), 573–596.

Bourdieu, P. (2000). 'Pascalian Meditations'. Retrieved from http://books.google.co.in/books?id=Or0tmdjsiKsC&pg=PA167&lpg=PA167&dq=P.+Bourdieu,+Pascalian+Meditations+%282000%29,&source=bl&ots=Gemd35KG03&sig=PEtnrUaz24Yj4s6uQfBkbQiNRo&hl=en&ei=kcVQTeqsOcP4ca3CxaEH&sa=X&oi=book_result&ct=result&resnum=2&ved=0CCIQ6AEwAQ#v=onepage&q&f=false

Bryant, A. and Charmaz, K. (2007). *The Sage Handbook of Grounded Theory*. New Delhi: Sage Publications.

Coster, W. (2007). 'Social Constructions of Childhood', in Paula Zwozdiak-Mayers (ed.), *Childhood and Youth Studies*. Southernhay East: Learning Matters Limited, 3–12.

Dabla, Bashir A. (1999). *Impact of Conflict Situation on Women and Children in Kashmir*. New Delhi: National Institute of Public Cooperation and Child Development.

Davidson-Arad, B., Dekel, R. and Wozner, Y. (2004). 'Correspondence in Residents and Staff Members: Assessment of the Quality of Life of Children in Residential Care Facilities'. *Social Indicators Research*, 68, 77–89.

Denzin, N.K. and Lincoln, Y.S. (1998). *Strategies in Qualitative Inquiry*. New Delhi: Sage Publications.

Edmond, R. (2003). 'Putting the Care into Residential Care: The Role of Young People'. *Journal of Social Work*, 3(3), 321–337.

Eekelaar, J. (1986). 'The Emergence of Children's Rights'. *Oxford Journal of Legal Studies*, 6(2), 161–182.

Emihovich, C. (1986). 'Argument as Status Assertion: Contextual Variations in Children's Disputes'. *Language in Society*, 15(4), 485–500.

Family Health International (2005). *Qualitative Research Methods: A Data Collector's Field Guide*, (eds) Mack, N., Woodsong, C., MacQueen, K.H., Guest, G. and Namey, E. North Carolina.

Giske, T. and Artinian, B. (2007). 'A Personal Experience of Working with Classical Grounded Theory: From Beginner to Experienced Grounded Theorist'. *International Journal of Qualitative Methods*, 6(4), 70.

Goonesekere, S. (1998). *Children, Law and Justice: A South Asian Perspective*. New Delhi: Sage Publications.

Gordon, L. (2008). 'The Perils of Innocence, or What's Wrong with Putting Children First'. *The Journal of the History of Childhood and Youth*, 1(3), 331–350.

Goulding C. (1999). 'Grounded Theory: Some Reflections on Paradigm, Procedures and Misconceptions' (Working Paper No. WP006/99). Retrieved from http://wlv.openrepository.com/wlv/bitstream/2436/11403/1/Goulding.pdf

Heywood, C. (2001). *The History of Childhood*. Cambridge: Polity Press.

Institute of Jammu & Kashmir Affairs (2002). 'Impact of Armed Conflict on Children of J&K State'. Jammu: Puri, Balraj.

James, A. (2007). 'Giving Voice to Children's Voices: Practices and Problems, Pitfalls and Potentials'. *American Anthropologist*, 109(2), 261–272.

Jans, M. (2004). 'Children as Citizens: Towards a Contemporary Notion of Child Participation'. *Childhood,* 11(1), 27–44.

Karniol, R. and Koren, L. (1987). 'How Would You Feel? Children's Inferences Regarding Their Own and Others' Affective Reactions'. *Cognitive Development,* 2, 271–278.

Kelley, B.T., Thornberry, T.P. and Smith, C.A. (1997). *In the Wake of Childhood Maltreatment*. Washington DC: US Department of Justice, Office of Justice Programs.

Kelly, P., Mayall, B. and Hood, S. (1997). 'Children's Accounts of Risk'. *Childhood,* 4, 320–321.

Khair, S. (2001). 'Street Children in Conflict with the Law: The Bangladesh Experience'. *Asia-Pacific Journal on Human Rights and the Law,* 2 (1), 55–76.

Lewis, A. (2010). 'Silence in the Context of Child Voice'. *Children & Society,* 24, 14–23.

Lundy, L. (2007). 'Voice is Not Enough: Conceptualising Article 12 of the United Nations Conventions on the Rights of the Child'. *British Educational Research Journal,* 33(6), 927–942.

Madhosh, A.G. (2004). *Women and Children under Armed Conflict in Kashmir*. New Delhi: National Institute of Public Cooperation and Child Development.

Margolin, C.R. (1978). 'Salvation versus Liberation: The Movement for Children's Rights in a Historical Context'. *Social Problems,* 25(4), 441–452.

Marshall, T.H. (1950). *Citizenship and Social Class and Other Essays*. New York, NY: Cambridge University Press.

Maynes, M. (2008). 'Age as a Category of Historical Analysis: History, Agency, and Narratives of Childhood'. *Journal of History of Childhood & Youth,* 1(1), 114–124.

McDowell, K. (2011). 'Children's Voices in Librarians' Words, 1890–1930'. *Libraries & the Cultural Record,* 40(1), 73–101.

Médecins Sans Frontières (2006). *Kashmir: Violence and Health—A Quantitative Assessment on Violence, the Psychosocial and General Health Status of the Indian Kashmiri Population*. Amsterdam: CRIN.

Morantz, G. and Heymann, J. (2010). 'Life in Institutional Care: The Voices of Children in a Residential Care in Botswana'. *AIDS Care,* 22(1), 10–16.

National Children's Bureau London (2003). 'Guidelines for Research'. Retrieved from http://www.Ncb.org.uk/dotpdf/open%20access%20-%20phase%201%20only/researchguidelines200604.pdf.

O'Neill, O. (1988). 'Children's Rights and Children's Lives'. *Ethics,* 98(3), 445–463.

Oleke, C., Astrid, B., Moland, K.M., Rekdal, O.B. and Heggenhougen, K. (2006). 'The Varying Vulnerability of African Orphans: The Case of the Langi, Northern Uganda'. *Childhood,* 13, 267–284.

Pandit, N.R. (1996). 'The Creation of Theory: A Recent Application of the Grounded Theory Method'. *The Qualitative Report*, 2(4).

Povrzanovic, M. (1997). 'Children, War and Nation Croatia 1991-4'. *Childhood,* 4(1), 81–102.

Sloutsky, V.M. (1997). 'Institutional Care and Developmental Outcomes of 6- and 7-Year-Old Children: A Contextualist Perspective'. *International Journal of Behavioral Development*, 20(1), 131–151.

Smart, C. (2002). 'From Children's Shoes to Children's Voices'. *Family Court Review,* 40(3), 307–319.

Smart, R. (2003). *Policies for Orphans and Vulnerable Children: A Framework for Moving Ahead.* Washington: Future Groups International.

Sternberg, M. and Rosenbloom, M. (2000). 'Lost Childhood—Lessons from the Holocaust: Implications for Adult Adjustment'. *Child and Adolescent Social Work Journal,* 17(1), 5–17.

Strauss, A.L. and Corbin, J.M. (1998). *Basics of Qualitative Research.* London: Sage Publications.

The Philosophy of Childhood (2002). 'Stanford Encyclopaedia of Philosophy Online'. Retrieved from http://plato.stanford.edu/entries/childhood.

Thurman, T.R., Snider, L.A., Boris, N.W., Kalisa, E., Nyirazinyoye, L. and Brown, L. (2008). 'Barriers to the Community Support of Orphans and Vulnerable Youth in Rwanda'. *Social Science and Medicine,* 66, 1557–1567.

Tolfree, D. (1995). *Roofs and Roots: The Care of Separated Children in the Developing World.* Save the Children Fund. UK: Arena Publishers.

UNCRC (1989). Article 1, Part 1. Retrieved from http://www.ohchr.org / english/law/crc.htm#part1

United Nations (2000). Protocol to Prevent, Suppress and Punish Trafficking in Persons, Especially Women and Children, Supplementing the United Nations Conventions Against Transnational Organized Crime'. Retrieved from http://www.uncjin.org/Documnts/Conventions/dcatoc/final_documents_2/convention_%20traff_eng.pdf

UNICEF (2004). *The Framework for the Protection, Care and Support of Orphans and Vulnerable Children Living in a World with HIV and AIDS.* New York: UNICEF.

United Nations Committee on the Rights of the Child (2003). 'General Comment No. 5, UN/CRC/GC/2003/1'. Retrieved from http://www.ohchr.org/english/bodies/crc/co mments.htm

Uprichard, E. (2010). 'Questioning Research with Children: Discrepancy between Theory and Practice?'. *Children & Society,* 24, 3–13.

Weisman, M. (1994). 'When Parents are Not in the Best Interests of the Child'. *The Atlantic Online*. Retrieved from http://www.theatlantic.com/past/docs/issues/96apr/orphan/weisorp.htm

Wicks, A. and Whiteford, G. (2006). 'Conceptual and Practical Issues in Qualitative Research: Reflections on a Life History Study'. *Scandinavian Journal of Occupational Therapy*, 13(2), 94–100.

Yuksel, I. (2010). 'How to Conduct a Qualitative Program Evaluation in the Light of Eisner's Educational Connoisseurship and Criticism Model'. *Turkish Online Journal of Qualitative Inquiry,* 1(2).

7

A Human Rights Perspective on Education and Research in Science and Technology

Astha Saxena

Progress in science and technology may be viewed from epistemological, economic, legal, sociocultural and ethical perspectives, albeit historically it has been considered as an epistemological end itself. Much of the progress manifested in military applications more so in inter-war period. However, post-Second World War, besieged with the challenges of burgeoning population and economic growth, technical progress has been regarded as a means of extending the frontiers of production possibility and delivering products and services for insatiable human needs and wants. Of late, one witnesses growing awareness about the necessity of ethical and human rights perspective (HRP) on science and technological education, research and progress. This emphasis has been reinforced by a host of disasters such as Japan's Nuclear Reactor Peril (2011), Endosulfan tragedy in Kerala (2010) and death of four girls from cervical cancer vaccination (*The Hindu*, 8 April 2010). Emerging from here is the need to make human well-being, the prerogative of every scientific research such as to inflict least harm to any living species in any way. Although the goal appears to seemingly insurmountable, this is what we should strive for, as having an anthropocentric concern will not be truly liberating rather selfish.

However limiting, the purpose of the present chapter is to examine education and research in science and technology from a human rights perspective (HRP). As such, the present chapter represents a species of the genus of STS issues.[1] The STS discourse takes a contextual view of science and technology rather than the conventional, decontextualised view that considers developments in science and technology, independent of the context in which they take place. The chapter takes the position that even 'responsible' science and technology will not suffice; one has to take a rights perspective if at all science and technology has to serve the human purpose. In presenting our position, we rely on the case study of human genome project. The present chapter is an attempt to understand the complex but estranged relationship between current trend of researches in science and technology and their societal implications by looking at it from a human rights perspective (HRP). Is it not important to base these researches in a humane context so that they inflict least harm to the society. Can development be viewed from a narrow perspective of advanced technology production, massive material gains and increased security in terms of nuclear armament, as there could be many pitfalls in the application and utilisation of any technology. Holistic development commands happiness to all and calls for maintaining peace and harmony in inter-personal relationships. Moreover, the distribution of the rewards of such technology should follow an egalitarian approach that upholds the issue of human rights for equality. Another could be the impact or safety assessment of these researches on common population. Often these researches follow less stringent safety measures and testing procedures leading to deleterious consequences on humans. Often people are aware about the basic human rights, yet do not know how to use and apply them in a scientific and technological context.

With this background, the present chapter has the following objectives: (a) to present and highlight the human rights issues attached to researches in science and technology (by referring to a case study based of human genomic project; HGP), (b) to discuss the impact of various researches on the society and thus drawing interface between science, technology and society, and (c) finally to derive implications for the inculcation of these human rights issues in science education.

Conceptual Framework

Let us first define the concepts represented in this chapter so as to delve into the deeper inter-relationships among them.

Human Rights

Human rights are a set of inalienable rights bestowed to humans from the time of birth until death, and help in leading life to its fullest with peace and harmony and without any kind of fear. Textbooks define human rights as a tool or concept for thinking in real terms and as a means to express human thoughts (Freeman 2002). Such a view sounds quite mundane and redundant, as it does not give appropriate directions for the fulfilment of those inalienable human rights or critically evaluate the present circumstance. A more elaborative conceptualisation could define them as a set of those inalienable rights that can neither be given nor taken away from any individual irrespective of class, colour, creed, race, gender or religion. A set of those ethical principles that are applicable and abided by all, at the same time being subjective as each individual has one's own way of conceptualising and utilising these rights (O'Byrne 2003). However, since recent past, there has been a realisation for the inclusion of human rights components in the researches related to science and technology, which belong to the third-generation human rights (Dev, Dev, and Das 1996) that include environmental, cultural and developmental rights. The growing awareness about HRP in science and technology is evident from successive UN declarations including 1948, 1961, 1966, 1971, 1972, 1975 and 1998.

Education

Education is said to be an aspect of human being's life that separates him from animals, provides rationality and logic, helps in uplifting us from slumber, and illuminates and enlightens the mind. An effective education system aims towards development of both human soul and mind, by demolishing all kinds of vices such as jealousy, anger, envy and hatred, and fosters the ideals of secularism, brotherhood, democracy and righteousness. This is in consonance with the Article 13 of the International Covenant on Economic, Social and Cultural Rights (1966) which states, 'Education should be directed to the full development of Human personality and the sense of its dignity and shall strengthen the respect for Human Rights and Fundamental freedom'.

Science Education and Research

The philosophical aims of science education includes the acquisition of ability to find out reasons and logic behind day-to-day happenings, conduct experiments, identify a problem, collection of relevant data, generating hypothesis and arriving at conclusions, all these constitute the scientific method that is the characteristic of science education. The often neglected sphere of scientific aims is the sociological one, dealing with the applied aspect of science in society or more precisely technology.

Technology Education and Research

Technology is often being looked from an objective status, as well as a ladder towards development of any country. Technology education is being imparted with a major role in the emancipation of the society by solving various problems, besides industrial arts education aims at developing technical skills, vocational and creative skills as well as worthy use of leisure (Dugger et al. 1979). One of the aims of technology education is also to establish beliefs and values based upon the impact of technology and the way it alters the environment (Snyder and Hales 1981).

By studying and analysing the afore laden concepts in the present chapter, it can be proposed that science and technology education as well as researches cannot be looked at in isolation from the society, rather have to be based in such a way that they do not pose any harm to the society for which the principles of science alone are not sufficient to put a check, rather a code of human rights has to be evolved that put these researches in a humane backdrop. This calls for an integrated approach in science education taking into account the human rights component so as to portray their significance in understanding the complexity of relationships amongst these three components of science, technology and human rights, and at the same time aiming towards a righteous path for development.

Review of Related Literature

Science education has generally been viewed from an objectivist viewpoint devoid of human element, however recent researches in the area of science education strive towards their renewal as well as inclusion in the curriculum. These researches pertain to the domain of STS (Science, Technology and Society) that adopts a humanistic approach in dealing with the recent science and technology researches. A humanistic approach involves making judgements about the practical utility of a particular technology, observance of humanistic values, taking in students' views and opinions and making them the centre of classroom transactions (Aikenhead 2006). The theory of sustainable science and technology development also values human survival as well as well-being, the top-most priority of any research endeavour, hence require an integration of society component in science and technology researches (Miller et al. 2008). The STS perspective is helpful in this regard, as it helps in gauging the intricate relationship between science, technology and society. Societal perspective here encompasses the governance and political system that can offer a way for implementing a humane perspective in research by way of issuing certain human rights laws.

From the socio-political perspective, science education derives its humanistic dimension from Freire's idea of 'critical pedagogy' and 'pedagogy of the oppressed' (1970) where the 'banking concept' in education is highly criticised, whereas a dialogue is suggested to have a democratic way of teaching-learning, thus challenging the unequal status and prevalence of authority in the present globalised scene. Freire's ideology can, thus, be extended to researches in science and technology in a way that offers an egalitarian distribution of the benefits derived from scientific research and adapting with the Marxian philosophy that favours the upliftment of the poor and the needy from the fruits of technology. Such an approach also saves us from engaging in destructive researches and places the human element at the top priority of any research organisation (Dos Santos 2008). Often technological prowess takes the shape of a socio-political debate between the power structures of our society, and to resolve such struggles requires training in both STS and scientific and technological literacy for a responsible citizenship. An example of such debate can be quoted as:

> Is it possible that the literature on scientific literacy still has to take into account that scientific literacy is not only concerned with knowledge sharing, but also, and perhaps mainly, with power-sharing? To introduce that dimension into the debate would mean confronting institutional, political, and economic issues. (Fourez 1989, p. 107)

Many researchers have since then introduced this component of social debate in science education so as to evoke a critical thinking process amongst learners regarding any technology and its use and have recommended active discussions in the areas focussing on socio-scientific issues (SSI) (Ratcliffe 1997; Ratcliffe and Grace 2003). Hence, discussions and debates on these SSI can serve as an important medium to bring to the fore the human rights issues that often take a backseat in the conventional science curriculum. A similar attempt has been made in the present chapter by discussing the 'human genomic project', another SSI along with the associated human rights issues.

The importance of human rights in science education is highly advocated as a means to generate awareness about the disturbed balance between the political aims and scientific aims leading to subjugation of the autonomy of the scientists and researchers to pursue research in the favour of mankind as well as science and also publish their researches and share opinion with those in the West without the fear of reprimand or persecution (Hannibal 1992).

Thus, the researches discussed above give a clear indication of the importance for the provision of human rights in each and every science and technology research, so as to save them from taking a destructive route and also bringing equality in the accessibility of technology irrespective of caste, class, gender or religion. Such an integrated and interdisciplinary approach in sciences would help in linking sciences to the daily life of the learners as well as lessen its alienating impact. The effective measures in science education that help in bringing about this kind of revolutionary change can be done by the inclusion of SSI as well as structuring discussions and argumentations around these issues facilitated by the teacher so as to promote a dialogue and expression of students' opinions.

Hypothesis and Methodology

The hypothesis of the study is that 'researches in science and technology need to have a human rights component for creating a welfare society, where each individual enjoys the rewards of technological innovation without experiencing any harm'.

The present study relied on the case study method due to the in-depth and comprehensive nature of the approach that allows the researcher to do a detailed analysis of the various human rights issues attached to the present case in hand, as well as delve into the intricacies of the inter-relationships between researches in science and technology and their societal impact. This discussion, in a way, reiterates the importance of human rights in planning and implementation of scientific and technological researches, further, justifying the place of human rights in science education and deriving implications for curriculum makers, textbook writers, and school and university environment.

HGP and Associated Human Rights Issues

Human genome refers to the entire set of genes contained in the chromosomes of an organism. It includes the information about the arrangement and sequencing of those genes as well as marking their location by the procedure of gene mapping. This information is highly significant and vital for understanding the mechanism of gene function or to diagnose any malfunctioning gene and other medical and therapeutic purposes. This whole research came to be known as HGP, initiated for the first time under the directorship of James Watson in the year 1989. However, the sequencing of the complete human genome had been completed by the year 2003; it had raised a volley of concerns and doubts regarding the potential usage and plausible threats associated with this coded genetic information of every human individual. All of this led to the provision and declaration of a new set of human rights adopted by the General Conference of the United Nations Educational, Scientific and Cultural Organization at its twenty-ninth session on 11 November 1997, endorsed by General Assembly resolution 53/152 of 9 December 1998 referred to as Universal Declaration on the Human Genome and Human Rights.

Issue of Privacy and Confidentiality of Genetic Information

Once the genetic code of every human being becomes accessible and visible, it can lead to the determination of various genetic predispositions of that person towards a particular disease, a faulty behavioural trait or any kind of environmental susceptibility. This can be in a way useful for that individual in terms of timely diagnosis and treatment, but on the other hand could also be used as a basis for discrimination. This has been sometimes used as a pretext by the employers for screening the most efficient and genetically sound employees and also by many health insurance companies to increase their premium amounts in case the person's genome depicts a susceptible gene. In order to curb such a malpractice and misuse of genetic information, Article 6 of the Universal Declaration on the Human Genome and Human Rights states, 'No one shall be subjected to discrimination based on genetic characteristics that is intended to infringe or has the effect of infringing human rights, fundamental freedoms and human dignity'.

Issue of Altering the Genome and Playing with Nature's Diversity and Gene Pool

Once the technique for inserting the right kind of gene at the right place becomes effectual in human beings, then it would take no time in treating the whole array of genetic disorders owing to single nucleotide malfunction or mutation. For instance, sickle cell anaemia is one such disorder in which due to the mutation of the gene that codes for the protein, haemoglobin leads to abnormally shaped red blood cells with decreased oxygen-carrying capacity. But, on the other hand, this technique can also lead to gene selection, or trait selection for favourable traits such as intelligence, blue eyes, athletic abilities and so on. Also, how fair is it to oodle out funds for such researches and gene enhancement techniques when we know that traits such as intelligence and athletic abilities or any other behavioural trait is multi-genetic, that is, determined by multiple genes and environment. This would again lead to the creation of a divide between the haves and have nots, and Article 12(a) of the Universal Declaration addresses this point as, *'Benefits from advances in biology, genetics and medicine, concerning the human genome, shall be made available to all, with due regard for the dignity and human rights of each individual'*.

Issue of Risking Human Life

Sometimes cases have been reported about the deleterious impact of genetic modification or gene transfer processes, leading to even death in the extreme cases. This raises an issue on the reliability and safety of such molecular biology techniques and their side effects on human health and life. Is it fair enough to conduct gene transfer experiment on humans when there happens to be no antidote or drug that could reverse its effect? Keeping this aspect into consideration, the Article 5(a) and Article 8 of the Universal Declaration on Human Genome and Human Rights states, *'Article 5(a): Research, treatment or diagnosis affecting an individual's genome shall be undertaken only after rigorous and prior assessment of the potential risks and benefits pertaining thereto and in accordance with any other requirement of national law'*. Also *'Article 8: Every individual shall have the right, according to international and national law, to just reparation for any damage sustained as a direct and determining result of an intervention affecting his or her genome'*.

Issue of Informed Consent of the individual

It is being expected out of the medical professionals and Biotech engineers to take the consent of the individual person in all his consciousness for carrying out a genetic screening or any kind of test. This is in relation to adhering to the norms of bioethics as well as for preserving and protecting the privacy and dignity of the individual. However, such norms are often being refuted for the sake of diagnosis of deadly diseases such as phenyl ketone urea, Down syndrome cases or in cases where the patient or individual is not in a state to give his/her consent such as dementia and comatose patients, newborn infants or mentally disturbed subjects. This raises an issue about the human rights of such individuals, and has been included under Articles 5(b), 5(c), and 5(e) of the UNESCO declaration as, '*5(b): In all cases, the prior, free and informed consent of the person concerned shall be obtained. If the latter is not in a position to consent, consent or authorization shall be obtained in the manner prescribed by law, guided by the person's best interest*'.

Issue of Patenting Genetic Information

Since the time of sequencing of the entire human genome, efforts have been made by many other private companies, to sequence a particular gene and patent its information and usage. This is simply because the funds required in such researches are usually huge and unaffordable for the US Government federal grants. Thus, big multinationals want to derive benefit from such endeavours, thereby being least bothered about the fact that such a basic information about one's genes should be available to all free of cost and without any discrimination. Article 4 of the UNESCO's declaration on Human Genome and Human Rights clearly dictates, '*The human genome in its natural state shall not give rise to financial gains*'.

The prevailing issues on the human rights component of the HGP clearly imply the depth and seriousness of the issue. From the above-mentioned points of reference, the following strands of discussion and debate emerge.

Science and Technology Angle

These researches including the one mentioned in the present chapter, HGP, and other related studies on reproductive cloning and genetic modification of crops are no doubt magnificently creative and can help any country climb the ladder of development with a fast pace. However, this development should not be at the cost of health and life of the country's or world citizens. This has also been stressed in the 1975 Declaration on the Use of Scientific and Technological Progress (Article 2) in the Interests of Peace and for the Benefit of Mankind as, 'All States shall take appropriate measures to prevent the use of scientific and technological developments, particularly by the State organs, to limit or interfere with the enjoyment of the human rights and fundamental freedoms of the individual as enshrined in the Universal Declaration of Human Rights, the International Covenants on Human Rights and other relevant international instruments'.

Globalisation has had a retrogressive impact on the human rights provision in terms of leading towards more inequalities due to privatisation and concentration of power in the hands of very few influential technocrats and multi-millionaires who own most of the advanced technology or patent it so as to keep it out of reach of the common man. Looking at this problem from a human rights perspective (HRP), the right of access at a minimum entails the 'freedom and opportunity to derive benefit from scientific and technological advancement be broadly diffused within a nation irrespective of race, colour, sex, language, religion, political or other opinion, national or social origin, property, birth or other status' (Article 2.2, ICESCR).

Privatisation and Commercialisation of Scientific Research

Scientific research can be categorised into core science researches related to the generation of knowledge component and applied scientific research that is usually dependent on societal demands. The previous is means driven, while the latter is end driven. Owing to the increasingly materialistic and profit earning scenario, the researchers in both the spheres are yearning to convert their scientific piece of work into money-making feat. This is actualised usually in collaboration with the big multinationals and biotech companies who employ scientists and cajole them to conduct such researches which earn maximum benefit. Many-a-times such researches are promoted that are detrimental to the of society as a whole, although appear to be needful, for example, the production of an insecticide, Endosulfan by an Israeli agro-chemical industry, produced great threats to human health and environment. Even after issuing a ban on its usage, it is still being used in many parts of India and China. Hence, a need arises at this point to carefully analyse and scrutinise the possible threats or harms that a new technology can pose, the absence of such a provision again leads to the violation of the human rights for safety of life. A human rights approach as articulated by Chapman (1999) clearly dictates a provision for the safety from any kind of deleterious impact of any science and technology research on the individual or a collective group.

Intellectual Property Rights Pertaining to Researches in Science and Technology

Any scientific research is the reward of indomitable hard work, diligence and creativity which must be acknowledged. One way of doing it is by means of print media or publication of such researches in science and technology journals and periodicals such as *Nature* and *Science*. The principal of universality and communism in *Science* also states that scientists should share the results of their research amongst fellow scientists. However, things change when a scientist writes a book or a publisher publishes it, as it then takes the shape of an intellectual property which needs to be protected and not be reproduced in any form by any other authority.

Shifting Power from Government to Transnational Companies to Guide the Research

With globalisation and ensuing privatisation, the control over major decisions with regard to science and technology researches has been taken over by the multinationals and biotech companies which see their profit or profit of a particular group in every decision rather than thinking in terms of benefit for the whole humanity. This snatches away the right of every citizen to participate in the democratic decision-making process and leaves them on the mercy of these techno-giants who do not hold any reverence or philanthropy for fellow beings and satisfy their own selfish motives. This is a clear infringement of Article 15.1 (b) of

ICESCR, which entails a right of choice in determining priorities and making decisions about major scientific and technological developments.

Breach of Human Values and Ethics

Besides violating innumerable human rights, some of the science and technology researches also hamper the basic human values such as truthfulness, trust and responsibility towards fellow beings. This kind of reciprocal relationship between development via science and technology and eroded human values has been rightly quoted in Jacques Ellul's (1964) pioneering work, 'The Technological Society'.

Summarisation of Case Study

The above case study illustrates the involvement of human rights issues in researches related to science and technology. It highlights the point that a single research initiative such as HGP can have many dimensions and shades to it. Analysing it from a socio-political and ethico-legal dimension gives it a real-life context and simultaneously deepens the level of understanding. The discussions and debates around such contentious issues are highly conflicting and often blur our vision of progress and development via science and technology route. Everything goes fine if in the interest of human well-being and welfare is taken care without the violation of any of the human rights. Thus, every research or technological innovation should be well planned, field-tested, should abide by all the safety standards and only then be introduced into the market. At any point if at all there appears to be any negative result, then such research should be banned or discontinued. Thus, scientists and researchers involved in any kind of research cannot be complacent about the research endeavour they are part of as they are bound to be responsible for what impact a particular research has on society as well as environment. Man has created technology and not vice versa, therefore man is responsible for controlling it and utilising it for the benefit of all. Here comes the role of ethics in decision-making so as to resolve any dilemma that arises in mind regarding the usage of a particular technology. Thus, training and development of ethical understanding is the foundation stone for building a human rights perspectives.

Human Rights and Science Education

Science education, inclusive of the various subject boundaries such as physics, chemistry and biology to be taken as broad themes, hardly receive a mention about human rights component, as they are considered to be a part of the social sciences curriculum. However, the social science curriculum does take into account the adoption and elaboration on the general civic and political human rights but largely misses upon the environmental and developmental human rights that constitute the third generation of human rights. More so, the next advanced level of human rights pertaining to human genome and gene technology has been hugely neglected or less understood both by science curriculum makers and curriculum translators (teachers).

The 20th century marked the era of industrialisation and with it came various molecular biology techniques, including sequencing of genome, DNA fingerprinting, gene mapping for a particular set of hereditary diseases and genetic modification of crops. Genetic technology is a buzzword still in the present century, and technology such as reproductive cloning and human genome sequencing raises grave issues on human rights, some of which have been discussed in the present chapter. Thus, all such issues in science and technology wherever there is a clash of values and the decision-making of which has a deep impact upon human survival, beneficence and welfare can serve as a food for thought for the framing and implementation of human rights.

Need for Human Rights in Science Education

If we look at the recent statistics, then it is clearly evident that there has been a drastic fall in the number of takers for science courses both at the higher education as well as undergraduate level. Although there could be many reasons for it, but the one that goes in consonance with the present chapter is the alienation with the subject due to the decontextualised approach in teaching-learning, imbuing disinterest amongst students. Although sciences are considered to be the subject that has evolved from nature, therefore the names such as life sciences, earth sciences and biochemical sciences has been given to different streams within science. However, the malady lies in the way science curriculum has been shaped and the way of transaction. Till students do not feel oneness with their subject, they would be least bothered about understanding it and would rather study it at the superficial level. Thus, one way of correcting it would be inculcation of human rights component in science curriculum. This will definitely help in connecting science and technology to human life and its cause. The students being educated this way can serve as volunteers and stewards for generating awareness amongst masses about the appropriate usage of a particular technology and also the scientific principle involved while simultaneously assessing and evaluating the impact of each and every technology so that they do not pose any harm to the society and its people.

Thus, the base of any science education has to be in basic human rights such as right to life for all human beings, right to freedom and right to development, so that we do not create insensitive scientists and self-centred technocrats. However, along with these basic or more general human rights, knowledge with regard to the more specific ones as enumerated in the present chapter pertaining to human genome also need to be imparted. This would definitely guide the students towards the ethically appropriate usage of such technology and will deter them from infringing any human rights in the future. This whole exercise is required to create a developed but at the same time non-violent and sensitive human society.

Educational Implications

One of the significant aims of education lies in understanding the meaning of being human, caring for fellow beings, inflicting least harm to others, practicing altruism and respecting life as is given by the almighty. But, how often is this aim being fulfilled, rather what remains ingrained in young minds is unhealthy competition for grades, denigrating fellow students, materialistic bent of mind, craving for all the worldly luxuries and disrespect for elders. This is the result of a structured curriculum that stimulates just the cognitive part of individual's mind (that too in a limited sense) and does not even touch the affective or to say emotional and aesthetic side of it. The current initiative in this regard has been made by a recent document on National Curriculum Framework for Teacher Education (NCFTE)-2009, that purports to inculcate this humane component in education.

Although currently negligible, but some realistic provisions can be created in science education for the incorporation of human rights. These can be done at different levels, however I would like to restrict my study to the senior secondary and undergraduate level as the issue being discussed—HGP—is being dealt at higher education level.

Role of Textbook

A content analysis of Class XII NCERT Biology textbook clearly depicts the absence of human rights issues. The focus is being laid just on the content representation and explanation of complex terms and concepts. A slight reference about ethical issues is being made and that too at some points, for instance GM crops. Talking about the Indian classrooms, where textbooks are being religiously followed by both the students and the teachers, it is very important to inculcate such an indispensable element within the context of science education. This will not only guide the students towards correct and ethically appropriate usage of technology, but will also help in widening their perspective of linking science to daily life. Textbook material can include some vignettes where certain human rights issues can be raised along with recent science and technology researches, for example, genetically modified crops, biotechnology and genetic testing. Hence, science education and its practices can become more humane and work towards the benefit of the whole society.

Role of Curriculum

The preliminary step towards the creation of a good textbook is the framing of an effective curriculum that takes into account the appropriate addressal of human rights issues in science education, that could be achieved via different pathways, and one of them could be redesigning textbook content, others can be classroom activities, pedagogy, co-curricular activities, and so on. Some of the effective classroom teaching learning activities in this regard would include more democratic approaches such as by way of discussion on human rights issues along with the main content, staging role plays where students can be given the roles of stake-holders such as a molecular biologists, ministers of centre and state for health and development in science and technology, human rights activists and so on, and thus a debate can be generated. Besides, other methods include giving tasks such as analysis of human rights documents pertaining to science and technology. Using local media such as folklore and street plays, arranging informal meetings with human rights activists, for example Dr Vandana Shiva, complementing these with broad-casting media such as radio and TV can help in creating awareness about these issues in an implicit way.

Role of Teacher Education Programmes

In order to develop sensitivity amongst students regarding the significance of human rights, it is very much required to prepare the teachers in this regard by way of pre-service and in-service programmes. A course work on HRE including the theory as well as pedagogical component can be designed placing more stress on the humane component of the subject.

Role of Classroom and School and University Environment

The classroom and school environment has to be more conducive so as to comply with the basic human rights that means an environment which is democratic, unbiased, safe, peaceful and respects child rights. Freedom of expression in classroom and liberty in practicing one's own way of learning, freedom to be oneself and respect for other cultures, religions, castes and tribes. A learner-centred and constructivist approach in teaching-learning also fosters the development of human rights perspective in a tacit way.

Conclusion

The present chapter delves into the virgin yet important area of human rights issues in STS followed by their inclusion in science education. The study draws inspiration from the real-life science and technology-related disasters that force us to think whether the dream of development and emancipation that is being visualised is actually being fulfilled by way of fruits of researches in science and technology? Is there a need to rethink upon certain aspects of science and technology from a point of view of a common man? Is there a need to re-establish the principle of equality in terms of deriving benefit from these researches? All of these questions give a clear indication towards the human rights issues that are often neglected in conducting and implementing many science and technology researches. These issues require both attention and appropriate addressal so that the strained equation between technology and development is balanced. This kind of a thinking and perspective needs to be engrained in the young minds as soon as they enter the real scientific world of understanding, for which education can fill the gap. Science education needs to broaden its sphere and has to move beyond basic scientific principles, laws and theories and has to include this human rights perspective at both the level of curriculum and day-to-day teaching-learning processes. Besides school and university education, scientists and researchers also have to be sensitised about the basic human rights that a particular research can violate. Whenever there is a problem, the effective way out could be to combat it from all possible angles, so as to minimise the chances of its reoccurrence. Therefore, in order to solve the problem of unfavourable repercussions of some science and technology researches, we need to target it from the research angle, educational angle, socio-political angle, legal or human rights angle, and finally an ethical angle. The inference that can be drawn is that the protection of human rights should be the top priority for any country, state or region and every necessary effort should be done in this regard by the governing authorities, by suggesting alternatives and in some cases completely banning a particular scientific research, which is demeaning for the societal interest. Decisions regarding the permission and sanctioning of grants for researches in science and technology need to be made with care and keeping the ethical principles of beneficence and utilitarianism in mind. The case presented in this chapter refers to the 'human genome project' and the human rights issues associated with it. The human rights associated with the present case are the third-generation human rights and are less known to the general public. Thus, it becomes the priority of our education system and other allied means of information dispersal to make the general populace aware about them and their emergence and need in the prevailing scenario. Linking human rights pertaining to science and technology researches with science education, a ray of hope can be seen for freeing our society from the hegemony of profit-making multinationals that make use of science and technology just for minting money that goes in the least interest of common public. This will also help in creating a scientifically literate and responsible citizenry.

Suggestions for Further Research

Human rights in science and technology education is an ever growing area that needs the attention of educationists and researchers working in related areas owing to the value it adds to the discipline. Sciences have generally been viewed from a purist and objectivist perspective, to which human rights can add a subjectivist dimension which is essential in making sciences liberating in a true sense. The following areas pertaining to HRE can be further explored by budding researchers:

(1) Developing a curriculum module for the inculcation of human rights in science education.
(2) Critical analysis of any of the human rights documents in the light of present demands of this century with regard to development and research in science and technology.
(3) Studying teachers' perceptions on the inculcation of the human rights component in science education.

Note

1. STS issues refer to the socio-scientific issues at the interface of science, technology and society. They have a sociological dimension, as different people have differing views regarding them, for instance amniocentesis, nuclear waste disposal and genetic engineering.

References

Aikenhead, G.S. (2006). *Science Education for Everyday Life: Evidence-Based Practice*. New York: Teachers College Press.

Chapman, A.R. (1999). *A Human Rights Perspective on Intellectual Property, Scientific Progress, and Access to the Benefits of Science*. Washington, DC: AAAS.

Dev, A., Dev, I.A. and Das, S. (1996). *Human Rights: A Source Book*. NCERT.

Dos Santos, W.L.P. (2008). 'Scientific Literacy: A Frierian Perspective as a Radical View of Humanistic Science Education'. *Science Education*, 93(2).

Dugger, W.E., Miller, C.D., Bame, E.A., Pinder, C.A. Giles, M.B., Young, L.H. and Dixon, J.D. (1980). *Report of the Survey Data*. Blacksburg, VA: Virginia Polytechnic Institute and State University.

Ellul, J. (1964). *The Technological Society* (translated by J. Wikinson). New York: Vintage Books.

Fourez, G. (1989). 'Scientific Literacy, Societal Choices and Ideologies', in A.B. Champagne, B.E. Lovitts, and B.J. Calinger (eds), *This Year in School Science 1989: Scientific Literacy*. Washington, DC: American Association for the Advancement of Science, 1–14.

Freeman, M. (2002). *Human Rights: An Interdisciplinary Approach*. Blackwell Publishers.

Hannibal, K. (1992). *Taking up the Challenge: Promotion of Human Rights*. American Association for the Advancement of Science, USA.

International Covenant on Economic, Social and Cultural Rights, henceforth ICESCR, adopted 16 December 1966, 993 U.N.T.S. 3 (entered into force 3 January 1976), G.A. Res. 2200(XXI), 21

Miller, C., Sarewitz, D. and Light, A. (2008). 'Science, Technology, and Sustainability: Building a Research Agenda'. National Science Foundation Supported Workshop.

Mohanty, J. (ed.) (2008). *Human Rights Education*. New Delhi: Deep & Deep Publications.

O'Byrne, D.J. (2003). *Human Rights: An Introduction*. India: Dorling Kindersley.

Ratcliffe, M. (1997). 'Pupil Decision-Making about Socio-Scientific Issues within the Science Curriculum'. *International Journal of Science Education*, 19(2), 167–182.

Ratcliffe, M. and Grace, M. (2003). *Science Education for Citizenship: Teaching Socio-Scientific Issues*. Maidenhead, England: Open University Press.

Rehman, M.M. and Rehman, K. (2000). *Human Rights & Human Development: Concept and Contexts*. New Delhi: Manak Publications.

Reichert, E. (ed.) (2007). *Challenges in Human Rights: A Social Work Perspective*. Jaipur: Rawat Publications.

Snyder, J.F. and Hales, J.A. (1981). *Jackson's Mill Industrial Arts Curriculum Theory*. Charleston: West Virginia Department of Education.

The Declaration on the Use of Scientific and Technological Progress in the Interest of Mankind, adopted in 1975. Available from http://habitat.igc.org/open-gates/a30r3384.htm

The International Covenants on Civil & Political rights and on Economic & Cultural Rights, 1966. Available from http://www.ohchr.org/english/ law/ccpr.htm

UNESCO. 'The Gene Letter'. *UNESCO Declaration on the Human Genome and Human Rights, July 1997*. Available from http://www.geneletter.org/0398/UNESCO.htm

Part IV

Human Rights and Persons with Disabilities

8

Learning Disability and the Indian School

A Study in Delhi

Jasleen Kaur and Neerja Sharma

For years, a particular developmental disability created confusion that was later debated and discussed at several academic forums worldwide to settle for a terminology. In 1963, for the first time Samuel Kirk used the term 'learning disabilities' to refer to children who showed problems in the areas of reading, writing, spellings and mathematics, but having average to very high range of intelligence quotient scores. Since then the condition has been termed learning disabilities in the United States and 'specific learning difficulties' in United Kingdom. It is recognised as a heterogeneous group of disorders due to problems in specific processing areas of brain and manifested as difficulties in reading, writing, reasoning and mathematical abilities. The term includes conditions such as dyslexia, dysgraphia and dyscalculia. Students with learning disability have average to above average intellectual capacity and yet struggle to keep pace with the work done in class and to be at par with peers in learning. There is usually a huge gap between the level of achievement of the student and his/her potential for achievement. A discrepancy of two years between ability and performance in academics is considered as a marker of learning disability. The definition of learning disability is based on exclusionary clauses wherein the discrepancy is not attributed to factors such as sensory impairment, mental retardation, emotional disturbances, cultural differences, economic disadvantages and inappropriate instruction. Often the terms dyslexia or reading disabilities are used synonymously with learning disability, however they are not equivalent (Karanth 2003).

The umbrella term, specific learning disabilities (SLDs), is preferred by most of the professional bodies working in this area in India (Malaviya 2010). India has adopted the following definition of learning disabilities given by the US Government in Public Law 94–142, which states:

> Specific Learning Disabilities means a disorder in one or more of the basic psychological processes involved in understanding or in using language, spoken or written, which may manifest in an imperfect ability to listen, speak, read, spell or to do mathematical calculations. The term includes such conditions as perceptual handicaps, brain injury, minimal brain dysfunction, dyslexia and developmental aphasia. The term does not include children who have learning problems which are primarily the result of visual, hearing or motor handicaps, or mental retardation, emotional disturbance or environmental, cultural or economic disadvantages. (Federal Register 1977, cited in Rehabilitation Council of India [RCI], 2007)

With this introduction to the area, the present chapter focusses on the legal and social aspects related to learning disabilities that are specific to the Indian context. The first section on justification of the study provides explanation as to why the study was required to be conducted. The section on review of literature provides glimpses of the few studies done in the area of learning disability in India and highlights some of the findings. Following this is a section on objectives which states the research goals that the study intends to meet. The participants, the procedure and the analysis of the data are being covered in the section on methods. The first subsection of the results and discussion section examines the legislations on disability and the governmental and non-governmental initiatives with respect to learning disability and the second subsection relates the findings. The findings, based on empirical data from an ongoing study, reveal how disability is addressed by the stakeholders, specifically in the sector of education. It also reports the varied perceptions about learning disabilities among teachers, parents, students with the disability and professionals working with them. It also shows how the awareness levels, stereotypes and attitudes of the people around the child with learning disability play a significant role in determining the actions they pursue for social inclusion. Before the conclusion, the chapter also proposes certain supportive reforms that can be made at several levels from the national level to the level of the teachers and parents.

Justification of the Study

There has been a gradual increase in awareness about the learning disability in the education sector. Several reforms in policy and initiatives in school education have been introduced by the government in the last decade. In the light of these changes, it was felt that there was a need to ascertain the status of learning disability. There has been a gradual policy-wise movement from the medical to the social models of disability but it is imperative to learn if the adoption of the social model has occurred at the level of stakeholders in the area of education. Therefore, both private and public schools and some professionals and parents of students with learning disability were made part of the study. Since India has ratified the United Nations Convention on the Rights of Persons with Disabilities (UNCRPD) 2006, some aspects related to its implementation for enabling students realise their full potential need to be considered with respect to children with learning disability.

Understanding Learning Disability

The recognition or awareness of learning disability is a more recent phenomenon in India. Its understanding, on a large part, is still dependent on Western literature, and the assessment and remedial interventions are also influenced by the practices in the West (Karanth 2003). The last decade has seen an increase in awareness of learning disability in India. With increasing awareness, there has been an increase in the number of children identified with learning disability (Thapa 2008), and therefore, there is a demand for developing appropriate policies and pedagogical interventions. Kapur (2008) has put the prevalence rate of learning disability to be about 10 per cent in English-medium schools. However, many state education bodies express doubts over the existence of learning disability (RCI 2007).

Although learning disability had found a place as a disability requiring special education in the National Policy on Education (NPE) in 1986 (Venkateshwarlu and Shah 2002), Jha (2010) has revealed that only private schools give admission to children with learning disability, while public schools admit only those with physical and sensory disabilities. Several researches have been conducted to understand the different aspects related to the disability, working towards its prevention and intervention. These have mainly focussed on children's self-perceptions and self-esteem (Iqbal and Gupta 2006; Tandon 2004), ecological factors related to learning disability (Pandey 2003; Singh and Dhanda 2008), integrated and inclusive education for the students (Madan 2002) and the experiences of children with learning disability (Mullick 1999).

In a study by Patel (2004), it was found that Gujarati-speaking children from higher castes attending private schools do not experience much difficulty in learning to read but children from SCs and STs, attending public schools, face problems in reading acquisition. Shrikanth's (2010) study of young adults with learning disability revealed that although a majority of the sample had not received special education services in school, most of them had received academic concessions in school. There are many features specific to the Indian context and learning disabilities that need to be seen in relation to each other. Facts of diversity in the Indian society by caste, socio-economic status, bilingualism and multilingualism as well as quality of schooling are context-specific issues that require focus (Thapa 2008). The present chapter discusses the status of learning disability in India with respect to current legislations and the situation in schools.

Thus, the major objective of the chapter is to understand the legal and social aspects related to learning disability specific to the Indian context. A specific objective was to explore the sector of education with focus on how public and private schools address the disability. The chapter also explored the perceptions of parents, teachers and other professionals about students with learning disability.

Methodology

According to the Ministry of Social Justice and Empowerment of the Government of India, there are three legal instruments on disability namely, the Persons with Disabilities (Equal Opportunities, Protection of Rights and Full Participation) Act, 1995; the Rehabilitation Council of India (RCI) Act, 1992; and the National Trust for Welfare of Persons with Autism, Cerebral Palsy, Mental Retardation and Multiple Disability Act, 1999. These legislations were analysed to examine their content.

The empirical study forms a part of a larger ongoing study on adolescents with learning disability. The larger study requires the researcher to contact several government and private sector schools of Delhi. It is a prerequisite of the study to locate students with learning disability in schools and to have interactions with them, their teachers and parents to collect data. A total of 25 private and 15 government schools in Delhi were first contacted either through personal visits or through telephone. These were English- and Hindi-medium co-educational schools, which were selected through purposive sampling and snowball sampling methods. Data was collected from one private school as part of the pilot study and from another private school as part of the main study. Teachers, special educators, counsellors and parents of students with learning disability were met at the school and interviewed. The responses of all the schools contacted were analysed. The qualitative data obtained through interviews was subjected to content analysis.

Results and Discussion

Before analysis of empirical data, a review and critique of the disability related laws, schemes and programmes is presented.

Indian legislations

The Indian legislations regarding people with disabilities come under the aegis of the Ministry of Social Justice and Empowerment of the Government of India. There are progressive disability policy frameworks which have been formulated for empowerment of persons with disabilities (PWDs). There are national laws such as the Persons with Disabilities (Equal Opportunities, Protection of Rights and Full Participation) Act, 1995; the RCI Act, 1992; and the National Trust for Welfare of Persons with Autism, Cerebral Palsy, Mental Retardation and Multiple Disability Act, 1999; state policies and sector specific policies. However, learning disability has not found a place in any legislation related to disability.

According to the PWD Act, 1995, disability means blindness, low vision, leprosy-cured, hearing impairment, locomotor disability, mental retardation and mental illness but it does not provide any reference to this prevalent condition of learning disability. The National Trust Act, as the name suggests, caters to people with autism, cerebral palsy, mental retardation and multiple disabilities, while learning disability does not fall under any of these categories. The RCI is a central statutory body which regulates the services provided to PWD, imparts training and certifies the personnel working in the field of rehabilitation and special education. It has also very recently recognised learning disability as a separate category of disability, however there was no mention of this disability in the RCI Act, 1992 (Malaviya 2010). India had ratified the UNCRPD 2006 in the year 2007 (United Nations 2011). The UNCRPD recognises learning disability among various disabilities but there is a need to make amendments in the Indian legislations for its recognition. This would be a crucial step in protecting and promoting the rights of persons with learning disabilities.

Various people and specific groups such as the Disability Rights Group have struggled to amend the PWD Act and include learning disability as a disability while it is under revision. Inclusion of learning disability in the act would extend all benefits, concessions and relaxations permissible under the act to persons with learning disabilities. Recently, Bhalla (2011) reported that the Indian Association of Paediatricians has prepared an Action Plan 2011 towards the inclusion of learning disability in the act as well as regarding other issues of identification, assessment, awareness and training of all the stakeholders. There is fresh hope for PWDs, specifically for people with learning disabilities, since a new legislation to replace the present PWD Act, 1995, has been drafted by a committee appointed by the Ministry of Social Justice and Empowerment of India. This legislation called the Rights of Persons with Disabilities Bill 2011, in harmony with the UNCRPD, includes SLD as a separate category of disability (Ministry of Social Justice and Empowerment 2011). According to it, SLDs refer to a heterogeneous group of conditions wherein there is a deficit in processing language, spoken or written, that may manifest itself as a difficulty to comprehend, speak, read, write and spell or to do mathematical calculations. The term includes such conditions as perceptual disabilities, dyslexia, dysgraphia, dyscalculia, dyspraxia and developmental aphasia.

National level organisations, the Census of India and the National Sample Survey (NSS) also make no mention of learning disability. Their reports have statistics for physical disabilities, mental retardation, speech and hearing disabilities. However, they do not give any statistics for people with learning disabilities. The statistics that are available in textbooks are based on either surveys done at places other than India or are mere estimations.

Schemes and Programmes

There have been certain attempts by the state in terms of various schemes and programmes as part of the implementation of the acts towards protecting and promoting the rights of PWDs. However, the scope of such initiatives remains narrow by either not taking learning disability into account as a disability or due to the improper implementation of the schemes and provisions. Some states such as Delhi, Maharashtra, Goa, Karnataka and Tamil Nadu have provided schemes and provisions for children with learning disability (RCI 2007). However, there have been reports of depriving the rights of students with learning disabilities even in these states.

The centrally sponsored Scheme of Integrated Education for the Disabled Children, introduced in 1974 with a view to provide educational opportunities to children with disabilities in regular schools along with other children without disabilities, has even after years of enforcement not been able to fill the gap (Department of Higher Education 2011). Moreover, many children with learning disability may have dropped out due to unsupportive environment of the schools. This scheme has been unsuccessful with the enrolment and retention of children with disabilities in regular school but stands as a backdrop for a new centrally sponsored Inclusive Education Scheme by the Ministry of Human Resource Development (MHRD). The scheme gives some hope in this direction by proposing to include children and youth with learning disabilities as its target group along with other disabilities.

Examination boards such as Central Board of Secondary Education (CBSE) and Council for the Indian School Certificate Examinations have recognised learning disability and have provided certain provisions to enable students with the disability to perform to their potential. Students with learning disability, under CBSE, are exempted from studying the third language, are given an extra hour during the exams and can have a scribe to write the answers. Similar provisions are also framed and provided by the Indian Certificate of Secondary Education.

Under the PWD Act 1995, the screening and identification of the disabilities becomes a duty of the state. Even though the act has not recognised learning disability, steps have been taken by some national level organisations towards facilitating the screening and diagnosis of the disability. The *Sarva Shiksha Abhiyan* (SSA), an initiative of the Government of India, which works towards the universalisation of elementary education, has provided a checklist for the screening of students with learning disability by teachers in schools (Sarva Shiksha Abhiyan 2011). This checklist is available in major regional languages of India apart from Hindi and English. The National Institute of Mental Health and Neurosciences (NIMHANS), Bangalore, has also developed an index for the assessment of SLDs in children. Department of Special Education at National Institute for the Mentally Handicapped (NIMH) too has developed screening checklists for assessing problems in English, Hindi and mathematics (NIMH 2003). In spite of these, there is lack of standard assessment procedures and indigenous tools for assessment in regional languages (Karanth 2003). Moreover, the awareness regarding learning disability, its assessment and interventions are restricted only to a few cities of India.

Learning Disabilities and Nongovernment Initiatives

It has been noted that most of the work in support of people with learning disabilities, especially with children, has been undertaken by NGOs and a few private institutions. The non-statutory initiatives particularly by the NGO sector are worth appreciation. Several examples are given later in the chapter. There does not exist any national body on learning disability. However, non-profit voluntary organisations such as Delhi Learning Disabilities Association, Madras Dyslexia Association, Maharashtra Dyslexia Association and Dyslexia Association of Andhra Pradesh have been formed privately, usually by groups of parents, educators and other professionals. These organisations work towards creating awareness about the disability in the education fraternity and work in advocacy for rights of people with learning disabilities. The organisations also provide remedial assistance, assessment and counselling services, as well as training programmes for professionals.

An example is Orkids, which was started by a special educator in 2000. It is a chain of multidisciplinary clinics intended to provide remedial intervention in academics to children with special needs, especially children with learning disabilities (Orkids 2011). It also provides services of assessment for disabilities, speech and language therapy, occupational therapy and teacher training. It has expanded its services over the years and now also offers a diploma, a certificate and distance learning programmes which can be attended by teachers, parents, psychologists and students of psychology and related fields. It augurs well for children with learning disabilities to have larger organisations such as the Tata group focussing on the special needs of children with learning disability. The group has held Tata Interactive Learning Disability Forum every year since 2006. It underlined the importance of early remedial action for children with special needs (Tata Interactive Systems 2011). The Information and Resource Centre for Autism and other developmental disabilities at Bangalore is a project which has started a one-year diploma course and a six-month Distance Education Certificate Programme in learning disability (*The Times of India* 2011).

Other private institutions and entrepreneurs also organise workshops for parents, teachers and other professionals. Since they are not supported by the government, the only disadvantage of such endeavours is that they usually cater to private school teachers and parents who can pay for such workshops.

Findings from the Empirical Study

Research studies on the brain have shown that learning disabilities are the result of damage caused to certain regions of the brain associated with particular skills required for reading and learning (Horowitz 2007). This damage usually takes place during the prenatal period. Learning disabilities are also known to have heritability (Thomson and Raskind 2003). Although there is growing awareness about learning disability, there are a number of misconceptions associated with the term and these are found to be held by the stakeholders and the society at large. For the present chapter, the researcher collated the responses of a few parents, teachers, students and professionals in the area with whom she had interactions with during the initial phase of the study. The interactions with the schools contacted for the larger ongoing study and the interviews with the subjects have been content analysed.

Schools

It was found during the explorations for identified students with learning disability that all the 15 schools under the Delhi government that were contacted have not identified children with learning disabilities in their schools. A regrettable fact is that several of these schools were not even aware of the term learning disability; however, some of them recognised it on being given the reference of the Hindi movie *Taare Zameen Par*. Most of the private schools showed awareness about the disability. The patterns of their work or lack of it with children who had disability were varied and as given below:

(1) Some of them were integrated or inclusive schools with special education services for children with learning disability. They were also providing support in terms of curriculum modifications, alternative evaluations and access to CBSE provisions;
(2) Some of the regular schools had mainstreamed students with learning disabilities and were providing support in the form of CBSE provisions but no special education services; and
(3) Some of them were regular schools that had consciously not given admission to children with disabilities and were not providing any support to those identified later with learning disability. Most of the time, students with learning disability were not identified or recognised in such schools even if the school had a counsellor.

Under the SSA and the Right to Education Act 2009, no child with special needs can be denied admission in mainstream schools. Although it has become mandatory for all schools to admit and provide education to all children with disabilities, the real picture is that due to lack of awareness and the belief that children with disability require special schools, only children with locomotor and physical disabilities such as speech, hearing and visual impairments are being admitted to schools. Additionally, when the students are given admission under the mandatory admission policy, they are at a disadvantage as the schools often do not have special educators or trained regular teachers to cater to their special educational needs. The schools were asked by this researcher about the type of disabilities that some of their students had. The usual responses were, '*kisi ka pair nahi hai, kisi ka haath nahi hai* ...' (Some don't have their legs, some don't have their arms ...), 'orthopaedic disability *ke bachche hain*' (have children with orthopaedic disability) and 'physically handicapped children'. Private schools do not have the obligation of following the government's policy regarding integration of children with disabilities in mainstream schools (Jha 2010). It should at least be evident in government's own schools. However, it was found that many of the schools contacted did not have any students with disabilities.

The regular schools, be it the private or public sector schools, have not been able to cater to the diverse needs of the children with disabilities. They do not have the requisite personnel and knowledge to screen and identify children with learning disabilities and carry out necessary interventions. Education of children with disabilities is believed to be a prerogative of the special schools. To give an example, a private school in Delhi was asked if there were any children with disabilities in the school, the reply was, 'Ours is a regular school, and we do not have spastic children'. This statement revealed two aspects of the nature of misconceptions of stakeholders: one, children with disabilities are to be found only in special schools; and two, disability equals to spasticity for some.

The students identified with learning disability in regular schools at times have to be moved to integrated or inclusive schools by the parents due to the hostile environment of the school. Sometimes it is not even the decision of the parents or children to change school as a *Times News Network* (2010) report from Delhi found that they are forced to leave school on grounds of their disability, depriving them of their fundamental RTE. In *Hindustan Times* (2011), news reports have also brought to notice the denial of admission by schools and colleges to students with dyslexia. Article 7 of UNCRPD states that in all actions concerning children with disabilities, the best interests of the child should be a primary consideration of all stakeholders (United Nations 2006). Being in a mainstreamed school and studying along with peers lies in the best interest of the child with learning disability as it contributes to his/her holistic development. Article 24 of UNCRPD on education also relates to the policy of no discrimination and equal opportunity to all students with disabilities. Therefore, a child with learning disability should not be excluded from the general education system.

An avoidable limitation of the Indian education system is that the evaluation of a child is always based on written examinations even though the child may be competent in answering questions verbally (NIMH 2003). This proves to be a major drawback for students with learning disabilities who already face difficulties in the tasks of reading, writing and spellings. The present study showed that a few private regular schools give concessions for spellings, but none of the school was found to offer oral evaluations. Although the examination boards have provided for certain provisions, there have also been reports of these provisions being denied to students with learning disability. Mahapatra (2010) reported that students have not been allowed to use calculators during examinations. A news report by Henry (2010) from Hyderabad illustrated that the education department was unable to provide scribes to dyslexic students for their examinations.

Schools often revealed an adverse side showing how unsupportive their environment was. For example, in a private school in Delhi, a child who showed difficulty in learning was detained in the same class stating that he was not able to cope with the curriculum. A similar report by Kumar (2010) came from a school in Chennai. Nair (2009) reported that the Delhi High Court had ordered the Delhi government, Municipal Corporation of Delhi (MCD) and the New Delhi Municipal Council to appoint two special educators in each school run by these bodies. The MCD had proposed to recruit special educators in schools run by the authority to meet the provisions under the RTE. However, the *Times of India* report (2011) indicates that no action had been taken so far towards the proposal. A professional in the field, commenting on the present plight of the Delhi government schools, said that one special educator or resource person looked after six schools. This, perhaps, accounts for the poor quality of education services for students with learning disability.

Most schools and other institutions catering to students with learning disabilities recognise learning disability on the basis of clinical or psychological reports for giving access to various provisions and relaxations. It has been a finding in this research that psychological reports of assessment given by clinics and professionals many a time use incorrect terminologies whereby learning disability is regarded to mean only dyslexia. Using the word dyslexia interchangeably with learning disability is technically incorrect (RCI 2007), as dyslexia is one of the forms of learning disability.

Even though in a small way, the situation is showing improvement and continuous affirmative action and innovations are being undertaken by various organisations. Nair (2010) reported that at the University of Delhi, there is reservation of seats for students with dyslexia for various courses. Some of the supportive schools from the private sector informed this researcher that they provide exemption from third language to students with learning disability. Students with learning disabilities either get CBSE provisions or they can give their examinations through the National Institute of Open Schooling (NIOS), an autonomous organisation established by the MHRD, Government of India, as part of implementation of the NPE of 1986. NIOS provides relief and benefits to students with disabilities as they successfully complete their schooling with their choice of subjects and get extra years to complete their courses. Its special cell for the education of disabled also has the provision of a scribe, extended time and use of computers and calculators during examinations. There are a few integrated and inclusive schools in Delhi that prepare students with moderate to severe learning disability for the NIOS examinations rather than the CBSE or other board examinations.

It was observed in the two schools that students with learning disability were often rejected by their peers due to low academic performance and also due to certain 'problem' behaviours they showed. On the brighter side, there are schools that intervene in the classrooms and try to create a positive environment by educating their peers. Therefore, it is the school's duty to foster an environment of respect and positive feelings among the peers towards children with learning disabilities irrespective of their academic performance.

Teachers

Children with learning disability appear normal in many skills and daily activities but they display difficulties in their ability to read, write and learn in the classroom. This often perplexes the teachers and parents who are unaware of the condition. Interaction with a few teachers at private inclusive schools in Delhi revealed that they often had doubts whether the child had the learning disability syndrome. Some of them held the view that students who do not want to study bring a report from the clinics to get relaxations and provisions at the schools.

Both public school and private school teachers feel similarly challenged. Lack of material resources, high student-teacher ratio and different learning styles and rates of learning of students which the teachers have to take into account to plan lessons are some of the challenges that they have to encounter every day in the classroom which were communicated to the researcher. According to one of the school counsellors, the result is that teachers often do not want to accept one more challenge of working with children with disabilities in their classroom and the children are transferred to the counsellor or the special educator for work. Sometimes teachers ignore the child who shows difficulties or they blame and scold the child assuming that the child is just being careless or is disinterested in studies.

School counsellors and special educators from the schools who participated in the study reported that the child is often described as 'not interested in studies', 'is interested in everything except academics', 'difficult child', 'stubborn', 'defiant', '*dhyann idhar udhar rehtaa hai iska*' (lacks attention and focus), '*samajhta hai lekin likhta theek se nahi hai*' (understands but cannot write properly), 'slow learner', 'duffer', 'careless' and so on. Most of the time, these phrases are loosely used by teachers and parents for students with learning disabilities and are always derogatory towards the child. Almost mimicking the teacher, the classmates ridicule the child using similar labels. When the child communicates his/her difficulties, many times teachers and parents believe that he/she is making excuses for something he/she does not want to do.

Students with learning disability are found to be at the mercy of their teachers. The teachers' beliefs, attitudes and awareness about the disability have implications for the students' well-being. It was inspiring to find that in one government school, a teacher was aware about learning disability and was screening children for the disability. After the screening, she used to discuss the issue with the parents and was helping them to go for the child's psychological assessment. There was another fine example from a government school. The principal, in spite of being unaware of the disability before the researcher met her, got motivated to screen and identify the students with learning disability in her school to support the researcher in her work.

Adolescents

After observations of and interactions with students with learning disability, it was found that they usually have to put in longer hours of study which in turn reduces their leisure intervals in school such as lunch breaks/activity time. They take much longer to finish academic tasks and most of them usually do extra work of studying the basics of language along with the class curriculum and end up being more exhausted than their classmates. After going back home from school, students have sessions lined up with tutors, special educators and even with parents. As a result, they spend less time in social interactions with peers at school and neighbourhood. They are often deprived of opportunities for play, fun and leisure. They may start losing interest in academics and that may extend to other areas also (Tandon 2004). Participation in cultural life, recreation, leisure and sports is one of the fundamental rights of all children including those with disability (United Nations 2006) and children with learning disability are often denied this right.

Our society places undue emphases on children's academic achievement, therefore, children with learning disability are at a disadvantage as they perform comparatively poorly in academics. Additionally, education stresses on 'knowing' rather than 'learning', theory rather than application, which does not facilitate true learning considering the kind of difficulties children with learning disability face (RCI 2007). Furthermore, because academics are valued so highly, it is often a myth among students with learning disability, their parents and teachers that such students have limited career opportunities.

Parents

It has been seen that some parents leave all remedial activities to the school and often blame the school and its teachers for their child's difficulties. On the other hand, there are parents who struggle a lot for getting their child admitted in a mainstream school, of working towards the child's promotion to the next class and being given concessions that he/she deserves.

Sometimes parents, having identified that the child has learning disability, try to understand the strengths and limitations of the child. They try to promote what their child is good at and work on his/her limitations. Such actions, attitudes and beliefs are positive as they are conducive to the child's development. If the parents lack insight about the child, the aforementioned labels are often used for the child without even identifying his/her strengths. Such parents often are unaware and of the view that their child cannot do anything because he/she is unable to score well in academics. Significantly, in India, parents can be quite overbearing towards their child and take most decisions on his/her behalf. When the child has learning disability, parents have greater difficulties in accepting his/her competencies or lack of them.

Learning disability, during data collection, was found to have a stigma attached to it. The researcher discovered that only the immediate family of the child was aware of the disability. That he/she had a disability was hidden from even the child's grandparents and the joint family living in the same household. This is something which is, perhaps, peculiar to Indian families. Due to irrational beliefs and lack of awareness, disability is often considered a matter of shame. Learning disability is often confused with intellectual disability and that is stigmatised. The parents' expectations from their child with disability were found to depend on their beliefs and attitudes. One set of parents was found to be supportive providing a lot of opportunities and encouraging the child to take part in several recreational activities so that she can find a niche for herself. Another family was of the view that the child must learn basic functional academics and did not expect her to have a career. Parents' education and awareness in both the cases did not change the fact that the knowledge about the child's disability was not shared with even the closest of relatives. If the child is referred to a counsellor in school, or a clinic for assessment and is being taught by a special educator, it brings a lot of discomfort to the parents as these activities carry the burden of stigma to family's prestige.

Supportive Reforms

Considering the state of government initiatives and the sector of education with respect to children with learning disabilities, there are several levels at which action needs to be taken for helping them realise the outcomes of their rights. At the national level, legal reforms must be introduced for which the government has taken a step by revising an existing legislation (The Rights of Persons with Disabilities Bill, 2011) to replace the older one (PWD Act 1995). The action should necessarily include appropriate implementation of the laws and policies. A non-profit body on learning disability can be formed at the national level for advocacy of the rights of persons with learning disabilities and also to keep vigilance over the concerned organisations. There is a paucity of counsellors and special educators who should be recruited for supportive work in every school. The RCI must look into the matter of creating a resource pool of persons with suitable training and certification for assessing children with the disability and providing special education facilities when required. Standard components about the various aspects of the disability such as screening, identification and intervention must be developed to guide government and private institutions working in this area across the country.

As research in the various areas of disability is inadequate, the understanding of learning disability is dependent on Western research and literature. The state must sponsor and support research initiatives. Chapter IX of the PWD Act 1995 directs the state to promote research on issues related to disability, but it has been a personal experience of the researcher that the Directorate of Education in Delhi denied permission to conduct research in schools under its jurisdiction on grounds of its policy of not allowing research scholars to work in government sector schools.

Media has always had a powerful impact on the masses. The movie *Taare Zameen Par* was an excellent initiative. The government school teachers reported that they were shown the movie and many of them are now aware about the disability. It was found that most of the teachers recognise the disability not by the term but by reference to the Bollywood movie. Similar media initiatives must be supported by the government, and short documentaries must be made and shown to teachers and public. Media can play a role in promoting positive models of education of children with disability, and more importantly, this would help in understanding disability with an informed perspective.

At the state level, what is of most significance is the implementation of the laws by the governments. The state governments must form bodies which would ensure that the provisions by the government are accessible for all persons with learning disabilities. They should attempt to form advocacy groups which would have a role in ensuring inclusion in schools. There is a need to set up family-friendly clinics with trained professionals for the assessment of the disorder. States must work towards pre-service and in-service teacher training to enable them to screen and identify children with learning disability in the classroom as well as to enable them to work to the best of their ability. Universities and institutes offering teacher training courses such as Bachelors of Education and Nursery Teachers Training must modify their curriculum to include components on learning disabilities and hands on experience.

Students with learning disability may not require job reservations but appropriate pedagogical interventions are crucial for their growth. Hence, the government bodies for education such as directorates of education, examination boards and private and public sector schools have a major role in helping the children with learning disabilities experience stigma-free education. Schools must be prepared to reflect on their own attitudes towards children with learning disability. They must ensure that the rights of children for quality education are not compromised by either denial of admission or by asking the child with the disability to leave school. Every school needs to have a flexible curriculum and alternate evaluation procedures keeping in view the child's strengths and weaknesses. It is of utmost importance that the school changes its environment and perspective to suit the child with special needs rather than expecting the reverse. Training of in-service teachers at the school, having counsellors and special educators are some of the good practices the schools can adopt to support children with disabilities. Providing access of the provisions and schemes available through the boards of education to students with learning disability is an important duty of the schools. At the interpersonal level, the school must try to inculcate in every child respect for every other child irrespective of his/her academic performance, behaviour and other individual characteristics. As students with learning disability are found to have low self-esteem and low confidence, taking care of their socio-emotional health should be a prime concern of the teacher in the classroom as well as other personnel. The peers of the child with learning disability can be resources in the form of peer tutors. It is also the school's responsibility to help make parents aware of parent-support groups/organisations which conduct workshops, seminars and lectures for awareness and counselling.

At the classroom level, instructional adaptations must be made to support students with different learning styles. Teachers can look into the management of classroom in a way to enable students with disability. Technology can be brought into the classrooms to make the teaching-learning process interesting. Expectations from the child need to be revised and belief in child's strengths need to be brought about at both the teacher and parent level. The school and family networking holds importance as parents can become partners and the collaboration would mean giving similar messages to the child who has learning disability (Malaviya 2010).

Conclusion

Lack of information, scarce human resources and adverse attitudes in society pose challenges to the recognition of rights of persons with learning disability. The legal space and sense of equity that people with learning disability deserve have not been accorded to them due to these barriers. Additionally, in the absence of policy favouring children with learning disability coupled with unsympathetic environments, children's rights cannot be protected and promoted. Since India has ratified the UNCRPD, it is the state's duty to formulate programmes and schemes for promoting the fulfilment of the rights of children with learning disability and work towards the implementation of its policies.

Reforms are underway for the social inclusion of children with disabilities in the sector of education through measures such as mainstreaming in regular schools using the scheme of inclusive education, although a shift towards the social model is far from discernible. Myths and misconceptions of teachers and parents give evidence of learning disability in the classroom being unacceptable and hence a challenging notion. It seems plausible that schools have to work towards a rights-based model of disability to understand, accept and educate children with learning disability.

References

Bhalla, J.S. (2011, November 22). 'Include Learning Disabilities in Disability Act, Say Docs'. *Hindustan Times.* Retrieved from http://www.hindustantimes.com

Department of Higher Education, Ministry of Human Resource Development (2011). 'Inclusive Education Scheme'. Retrieved from http://www. education.nic.in/iedc_sch_draft.asp

Henry, N. (2010, January 31). 'Crippling Blow to Dyslexics'. *The Times of India*. Retrieved from http://timesofindia.indiatimes.com

Horowitz, S.H. (2007). 'The Neurobiology of Learning Disabilities'. Retrieved from http://www.ncld.org/ld-basics/ld-explained/basic-facts/the-neurobiology-of-learning-disabilities

Iqbal, N. and Gupta, P. (2006). 'Self-Esteem and Adjustment of Children with Learning Disabilities'. *Disabilities and Impairments*, 20(1), 37–44.

Jha, M.M. (2010). *From Special to Inclusive Education in India: Case Studies of Three Schools in Delhi*. Delhi: Pearson.

Kapur, M. (2008). 'Profiles of Academic Skill Deficits in Indian Schools', in K. Thapa, G.M.V. Aalsvoort and J. Pandey (eds), *Perspectives on Learning Disabilities in India: Current Practices and Prospects*. New Delhi: Sage Publications, 171–180.

Karanth, P. (2003). 'Introduction', in P. Karanth and J. Rozario (eds), *Learning Disabilities in India: Willing the Mind to Learn*. New Delhi: Sage Publications, 17–29.

Kumar, D.S. (2010, June 11). 'Not Promoted, 8-yr-Old Dyslexic Stays Home'. *The Times of India*. Retrieved from http://timesofindia.indiatimes.com

Madan, A. (2002). 'Paradigms for Integrated Education of Primary School Children with Learning Difficulties in Delhi'. (Unpublished doctoral dissertation), Department of Home Science, University of Delhi.

Mahapatra, D. (2010, March 19). 'Denied Calculator in Boards, Dyslexic Student Noves SC'. *The Times of India*. Retrieved from http://timesofindia.indiatimes.com

Malaviya, R. (2010). 'Inclusion of Children with Specific Learning Disability (SLD): Pedagogical Issues and Supports', in A. Siddhu, N. Sharma, P. Sundaraj, V. Kapur and S. Guglani (eds), *The Social Ecology of Disability*. Delhi: Academic Excellence, 150–167.

Ministry of Social Justice and Empowerment (2011). 'The Rights of Persons with Disabilities Bill, 2011'. Retrieved from http://www.socialjustice. nic.in/pdf/draftbill-pwd.pdf

Mullick, Y. (1999). 'The Experience of Being a Child with Learning Disability'. (Unpublished master's dissertation), Department of Child Development, Lady Irwin College, University of Delhi.

Nair, H.V. (2009, September 17). 'Special Tutors for Special Students'. *Hindustan Times*. Retrieved from http://www.hindustantimes.com

Nair, H.V. (2010, March 11). 'Delhi University Reserves Seats for Dyslexic Students'. *Hindustan Times*. Retrieved from http://www.hindustan-times.com

National Institute for the Mentally Handicapped (2003). *Educating Children with Learning Problems in Primary Schools: Resource Book for Teachers*. Secunderabad, Andhra Pradesh: NIMH.

Orkids (2011). 'About Us'. Retrieved from http://www.orkidsped.com

Pandey, M. (2003). 'Effect of Ecological Factors on Learning Disability'. *Disabilities and Impairments*, 17(2), 123–131.

Patel, P.G. (2004). *Reading Acquisition in India: Models of Learning and Dyslexia*. New Delhi: Sage Publications.

Rehabilitation Council of India (2007). *Status of Disability in India*. New Delhi: Rehabilitation Council of India.

Sarva Shiksha Abhiyan (2011). 'Guidelines on Assessment of CWSN'. Retrieved from http://www.ssa.nic.in

Shrikanth, K.P. (2010). 'Young Adults with Learning Disabilities: A Follow-up Study'. *Disabilities and Impairments*, 24(1), 53–62.

Singh, C.K. and Dhanda, B. (2008). 'Children with Learning Disabilities in Relation to Different Ecological Factors'. *Disabilities and Impairments*, 22(1), 24–28.

Tandon, P. (2004). 'Constructing the Self: Voices of Children with Learning Difficulties'. (Unpublished master's dissertation), Department of Child Development, Lady Irwin College, University of Delhi.

Tata Interactive Systems (2011). 'The Tata Interactive Learning Disability Forum 2011'. Retrieved from http://www.tatalearningforum.com/TLDF/index.htm

Thapa, K. (2008). 'Learning Disabilities: Issues and Concerns', in K. Thapa, G.M.V. Aalsvoort, and J. Pandey (eds), *Perspectives on Learning Disabilities in India: Current Practices and Prospects*. New Delhi: Sage Publications, 23–47.

The Times of India (2011, December 12). 'MCD Schools Still Waiting for Special Teachers'. *The Times of India*. Retrieved from http://timesofindia.indiatimes.com

Thomson, J.B. and Raskind, W.H. (2003). 'Genetic Influences on Reading and Writing Disabilities'. In H.L. Swanson, K.R. Harris, and S. Graham (eds), *Handbook of Learning Disabilities*. New York: The Guilford Press, 256–272.

TOI (2011, July 21). 'Speed News'. Retrieved from http://timesofindia.indiatimes.com

United Nations (2006). 'Convention on the Rights of Persons with Disabilities'. Retrieved from http://www.un.org

United Nations (2011). 'Conventions and Optional Protocol Signatures and Ratifications'. Retrieved from http://www.un.org/disabilities/countries. asp?id=166

Venkateshwarlu, D. and Shah, B. (2002). 'Concept of Learning Disability'. *Disabilities and Impairments*, 16(1), 29–36.

9

Equal 'Human' Status to Women and Girls with Disabilities

Gender-Disability Dimension of Human Rights

Deepshikha Singh

Women and girls with disabilities face discrimination on daily basis irrespective of their background. This includes discrimination in the enforcement of laws, denial of equal opportunity in education and employment, exclusion of women with disabilities in political representation, deprivation of reproductive rights, cultural and social norms that reinforce stereotypes, and physical, sexual and psychological violence to subordinate and ostracise females with disabilities. Although there is an increasing trend of women with disabilities coming out of isolation and establishing advocacy groups, their status in developing countries remains miserable. The social experiences of women with disabilities have been ignored by both the women's rights mechanisms and disability rights mechanisms. Even disability studies and women studies do not sufficiently deal with the extreme marginalisation of women and girls with disabilities. The 'disability' within women studies is used synonymously with the general identity of being a 'woman' and the experiences of women with disabilities have lost its concern for women's rights in general. Similarly, disability studies have traditionally used a gender blind approach to examine the lives of people with disabilities and have neglected to explore the influence of gender in the lives of men and women with disabilities. The lack of gender-disability analysis of the policies and practices for women and the disabled makes it difficult to meet the specific requirements of women with disabilities.

Rationalising the Problem

Women with disabilities have been largely neglected for research, state policies, disability and women movements, education, work and employment, health and rehabilitation programmes. In India, there is the lack of sufficient data on women and girls with disabilities in both the national statistics on women and that on disabled. The gender-segregated data on disability is limited to only prevalence by location and types of disability. The limited data available on women and girls with disabilities is a challenge for research. The lack of extensive research on issues of women with disabilities has allowed challenge to continue and left gaps in the evidence to support the needs for laws, policies and programmes. Hence, women with disabilities live in isolation with their voices remain silent in the policy debates. The sidetracked issues of human rights violations of women with disabilities justifies the emergent need to study the multiple disadvantages experienced by this group ranging from basic human rights violations to research paucity.

In this chapter, various significant literatures have been reviewed to highlight the intersectional discrimination and violations faced by women with disabilities. The main aim of this chapter is to examine the policy of government on 'women' and 'disabled' with the lens of gender-disability dimension in order to elicit specific gaps in the policies leading to the exclusion of women with disabilities. The first section of the chapter throws light on the gender-disability dimension of human rights through a discussion of the contributions of various international human rights instruments for specifically advocating the human rights of women with disabilities. The second section of the chapter covers the review of literatures, the policy analysis and specific policy recommendations to redress for human rights violations in case of women with disabilities.

Gender-Disability Dimension of Human Rights

Disability is a human rights issue because people with disabilities experience inequalities, subject to violation of dignity and denied autonomy. A range of international documents have highlighted that disability is a human rights issue, including the World Programme of Action Concerning Disabled People (1982), the Convention on the Rights of the Child (1989) and the Standard Rules for the Equalization of Opportunities for People with Disabilities (1993). UNCRPD (2006)—the most recent and the most extensive recognition of human rights of PWDs—outlines the civil, political, social and economic rights of PWDs. Exercise of human rights in case of PWDs includes the provision of accessibility, protection and safety in situations of risks and emergency, RTE, right to health, protection of integrity, respect for the family, habilitation and rehabilitation, participation rights, right to work and employment on equal basis, adequate standard of living and social protection, right to vote and reservation (CRPD 2006).

The disability discrimination is based on the definition in Committee on the Rights of Persons with Disabilities (CRPD), Article 2:

> any distinction, exclusion or restriction on the basis of disability which has the purpose or effect of impairing or nullifying the recognition, enjoyment or exercise, on an equal basis with others, of all human rights and fundamental freedoms in the political, economic, social, cultural, civil or any other field. It includes all forms of discrimination, including denial of reasonable accommodation.

Similarly, the Convention on the Elimination of All Forms of Discrimination against Women (CEDAW) defines gender-based discrimination in Article 1:

> any distinction, exclusion or restriction made on the basis of sex which has the effect or purpose of impairing or nullifying the

recognition, enjoyment or exercise be women, irrespective of their marital status, on a basis of equality of men and women, of human rights and fundamental freedoms in the political, economic, social, cultural, civil or any other field.

Women and girls with disabilities experience disadvantages and discrimination based on the combination of both disability and gender-based discrimination, known as 'intersectional discrimination'.

The Vienna Declaration and Programme of Action is a human rights declaration adopted by the consensus at the World Conference on Human Rights on 25 June 1993 in Vienna, Austria. Though there is a lack of gender-disability analysis, the Vienna Declaration reaffirms the human rights of women and PWDs in separate sections. The CEDAW with its strength to fight all forms of discrimination against women is a valuable tool for advancing the rights of women with disabilities. CEDAW General Recommendation No. 18—Rights of Women with Disabilities 1991—recommends state parties to the CEDAW to provide information on disabled women in their periodic reports and on measures taken to deal with their particular situation, including special measures to ensure that they have equal access to education, employment, health services and social security and to ensure that they can participate in all areas of political, social and cultural life. CEDAW General Recommendation 24—Women and Health 1999—analyses the right to health in the context of women with disabilities and also acknowledges that cultural or traditional practices carry a high risk of causing discrimination.

Article 12 (1) (25) of CEDAW reports:

> Women with disabilities, of all ages, often have difficulty with physical access to health services. Women with mental disabilities are particularly vulnerable, while there is limited understanding, in general, of the broad range of risks to mental health to which women are disproportionately susceptible as a result of gender discrimination, violence, poverty, armed conflict, dislocation and other forms of social deprivation. State parties should take appropriate measures to ensure that health services are sensitive to the needs of women with disabilities and are respectful of their human rights and dignity.

Key tools for disabled women's rights advocacy is the Beijing Declaration and Programme for Action of the Fourth World Conference on Women in 1995 (Beijing Platform for Action), which put concerns of women with disabilities on the international women's agenda. Accordingly, governments need to reaffirm the entire scope of the human rights of women and girls with disabilities, including the implementation of the Beijing Platform for Action, in order to achieve the internationally agreed development goals as well as those contained in the UN Millennium Declaration.

The Biwako Millennium Framework for Action (2002), a policy framework that promotes an inclusive, barrier-free and rights-based society for people with disabilities in the Asia and the Pacific region emphasises issues of women with disabilities and finds that they are subject to discrimination, denied access to health services, education, training, and employment, are at high risk of abuse and do not participate in community activities.

CRPD (2006) and the entry of its Optional Protocol in May 2008 marked the beginning of a new era for the rights provision of PWDs. Article 6 of the convention separately discusses women with disabilities.

Article 6 of the convention states that:

> State Parties shall take all appropriate measures to ensure the full development, advancement and empowerment of women, for the purpose of guaranteeing them the exercise and enjoyment of the human rights and fundamental freedom set out in the present Convention.

Although many international human rights documents have mentioned the human rights of girls and women with disabilities, there is a need of intersectional analysis for protecting and promoting the human rights of women and girls with disabilities. When human rights frameworks and institutions talk about disability and gender in isolation from each other, they risk entrenching discrimination against women with disabilities (HREOC 2001). Human rights mechanisms should respond effectively and sufficiently to the intersectional discrimination that affect a large number of sub-group including women and girls with disabilities.

Understanding the Disability

Various significant literatures have been reviewed to present the current status of women with disabilities. The available literatures show that women and girls with disabilities in every community all over the world experience intersectional discrimination due to their status of being 'female', 'disabled' and 'poor'. In 2003, the ESCAP Report indicated that girls and women with disabilities receive less care and support and are more likely to experience abuse resulting in their higher mortality rates (ESCAP 2003). The evidence drawn by a UNDP research shows that despite some helpful laws, policies and practices in some countries, compared to their disabled male or non-disabled female counterparts, women and girls with disabilities are less educated; experience high rates of unemployment, are more likely to be abused, are poorer; are more isolated; experience worse health outcomes and generally have lower social status (Stubbs and Tawake 2009). This shows that the status of women and girls with disabilities is dismal on various indicators of development. Poverty has exacerbating effects on the experiences of disability. Disability acts as a barrier to join labour force and derive adequate earnings. Lack of employment opportunities and poor participation in the labour force contributes to poverty. Poverty plays its devastating role when it gets coupled with gender and disability factor, that is, the females with disabilities face the worst consequences of poverty because of being female and disabled. The International Labour Organization (ILO) based study in Ethiopia, one of the least developed countries, highlighted the occupational status of women with disabilities. The key findings of the study indicated that most of the women were engaged in low value added trading activities; very few women were involved in profitable and productive activities; many of the women eke out a living, earning barely enough to survive and many of them have reported low profit and problems in accessing credit (ILO 2003). The ILO states that women with disabilities are at an increased risk of being sicker, poorer and more socially isolated than either men with disabilities or women without disabilities. The UN estimates that worldwide, only 25 per cent of women with disabilities are in the work force (International Disability Foundation 1999, as cited in Rousso 2003).

The status of women with disabilities in the developing countries is highly deplorable. They remain hidden and neglected with their human rights frequently violated and their voices suppressed. The recent World Health Organization (WHO) world report on disability shows that vulnerable groups such as women, those in poorest wealth quintile had higher prevalence of disability in the developing countries (WHO 2011). In a patriarchal society, gender exacerbates women's experience of disability and the sociocultural prejudices related to gender and disabilities are highly dominant. This greatly violates the human rights of women with disabilities rendering them as forgotten 'human'. Ghai (2008) noted that women with disabilities in Indian society encounter discrimination at several levels, each of which restrict their options and opportunities for equal participation in the economic, social and political life of society. Women with disabilities become double marginalised because of socially constructed roles for men and women. They face social rejection as they are considered as incapable of performing the socially constructed gender roles. Franklin (1977) researched on women with disabilities and noted that they are perceived as incompetent in performing the role of a wife, mother and homemaker because of their disability, even if they have the ability to do so. They are not considered marriageable because their disability is considered as a defect. They are less likely to be married than disabled men. Women with disabilities also do not get their potential marriage partners and they are married off to unmatched partners. They are also more likely to be divorced and abandoned. Child bearing, like marriage, is another issue where women with disabilities face discrimination. Women with disabilities are restricted to participate in community life because of the physical insecurity and over-protective nature of families for disabled girl or women. In many of the Indian communities, the presence of a disabled woman is considered as inauspicious in cultural events (Hema and Dreams 1996). A report of a consultative meeting on gender and disability concluded that:

> Girls and women are more likely to be excluded from education than boys with disabilities; they are less likely to be taken for health care and treatment for their impairment than boys, particularly when money is in short supply; their opportunities for family life are severely compromised, due to societal prejudices against marriage of disabled young women, which can lead either they being unmarried or their family having to pay large dowries to 'offset' the disadvantage of their disability; with limited education, employment opportunities are restricted and even if they are educated, discrimination makes it more difficult for young women to obtain and hold on to jobs; and in many of these contexts—family, school and work—disabled women and girls experience high rates of sexual abuse. as a consequence of a life marked by discrimination, disadvantage and often abuse, most disabled women and girls suffer from low self-esteem and confidence and poor self-image. (Khanna et al. 2004)

Disabled girls tend to receive less care than disabled boys and are more likely to die or be killed. Where men and women have similar impairments, women are more likely to continue working than their male counterparts and are less likely to seek medical treatment or to see themselves as disabled. Rousso (2003) noted that women with disabilities have limited access to rehabilitation services receiving only one-fifth of the rehabilitation in the world. Women with disabilities are more vulnerable to exploitations and violence of different forms such as rape, molestation, domestic violence and exploitation at workplace. Available data suggests that women with disabilities experience violence and abuse within the family, institutions and community at higher rates than their non-disabled peers. Moreover, the violence they face may be more chronic and severe, taking some unique forms such as withholding essential care. The disabled women are not able to assess violent situations, to defend themselves and/or flee, or report incidence of violence (Erb and Harris-White 2002; Ghai 2008; Mohapatra and Mohanty 2004). Mohapatra and Mohanty (2004) conducted a study in Orissa which showed that about 98 per cent of the disabled women surveyed were beaten at home, and 25 per cent of the mentally challenged women had been raped and 6 per cent of women with disabilities had been forcibly sterilised. Women and girls with disabilities are easy targets of sexual exploitation, particularly if they are visually impaired or mentally retarded. The social, physical and economic dependency of women with disabilities on others increases the vulnerability to exploitation and abuse. A fact-finding report highlighted the mass hysterectomies of mentally challenged girls in a state-run institution in Shirur, Maharashtra, which is a shocking evidence of abuse of reproductive rights of women and girls with disabilities. In a horrific case, in 1994, 11 hysterectomies were performed on intellectually disabled women between the ages of 13 and 35 years.[1] A UNDP (2007) study showed some important findings on women with disabilities in four states: Andhra Pradesh, Orissa, Chhattisgarh and West Bengal. The study indicated that the status of women with disabilities was low on most of the parameters such as marital status, education, employment, self-employment, microcredit, vocational training, disability certificate, aids and appliances, family support, decision-making and political participation, access to health services, access to schemes and knowledge about rights. The study has given useful insights about the socio-demographic parameters of women with disabilities, which were found to be low in most cases. The study reported the extreme violence faced by women with disabilities in different cases: a girl with cerebral palsy was found to be frequently raped by the villagers and she was blamed for the rape; a woman with mental condition is battered by her sisters-in-law; a woman with mobility condition was tortured and given electric shocks; a neighbour tried molesting woman with hearing impairment; married to a non-disabled, a woman with a mobility condition faced violence by her husband and deserted; hysterectomies are common to women with mental conditions; and cases of false promises to marry and desertions (UNDP 2007).

The available data on literacy indicates that women and girls with disabilities fare less well in the educational arena than either disabled male or non-disabled female counterparts. The National Sample Survey Organisation (NSSO) 2002 58th round data indicated that in India, women and girls with disabilities receive less educational opportunities. The mainstreaming of the girls with disabilities in regular schools and classrooms in India is still a distant dream for a majority of such girls especially those who belong to rural areas or having multiple disabilities. The NSS in India has shown that girls with disabilities had lower enrolment ratios than boys with disabilities (a) across region, that is, urban and rural, (b) be type of schooling, that is, regular and special schools and (c) by level, that is primary and secondary. Of all the disability categories, women and girls with disabilities were least likely to have received education, had the lowest enrolment ratio in schools, were the lowest proportion of employed persons and were the most likely to remain unmarried. The enrolment of girls with disabilities in the elementary education is low as compared to their male counterparts. District Information System for Education (DISE) data (2009–2010) indicates that the percentage of children with disabilities to total enrolment for the year 2009–2010 is 0.75 for primary level and 0.74 for upper primary level. The percentage of girls with disabilities to the total of such enrolment of children with disabilities is 48.46 at primary and 48.12 for upper primary in the year 2009–2010. The calculated Gender Parity Index (GPI) in case of disabled children is low as compared to the GPI of overall enrolment. In case of disabled children, the computed GPI is 0.94 for primary level and 0.93 for upper primary level (DISE 2011).

In India, large numbers of women with disabilities are unemployed or engaged in very low paid jobs. According to NSSO 2002 58th round data, the usual work activity status (activity status during last 365 days preceding the survey) for the disabled persons depicts that 62 per cent and 89 per cent males and females respectively in rural areas and 63.5 per cent and 90.5 per cent males and females respectively in urban areas were out of labour force. The overall employment scenario is worst for disabled women (NSSO 2003).

The two important national statistics on disability, that is census 2001 and NSSO 58th round survey reported that women with disabilities are fewer in number than men with disabilities. Some researchers have noted the underrepresentation of women with disabilities in national statistics. According to the NSSO 58th round survey in 2002, there are 18.49 million people with disabilities in India, out of which 10.89 million were males and

7.59 million were females, constituting 59 per cent and 41 per cent of males and females respectively. The 2001 census estimates that there are over 9 million women with disabilities constituting 3.5 of the population and 42.46 of the total disabled population. The prevalence rates for females were lower than that for males. Bacquer and Sharma (1997) noted that underrepresentation of women with disabilities in statistics could be due to relatively higher non-reporting of disabilities in the case of females. The underrepresentation of women with disabilities in statistics made them more vulnerable to isolation and abuse.

The findings from the review of literature shows that women with disabilities form the most marginalised sub-group and their status in social, economic, political, educational, cultural, familial and community-related parameters is dismal. They have poor participation level in early care, education, health, employment, training, support services, political participation, cultural events and in self-help groups. The underrepresentation of this group adds to the severity of their condition. Being hidden in the society, their voices are never heard especially in case of those who belong to poor socio-economic and poor sociocultural background. The cases of their human rights violations, especially the extreme physical and psychological violence cases are hardly addressed. The disadvantages of women with disabilities as indicated by the above-mentioned literatures direct the need of a stringent policy and plan of actions to protect the human rights of this highly disadvantaged group.

State's Policies for 'Women' and 'Disabled': Gender-Disability Analysis

Available information demonstrates that the equity policies and programmes for women and disabled in India do not specifically cater to the unique needs of women and girls with disabilities. There is a lack of gender-disability analysis in the state's policies for women and disabled. The recent report of the Working Group on Empowerment of Women for the XI Plan throws light on the status of women with disabilities in India:

> Although a rights-based approach has entered the disability rights movement, the specific concerns of women with disabilities have found a place neither in the government policies and programmes nor the voluntary sector. Ironically or expectedly, the disabled rights movement all over the world including India is male dominated. It may even be blatantly sexist. (p. 93)

The General Recommendations 18 and 24 of CEDAW provide recommendations to states for specific provision for women with disabilities to ensure equal access to education, employment, health services and social security. The available sources show that so far, no specific measure has been taken by the state to protect and promote the rights of women with disabilities. State mechanism has failed to provide the de-facto enjoyment of human rights to women with disabilities. There is the absence of information on women with disabilities in any of the government CEDAW periodic reports.[2]

States have enacted several specific legislations on gender-based issues to realise equality rights of women. These legislations include Dowry Prohibition Act, 1961, Child Marriage Restraint (Amendment) Act, 1979, Protection of Women from Domestic Violence Act, 2005, Commission of Sati Prevention Act, 1987, Indecent Representation of Women (Prohibition) Act, 1986, Immoral Traffic (Prevention) Act, 1956, Pre-Conception and Pre-Natal Diagnostic Technique Act, 1994, Medical Termination of Pregnancies Act, 1971, Equal Remuneration Act, 1976, Maternity Benefit Act, 1961, and National Commission for Women Act, 1990. However, these legal provisions have largely benefitted women in general, they have failed to respond to the unique needs of women with disabilities. Women do not form a homogeneous group and the needs of women with disabilities may be different from women in general. The sociocultural analysis is important while analysing the needs of women as a group. There is the absence of specific provisions for women with disabilities within state's legislations for women. Women with disabilities are quite often excluded from gender equity programmes. They require very different but specialised provisions within the policies for women in general.

The National Policy for the Empowerment of Women (GoI 2001b) prescribed several provisions for women empowerment including responsive judicial-legal system, equal and active participation in decision-making, poverty eradication, microcredit facility, education, health, nutrition, housing and shelter, protection from violence, promotion of girl child rights and strengthening the role of mass media for empowering women. These provisions have benefitted women in general but at the same time the policy failed to cover specific provision or prescription for addressing the unique needs of women with disabilities in any of its section. The policy commitments act as a significant weapon to combat discrimination and violence against women in general but how far these initiatives have empowered women with disabilities is still a question. The empowerment needs of women with disabilities may require some additional provision which the National Policy failed to incorporate.

There is the lack of gender-disability analysis in the educational policies too. Accessing educational rights is a fundamental problem faced by girls with disabilities. They face problem with regard to access to schools, enrolments in schools and availing the opportunity of vocational training. The NPE, 1986, and the NPE, 1992, mentioned special focus groups as having girls, SC/ST, OBC, minorities and disability, but failed to focus separately on the education of girls with disabilities who are the most vulnerable group being multiple disadvantaged. The SSA addresses the needs of vulnerable out-of-school children, including children with disabilities. However, SSA did not differentiate the experiences of girls with disabilities with those of boys with disabilities and, thus, failed to ensure the specific provision for girls with disabilities in schools.

In India, none of the Five-Year Plans focussed on the women with disabilities as a target group for bringing gender equity. The Tenth Plan (2002–2007) was committed to create an enabling environment for the PWDs so that they can enjoy their rights, enjoy equal opportunities and participate in development activities. The Tenth Plan failed to focus specifically on the rights, opportunities and services for women with disabilities. However, the Eleventh Plan, for the first time, considers the situation of women with disabilities in all its complexity, focussing on the need for an intersectional understanding of discrimination in order for policy to be effective. The Eleventh Plan considers the vulnerability of poor women to triple discrimination: poverty, gender and disability. It observes that:

> Women with disabilities face violations of their rights at every level. They are considered a financial burden and social liability by their families; they are denied opportunities, movement outside the home and access to education; they are viewed as asexual, helpless and dependent ... they [are] isolated and neglected with no home of a normal life. (Report of the Working Group on Empowerment of Women for the XI Plan, p. 93)

Not only is there underrepresentation of women with disabilities in women-specific policies, but there is also the absence of a single disability law specifically for women with disabilities. State patriarchy is highly visible in the disability policy documents. The existing legal framework on disability makes no specific provision for women with disabilities. The Persons with Disabilities (Equal Opportunities, Protection of Rights and Full Participation) Act, 1995, is an important landmark in ensuring equal opportunities for persons with disabilities. The act provides for preventive promotional aspects of rehabilitation such as education, employment and vocational training, job reservation, research and manpower development, creation of barrier-free environment, rehabilitation, unemployment allowance for the disabled, special insurance scheme for the disabled employees and establishment of homes for persons with severe disability. The PWD Act remains gender-neutral, and it failed to address the unique needs of women with disabilities in the areas of health, education, employment, rehabilitation, research and training. The PWD Act failed to recognise the intersectional discrimination on grounds of disability and gender. Similarly, other provision such as the National Trust for the Welfare of Persons with Autism, Cerebral Palsy, Mental Retardation and Multiple Disabilities Act, 1999, and the scheme of Integrated Education for Disabled Children, 1974, failed to focus separately on women and girls with disabilities.

The MHRD drafted the Action Plan for Inclusion in Education of Children and Youths with Disabilities in 2005. The action plan for the Inclusion in Education of Children and Youths with Disabilities has an objective of facilitating an access for girls with disabilities from the rural or remote areas to the government hostels. The action plan proposes to ensure that girls with disabilities are included in all programmes and that existing Mahila Samakhya, National Programme for Girls Education at Elementary Level and Kasturba Gandhi Balika Vidyalaya are also sensitised to the educational needs of girls with disabilities. There are serious lacunas in the implementation of these provisions. The National Policy for Persons with Disabilities (GoI 2006b), under the Ministry of Social Justice and Empowerment is the only policy where the women with disabilities are mentioned in a separate section. The policy envisages that special programmes will be developed for education, employment and providing other rehabilitation services to women with disabilities keeping in view their special needs. Special training and vocation facilities will be set up for them. Programmes will be undertaken to rehabilitate abandoned disabled women/girls by encouraging their adoption in families, support to house them and impart them training for gainful employment skills (National Policy for Persons with Disabilities, GoI 2006b). The National Policy mandates the separate mechanism to review annually the intake and retention of the girl child with disability at primary, secondary and higher levels of education. However, although it mentions specific provisions for women with disabilities, there is none that proactively target women with disabilities, particularly in the context of health and social attitudes.

Though the state's policies for 'women' and the 'disabled' are able to address the general needs of women with disabilities, they do not qualify to address their special needs. Few policy provision passes to safeguard the interests of women with disabilities, but they look more like 'patch work' rather than an integrated approach. Except a few, significant policies and legislations for women and disabled is marked by the exclusion of unique provisions for women with disabilities. The existing gender-equity policies and disability-equity policies lack gender-disability lens that restrict women with disabilities in successfully realising their human rights. The intersectional evaluation of current 'gender' and 'disability' policies, laws and programmes is important for promoting the rights-based approach of disability relevant to supporting women and girls with disabilities. Policy-makers need to be aware that women as well as the disabled are not a homogeneous group. Gender and disability forms sub-groups on the basis of several sociocultural factors.

Policy Recommendations

State and the civil society do not adequately take the causes of women and girls with disabilities. There is a lack of political will to safeguard the human rights of women with disabilities as they are considered as 'to be a few' in population and thus, do not form 'vote bank'. Government programmes consider women as one homogeneous group and disabled as another group. A specific programme for women with disabilities, cutting across all identities is not available. There is an urgent need to consider this highly marginalised group as a priority in all gender-specific and disability-specific policies. The rights of women with disabilities can be safeguarded by including them in the policy of social, economic and political empowerment.

The gender-disability (intersectional) analysis of existing legislations on disability and women would be highly significant for promoting and protecting the human rights of women with disabilities. State should establish a human rights mechanism that can effectively address the intersectional discrimination and promote a right-based approach in accordance with international human rights norms and standards. It is important for the government to legislate the elimination of all forms of discrimination against women and girls with disabilities, as part of either the current disability or women legislations. There is a need to harmonise policies and legislations for disability and to align gender-equality issues across all ministries and services.

There is a lack of sufficient data on women and girls with disabilities in both the national statistics on women and that on the disabled. The gender-segregated data on disability is limited to only prevalence by location and types of disability. The limited data available on women and girls with disabilities is a challenge for research. The lack of research on different issues relating to women with disabilities results in divagation from issues of human rights violations. National statistics offices should collect, update and use high quality data on women and girls with disabilities in close consultation with the women and disability departments. Data on women and girls with disabilities should be disaggregated by relevant indicators to inform policy and programme development. Data on women with disabilities should include indicators of age, education, employment, occupation, income, marital status, living arrangements and community participation.

Other Recommendations

The national disability coordinating committees should have a representative to look after the gender-equality issues and to provide advocacy and technical guidance on the concerns of women and girls with disabilities. There should be a separate wing for women with disabilities in the Disability Commissioners office. Also, the national women machinery should include women with disabilities as representatives.

There is a need of an integrated 'Empowerment Policy' for women with disability focussing on awareness, education, employment, health, vocational training, advocacy, women friendly rehabilitation, self-help groups, and social and political competency. Awareness and education will help women with disabilities to advocate for their own rights. They should be provided career-oriented education leading to income-generation, credit facilities and other forms of economic self-reliance making them self-dependent.

The health system should be revived to respond to the health and reproductive requirements of women with disabilities. The health system must be strengthened for the successful prevention, identification and intervention for all disabilities including mental illness and cerebral palsy. Reproductive health of women with disabilities has to be promoted by putting a strong check on the violation of their reproductive rights in the form of forced sterilisation, contraception and abortion. Health personnel should be trained in health issues that women and girls with disabilities experience at different stage of life.

Promoting self-help groups of women with disabilities will play a major role in empowering disabled women. This will prevent them from isolation, provide mutual support and encourage the community participation. It will give a sense of self-worth to them and make them economic self-reliant. Self-help group will educate the women with disabilities about their rights and opportunities, and reduce the chance of gender- and disability-based violence. Community-based rehabilitation can be the best way to address some of the complex cultural, economic and social factors that are related to expectations from traditional gender roles. The promotion of community-based rehabilitation programmes for women with disabilities may facilitate the public education and awareness generation efforts about the potential of women with disabilities with appropriate interventions, remove misconception about marital, domestic, and motherhood roles, and bring about changes in societal attitudes. The self-defence programme especially for young girls with disability has to be started in community settings to prevent the incidents of violence such as rape, molestation and domestic violence.

Lack of access to rehabilitation programme by women with disabilities must be addressed by including more women professionals in rehabilitation programmes. Rehabilitation system is male dominated which prevents a large number of women with disabilities to access the rehabilitative services. Involvement of more women functionaries in the delivery of rehabilitative services will encourage more women with disabilities to access the services. Women with disabilities should also be trained to be the functionaries and not only beneficiaries of disability service provisions. This will boost their confidence level and they can better respond to the needs of their counterparts.

Negative portray of women with disabilities in media places them in disadvantaged situations. Media can play an important role in propagating the positive images of women with disabilities by highlighting their achievements and by negating the 'beauty concepts' for promotion of brands. Gender mainstreaming should be included in the pedagogy of special education course, rehabilitation or women studies course by preparing special modules for women with disabilities. Rehabilitation Council of India, the agency responsible for standardising teaching and curricula in the disability sector, should initiate the special training courses to prepare the cadre of professionals to meet the unique needs of women with disabilities.

Notes

1. In the Guise of Human Dignity. Fact-finding report. Available at http://cssh.unipune.ernet.in/HumanRights/07%20STATE%20AND%20GENDER/12.pdf
2. CEDAW Initial Periodic Report (1998) and CEDAW Periodic Report II and III (2000). Ministry of Women and Child Development. New Delhi.

References

Bacquer, A. and Sharma, A. (1997). *Disability Challenges versus Response*. New Delhi, India: Concerned Action Now (CAN).

CRPD (2006). 'United Nations Convention on the Rights of Persons with Disability'. Retrieved on 27 July 2018 from www.un.org/disabilities/documents/convention/convention_accessible_pdf.pdf.

DISE (2011). *Elementary Education in India Progress towards UEE. Provisional Flash Statistics 2009–10*. New Delhi: NUEPA.

Economic and Social Commission for Asia and the Pacific (ESCAP) (2003). Hidden Sisters: Women and Girls with Disabilities in the Asia-Pacific Region. Bangkok: ESCAP.

Erb, S. and Harris-White, B. (2002). *Outcast from Social Welfare: Disability in Rural India*. London: Sage Publications.

Franklin, P. (1977). 'Impact of Disability on the Family Structure'. *Social Security Bulletin*, 40(5), 3–18.

Ghai, Y. (2008). Bills of Rights and Decolonization: The Emergence of Domestic Human Rights Instruments in Britain's Overseas Territories by Charles O.H. Parkinson, *Journal of Law and Society*, Vol. 35, No. 4, 576–578 (Book Review).

Hema, H. and Dreams (1996). 'The Situation of Women with Disabilities in India', in Driedger, D., Feika, I. and Gironbatres, E. (eds), *Across Borders*. Canada: Gynergy Books.

HREOC (2001). 'Issues Paper: Gender and Race Intersectionality'. Sydney.

International Labour Organization (ILO) (2003). 'Developing Entrepreneurship among Women with Disabilities in Ethiopia: Exploratory Surveys in Addis Ababa and Tigray Region'. ILO/Ireland Aid.

Khanna, R. et al. (2004). 'Consultative Meet to Design a Perspective Building Workshop on Gender and Disability: Report on the Proceedings'. Vadodara: Women's Health Training Research and Advocacy Cell, M.S. University, Baroda.

Mohapatra, C.S. and Mohanty, M. (2004). *Abuse and Activity Limitation: A Study on Domestic Violence against Disabled Women in Orissa.* Orissa: Swabhiman.

National Sample Survey Organization (NSSO) (2003). 'Disabled Persons in India'. NSS 58th Round. Government of India, New Delhi.

Rao, I. (2005). 'Equity to Women with Disabilities in India'. Strategy Paper. Disabled People's International. Retrieved on 18 December 2011, from http://www.dpi.org/lang-en/resources/details.php

Rousso, H. (2003). 'Education for All: A Gender and Disability Perspective'. Background paper presented for the Education for All Global Monitoring Report 2003/4 Gender and Education for All: The Leap to Equality. UNESCO.

Stubbs, D. and Tawake, S. (2009). Pacific Sisters with Disabilities: At the Intersection of Discrimination. UNDP Pacific Centre.

UNDP (2007). A Multi-state Socio Economic Study of Women with Disabilities in India. Bhubaneshwar: Shanta Memorial Rehabilitation Centre- Government of India-UNDP Study.

World Health Organization (WHO) (2011). World Report on Disability. Malta: WHO.

10

Disability Space in News and Entertainment Media in India

A Case Study

Santosh Kumar Biswal

Disability, according to the World Health Organization (WHO), is defined as an umbrella term covering impairments, activity limitations and participation restrictions. An impairment is a problem in body function or structure; an activity limitation is a difficulty encountered by an individual in executing a task or action; while restriction of participation is a problem experienced by an individual in involvement in life situations. Thus, disability is a complex phenomenon, reflecting an interaction between features of a person's body and features of the society in which he or she lives (World Report on Disability 2011). Thus, a disability may be physical, cognitive, sensory and emotional or some combination of these.

According to the Persons with Disabilities (PWD) or Equal Opportunities, Protection of Rights and Full Participation Act, 1995, 'Disability' includes blindness, low vision, leprosy-cured, hearing impairment, locomotor disability, mental retardation and mental illness. The act further defines a 'person with disability' as suffering from not less than 40 per cent of any disability as certified by a medical authority. Under PWD Act 1995, the disabilities mentioned above have been included in order to enable the persons suffering from disabilities to derive certain benefits/concessions provided by the state government/UTs administration/central ministries/department and local authorities. The new definition of disability includes persons with any impairment that has a 'substantial and long-term adverse effect' on the ability of a person to carry out normal day-to-day activities (National Human Rights Commission 2005).

The number of PWD has touched to around 40–90 million (Bakshi 2010). India is accommodating the largest population of disabled people in the world. According to the NSS of India, for estimations in the last three decades, that is, 1981, 1991 and 2001 there were 12 million, 16.15 million and 18.49 million people respectively and constituting 1.8 and 1.9 per cent of the total population (Klasing 2007). Despite huge population and unlimited sufferings on their part, PWDs have become the most politically invisible and underrepresented groups in the country. Unlike other minority groups, disabled people are subjugated and unable to form special groups to take part in the politics at either the state or national level (Karna 2000).

Programmes for PWD under the National Policy for Persons with Disability include extending rehabilitation services to rural areas; increasing trained personnel to meet needs; emphasising education and training; increasing employment opportunities; focussing on gender equality; improving access to public services; encouraging state governments to develop a comprehensive social security policy; ensuring equal opportunities in sports, recreation and cultural activities and increasing the role of civil society organisations as service providers to PWD and their families. The policy recognises the need to replace the earlier emphasis on medical rehabilitation with an emphasis on social rehabilitation (Bhas 2006).

No doubt, the Persons with Disabilities or Equal Opportunities, Protection of Rights and Full Participation Act (PWD Act) of 1995 has heralded a new dawn in the lives of disabled people in India. However, the PWD Act adopts a narrow definition of disability and confines it to 'blindness; low vision; leprosy-cured; hearing impairment; locomotor disability; mental retardation;

and mental illness'. Disabled rights groups are demanding a new law instead that would guarantee civil and political rights to disabled people and expand the definition of disability. They are arguing for a complete overhaul in the PWD Act (Raha 2010).

Many people with disabilities do not have equal access to health care, education and employment opportunities, do not receive the disability-related services that they require and experience exclusion from everyday life activities. Following the entry into force of the UNCRPD, disability is increasingly understood as a human rights issue (World Report on Disability 2011). Inadequate legal framework, lack of financial and skilled human resource to carry on activities, lack of training and capacity building activities, absence of large networks of disability groups to share resources with each other and low level of awareness among disabled and public sphere are the impeding factors for the advancement of disabled people (Enabling Access to Education through ICT, 2010). It is evident from the international development literature that the linkages between disability and poverty have been increasingly recognised (Yeo 2005). PWDs suffer more in terms of having access to clean water or adequate nutrition. The problems multiply at the time of illness and they have limited scopes physically and financially to afford treatment. Poor financial back-up and over-dependence on others result in vicious circle of poverty and social exclusion (Elwan 1999; Yeo 2005).

A study conducted on a sample of super 100 companies by National Centre for Promotion of Employment for Disabled People found that corporate India has largely ignored the statutory reservation for disabled persons, violating the Disability Act 1995 by employing only a handful of disabled employees. The respondent companies were Castrol India Limited, with a workforce of 1,300; Colgate Palmolive India Limited, with a workforce of 1,300; EID Parry India, with a staff of 4,700; and the Bombay Dyeing and Manufacturing Company Limited, with a workforce of 10,000. It is surprising to note the extremely low percentage of disabled employees in the multinational companies despite strict laws favouring disabled workforce (rediff.com 2000).

Almost no cities in India are disabled-friendly, for instance public places such as government offices, parks and hospitals. In

Indian cities, the environmental barriers are so severe (few sidewalks, pedestrian traffic signals, curb cuts or ramps) that most people with disabilities face a hard time to go out in public. Bangalore is a case in point. Bangalore, known as garden city, has only three parks, which are wheelchair-friendly or 'inclusive' out of 710 parks (Francis 2011). Whether going to a movie, visiting friends, getting to school or work or seeing the doctor and riding the bus or train is a daily necessity, everyone, regardless of their abilities and disabilities, has the right to use public transport with dignity and independence. However, the disabled often get a raw deal when travelling (Menon 2007).

Covering the sociocultural dimension of media in addressing disability, Meenakshi Sinha (2011) claims that marriage proposals for disabled people are limited for non-resident Indians from the United States, United Kingdom, Canada, Middle East, South East Asia, Australia and New Zealand. This was revealed from an online survey conducted by matrimony site. Activist Javed Abidi criticised the polls like this should not stereotype disability. However, such kind of event is degrading the confidence level of disabled people.

Disability is a development issue because of its bidirectional link to poverty: disability may increase the risk of poverty, and poverty may increase the risk of disability. The onset of disability may lead to the worsening of social and economic well-being and poverty through a multitude of channels including the adverse impact on education, employment, earnings and increased expenditures related to disability (Jenkins and Rigg 2003).

Media and Society

Mass media plays vital roles in shaping public perceptions on a variety of important issues through the information emanated from its various channels. They also play a larger role in shaping modern culture and public opinion by selecting and portraying a particular set of beliefs, values and traditions. Media attempts to shape reality to be more in line with that interpretation, by portraying a certain interpretation of reality (Lorimer and Scannell 1994; Webb 2008).

News media comprises newspapers, magazines, journals; roadcast media including radio and television; and new media ncluding online newspapers and news blogs. News media aims t delivering news, views and other informative programmes to ne audiences through the programmes such as news, debates nd discussion. It makes frequent attempts to create interactive essions among the public, government and corporate bodies in rder to break the deadlocks on various programmes and olicies. News media through its information tries to shape the ublic opinion.

Entertainment media aims at entertaining the audience nrough soap operas, cartoon series, reality shows and movies. ccording to an Ernst & Young report, 'Spotlight on India's Enter-inment Economy', media and entertainment industry in India corded revenues of US$ 16.3 billion in 2010 and is expected to e in excess of US$ 25 billion in the next four years. Factors such economic liberalisation, double-digit annual growth, st-growing middle class and a huge volume of demand for isure and entertainment have enticed global media companies scale up investments in India. India is a place with different ltures, languages and content preferences. These markets ovide conducive scopes for global media and entertainment mpanies to deliver localised content (www.ibef.org 2011).

The current study is apt to the social responsibility theory of edia—a part of normative theories—which states that freedom press is subject to the responsibility of the society. dependence is desirable as long as it obligates the needs and mands of the society. In this connection, media should perform e role of public stewardship and act as a watchdog against vernment or private misappropriation of power. Media must be countable to the society regarding all its functions. However, dia at present is biased, class-oriented and advertisement-ven, leaving the disabled people in sheer deprivation.

Onus is on media in constructing and reforming opinions and tudes in the society. It has to strike a proper balance among ormation, education and entertainment. According to Press ncil of India, Chairman Markandey Katju (2011) asserts:

> No doubt, the media should provide some entertainment also to the people. But if 90 per cent of their coverage is devoted to entertainment, and only 10 per cent to all the socio-economic issues put together, then the sense of priorities of the media has gone haywire.

Coverage of disabled related issues in media occupies the least, as media has become 'lapdog' instead of 'watchdog'.

Background

Needless to mention, media has become part and parcel of our everyday life. Media as an industry has been instrumental in disseminating information to the people. However, media does not always address all issues and bother for society's benefit at large. The problem of disability is a case in point. Media is adding woes, continuing discrimination towards disabled people. The disability portrayal as a sin, evil and tragic has been grossly disseminated throughout society by religious teachings and beliefs. Unfortunately, with little or almost no representation of disabled people in the media outlets and their workforces, and with the tradition of segregation of disabled people, attitudes and beliefs about disability have been left unchallenged. Media has been accused of on various grounds. Media still adopts the medical model of disability and it stresses on impairment more than the individual (*Media Representation of Disabled People* 2006).

Stereotyping the character of disabled people, mass media project them as pitiable and heroic. It creates a social dichotomy in the society and call instead for its supporters to 'Piss on Pity' instead of inclusive approach (Mickey 2005). This plight increases manifold as society takes disability from medical model perspectives. Disability rights activists criticise medical model of disability and media's role in this concern (Hershey 2001). It is seen that media channels are sidelining and emphasising less priority to the issues pertaining to women and marginalised classes such as low castes, religious minorities, economic awkward people, people with disabilities and the like.

Pinto and Sahur (2001) explore that there is a noticeable lack of coordination between media professionals and those working for the disabled, causing misrepresentation of disabled people from the society. Media is less bothered for the involvement of media in the cause of disability welfare. It is seen that there is no special approach suited to cover and address the issues pertaining to disability. They also point out that media is all the time busy in covering political affairs and attempting to please the ruling political party or bureaucrats for vested interests. As a result, it is failing to pay due attention to audiences' needs for information and the media's moral responsibility to help in policy formulation and implementation. Even though there are few media initiatives for the cause of disability needs, there is a marked indifference to the cause of integration of people with disabilities into mainstream society. In addition, integration has not even been identified as a goal. Giving instances of apathetic attitude of media, they further underline that All India Radio broadcasts a few programmes on disability awareness.

Coming down heavily on mainstream media, Starkey and Lay (2006) slam that language used in mainstream media to address disability is still derogatory and negative. They accuse that media uses very strong negative language. Some negative connotations are very grave and offensive. Views on disability vary with geography and culture, over time, and among individuals. Terms such as 'retard' and 'lame' are deliberate insults; others, such as 'wheelchair-bound', are inherently negative; still others, such as 'Mongolism', are based on stereotypical ideas of certain groups of individuals with disabilities. If these types of language were being used without check, this would keep sending wrong messages on disability to the society.

There has been a significantly increased use of pejorative language to describe disabled people, including suggestions that life on incapacity benefit had become a 'Lifestyle Choice' (Briant, Watson, and Philo 2011). Reiterating the theme of media's negligence in covering disability, Sengupta (2006) depicts this as a vicious cycle since the ideas communicated by media are derived from established social stereotypes, and these stereotypes are further strengthened and reproduced via representations in the media.

Joseph (2005) opines that it is generally true that occasions such as the International Day of Disabled Persons (instituted by the UN in 1992) usually generate more media coverage for such issues than can be expected through the rest of the year. Even though sometimes newspapers cover news on the disabled, they do not get due weightages. They do not publish on the front pages. The media do go beyond routine coverage of events, they tend to focus on individuals who are physically or mentally challenged and to portray them as either heroes or victims.

Sundar (2005) confirms that few movies have been made on disability in India. Of those, little is made on women disability. It has always been the male character who is shown with afflictions of some sort, with the female—in the form of the mother, sister, girlfriend or wife—providing tender support and caring. It has led to gender discrimination in addressing disability issue too. Sundar also cautions that mainstream Indian cinema rarely addresses the issue of disability, and it is still rare to find a film on the plight of the disabled woman.

Owing to bring justice for disability classes in terms of socio-economic parameters, disability should be given due prominence. Studies on disability need to be initiated in the media and academic circles as well in a view to reinstate the citizenship and identity, which can flourish the disability culture. In order to stop misrepresentation of disability and the experience of people with disabilities, there ought to be code of practice for the media barons and media users, which can ensure correct representation of the lives of disabled people.

With this understanding, the present chapter is based on the following objectives: (a) to understand the nuances of representation of disability in news and entertainment media, (b) to study the media coverage from disability perspectives and (c) to study the socio-economic conditions of disabled people.

Significance of the Study

From the above review of literature, it has found that no sufficient study has been carried out on the present subject, that is, representation of disabled people in news and entertainment media in India. As the media is broadly divided into two parts—news and entertainment—it is essential to analyse these two media segmentations. Generally, it is seen that all the news media do cover on regular areas such as politics, business, sports and civic news. In entertainment media also, there is a lack of proper representation of disability characters. The entertainment media often find it fancy to represent the disability characters in serials and films. In a view to assess the importance paid to disability people, one of the marginalised classes in the society, the present study is of paramount importance. Moreover, the study on the problems of disability means to expose the neglected sides of the society, paving the ways for betterment of the same.

As *The Hindu* is a national English daily, wide-circulated and popular for authentic journalism, the researcher has chosen this newspaper to understand and analyse the disability representation in news media in India. On the other hand, Bollywood movies play a vital role in entertainment media in India. So, the film *My Name is Khan*, a movie made in the year 2010, has been taken for understanding, analysing and measuring disability.

Theoretical Framework

Based on the works in 'Four Theories of the Press' by Siebert et al. (1956), McQuail (1987) frames six normative theories of the mass media. The normative theories reflect how media should be, what is to be expected of them rather than what necessarily happens in practice and it is out of the political, cultural and economic context that the normative principles arise. The current study is apt to the social responsibility theory of media—a part of normative theories—which states that freedom of press is subject to the responsibility of the society. Independence is desirable as long as it obligates the needs and demands of the society. In this connection, media should perform the role of public stewardship and act as watchdog against government or private misappropriation of power. Media must be accountable to the society regarding all its functions. However, media at present is biased, class-oriented and advertising-driven, leaving the disabled people in sheer deprivation. Coverage of disabled-related issues in media occupies the least, as media has become 'lapdog' instead of 'watchdog'.

Methodology

The current study has attempted to explore the disability representation in news and entertainment media through content analysis and discourse analysis. To explore disability representation in news media and entertainment media, the English Daily *The Hindu* and Hindi movie *My Name is Khan* have been selected respectively. To carry out this study, quantitative and qualitative research methods have been used. Content analysis and discourse analysis have been adopted to collect and analyse the data.

Here the researcher has attempted to explore the disability representation in *The Hindu* through the content analysis methodology. The data from main and supplementary pages published from 1 January to 31 December 2010 have been carefully collected and analysed. Here print and e-paper editions of the English daily have been taken into consideration. In a view to analyse critically, the content coverage concerning the disability, the researcher has divided into various aspects such as types of disability covered; placement and nature of content; and placement of geographical coverage. Published photographs supporting disability issues have also been taken into research.

The movie *My Name Is Khan*, released in the year 2010, is a landmark in the entertainment media in India. For this movie, discourse analysis has adopted to analyse the disability character played by Shah Rukh Khan. Various signs, symbols, dialogues and songs from the movie have been taken into consideration to understand and analyse disability representation in entertainment media.

Analysis of *The Hindu*

Started in 1878 as a weekly, *The Hindu*, the popular English daily, became a daily in 1889. It is being published from Chennai, Coimbatore, Bangalore, Hyderabad, Madurai, New Delhi, Vizag, Thiruvanathapuram, Kochi, Vijayawada, Mangalore, Tiruchirapalli and Kolkata and its readership is touching the mark of about 4.06 million. Apart from regular news coverage, it is bringing out a number of supplements such as Metro Plus, Business Review, Education Plus, Young World, Book Review, Job Opportunities,

NXG, Science, Engineering, Technology & Agriculture, Friday Features, Metro Plus Weekend, Cinema Plus, Property Plus and Weekly Magazine. Owing to keep its reader intact, the group publishes *The Hindu Business Line*—business daily; *Sportstar*—weekly sports magazine; *Frontline*—fortnightly magazine; *Survey of Indian Industry*—an annual review on Indian industries; *Survey of Indian Agriculture*—an annual review on Indian agriculture; and *Survey of the Environment*—an annual review of the environment.

When the data from *The Hindu* was collected from 1 January to 31 December 2010, 26 contents on disability were found. The whole data has converted into various categories such as types of disability covered; types of content covered; placement of content, nature of content covered; distribution of contents on the various problems faced by PWDs; category of reported content; content covered geographically and photograph published.

The current analysis concentrates on what has been represented, that is, what kind of stories have been included and what kind of stories have been dropped; and how has been the representation, that is, in terms of form, language, tone of representation or voice and region pertaining to contents on disabilities. This analysis shows the representation of disability in media which is institutionalised within our social psyche, emanated from our attitudes and policies directly or indirectly and demand for justified disabled rights. On the contrary, some intellectuals associated with disability claims that with the communication of such miserable data through various channels of mass media and facts on disability, it will further deteriorate the conditions of disabled by strengthening social stereotypes through media itself. Here, the role of media is not just to show the issue in the limelight but also to attempt that society's institutionalised bias should not be merely represented.

Kinds of Disability Represented

It is unfortunate to find that 45 per cent reports do not indicate which type of disability is covered. When the media is not mentioning the kind of disability and by writing for the words such as 'physically challenged', it reflects the casual kind of reporting in the newspaper. Thanks to its gross negligence, reporting is not factual and becomes superficial in nature. In the whole one year, there is no coverage on hearing impairments as if there is no such disability. However, 35 per cent of reports indicate mental disability. It is a praiseworthy work on the part of newspaper after lots of campaign from much organisations. Media used to cover less on mental disability previously, resulting in scanty awareness among the public.

Disability as an Event

Despite repeated criticism from various quarters associated with disability rehabilitation, newspapers continue to cover the highest number of content on event theme rather than serious stories. With this poor number of reporting, again 47 per cent is event based. The 15 per cent are only problem portrayal and 31 per cent are half-hearted solution for the PWD. Several inaugural events have turned fancy and have extravagantly misused the scope of media exposure. Such kind of event-centric contents drag the readers' attention more on the context of disability and develop the notion of disability as distant from mainstream society. However, event-based news, such as '102 Physically Challenged Persons get Jobs at *Mela*' on 29 March 2011 in *The Hindu*, is a special kind of publication which encourages other disability person to exploit employment opportunities.

Language and Media

The news stories such as 'Government Jobs Elude Persons with Disabilities' on 3 December 2010 covers only injustice done to person with disability, and not any solution, and further distorts the confidence level of person with disability. The frequent derogative terms such as blindness, deaf and dumb, lame, pity, sympathy, discouragement, liability, tryst, tragedy and *karma* are sending wrong messages to the non-disabled society. On the other hand, media often make colour and fancy and turn a casual event to an important happening by using the terms such as ambitious plan, beneficiaries, experiment and self-reliance. There should be judicious use of these terminologies, otherwise these would create false consciousness among the person with disabilities.

Disability and Skewed Geographical Media Coverage

Classification of total disabled population by residence shows that nearly 75 per cent of total disabled lives in rural areas, whereas most of the governmental and non-governmental organisations working for disabled are urban based (Chauhan 2011). Media is found biased and injustice in covering PWDs in rural areas. The 46 per cent content on disabilities is from urban areas and 15 per cent on disabilities from rural area. However, 39 per cent is not specified as whether urban or rural. It is unfortunate that there is no coverage on disabilities from exclusive rural areas. Content covered on disabilities geographically is absurd and needs immediate correction.

Media's Pitiable Editorial Priority and Disability

As of now, media has only sporadically focussed on disability issues. Media rarely views disability issues as 'newsworthy'. The 50 per cent content covered are on casual/isolated stories, but only 12 per cent are follow-up stories. Less follow-up stories rightly enunciate the theme 'out of sight is out of mind'. Even though the number of contents covered is dismal, again their placements in the newspaper have taken a backseat. Eleven per cent and 66 per cent content appear in the front and middle pages respectively. Supplementary pages constitute only 4 per cent coverage. Only 19 per cent of disability coverage makes to the editorial and open page write-ups. And maximum editorials are only for the support of disability enumeration in the census 2011. There is no letter to the editor, which shows the feedback of the readers. It tells directly that there is less awareness on PWDs among the common people. Several claim that as census 2011 was in process, reports on PWDs appeared in the front page and editorial pages. In addition, it is seen that those who cover the disability issues are the journalists with the specialisations of politics, education, crime or sports which leads to misrepresentation of disability in the media. If the journalists are not fully aware of disability movements and rights, how can they report in an appropriate way. This clearly points out the apathetic attitude of media towards addressing disability issues.

PWD as a Victim or Super-Achiever

Disability coverage on heroic act or falling prey to situations is often lengthy. Media try to prove that their media contents are realistic, mass oriented and paves way for such kind of social inclusion. As a result, it creates a social dichotomy in the society, leading to social unrest. However, frequent criticism of media on this ground has led to fall in such kind of reporting. Repeated coverage on heroic and victim character of disability has reduced significantly. Seven per cent contents are heroic stories on disabilities.

Pictorial Representation

Pictorial representation of disability suffers the most in the newspaper. Only 14 photographs appeared throughout the year 2010. Approximately 28 per cent, 50 per cent and 21 per cent are found relevant, superficial and stereotypical, respectively, in nature. The event-based story on 27 March 2010 carrying the headline 'Sneha Kiran to Get a New Building Soon' seems fancy poster. However, the photograph carrying caption *ENABLING EXERCISE: Children are trained through multi-sensory teaching and periodically evaluated for their skill levels* by K. Pichumani is argumentative for the news story 'Catering to the Special Needs of Children' on 13 February 2010.

Analysis of *My Name Is Khan*

Bollywood, the Hindi film industry, is known to bat for the underdog and Shah Rukh Khan is found to explore the illness plaguing the human mind in *My Name Is Khan* (MNIK). Similarly, the audiences have seen Hrithik Roshan in *Koi Mil Gaya* and Anil Kapoor in *Yuvvraaj*. MNIK, a 2010 Indian Hindi drama film, is produced by Hiroo Yash Johar and Gauri Khan and directed by Karan Johar and distributed by FOX Star Entertainment. This was the first time that a Bollywood company was tying up with a mainstream Hollywood studio. The film marked the first instance of a film using the Roadblock advertising technique to market a film, in which the three-minute trailer was aired on all leading television channels simultaneously. Karan Johar, Shah Rukh Khan and Kajol bagged Best Director, Best Actor and Best Actress respectively in 2011 Filmfare Awards (Guha 2010)

MNIK is a film made with sincerity and sweat, ambition and conviction and has three major components: love story, Islam and a mild form of autism. The film is all about Shah Rukh Khan starring as Rizwan Khan, a man with Asperger syndrome, who is mistaken for a terrorist while travelling in the United States. Asperger syndrome, milder form of autism, impairs Rizwan's social communication skills and gives him some decidedly odd behaviour patterns. He cannot stand before loud sounds or the colour yellow and he rotates stones obsessively. He is married to Kajol starring as Mandira. After 9/11 blast, their happy family is separated because of 'Khan' tag. Therefore, he decides to meet the US President to tell him a message 'My name is Khan, and I'm not a terrorist'. After long struggle, he meets the President and sends the message. Later his family gets reunited.

One popular dialogue in the film is 'My name is Khan, and … I'm not a terrorist'. This dialogue seems simple, yet it is the base of the film. The whole film revolves around this theme. It tells the religious differences prevalent in the United States. Another popular dialogue is: *'Meri ammi kaha karti thi ki duniya me sirf do kisam ke insaan rehte he, ek accha insaan aur doosra bura insaan … Mein accha insaan hoon, mein acche kaam karta hoon'* (My mother used to say that there are only two types of people in this world: good people and bad people. I am a good person, I do good deeds). This is a positive attitude of a person with disability shown in the film. This dialogue teaches us a lesson that people are known by their deeds they do and is divided accordingly and not based on religion or other traits.

When the film is looked into, some positive aspects towards disability are found. Those aspects are inspiring and motivating. In the very beginning of the film, Rizwan's mother is praising and guiding him even though she is not aware of the symptoms and behaviours of Asperger. Some of the scenes of Rizwan and his mother indicate that disabled can do wonders if they are properly guided. The film also says that they can take care of themselves and can be differently abled. In fact, his disease was detected by his brother Zakir's wife Hashina, who is a professor in Psychology.

In one scene, Rizwan's brother is encouraging as he states, 'I got success, because I worked hard. Now it's your time to work hard'. The scene underlines that disability persons have equal potentialities and they can too succeed. This film is issue-based, not hero-based. Heroism is underplayed, and the magnitude of heroism has justified. Even though superstar Shah Rukh Khan plays the role of the disabled person, he is not found as extraordinary person. Thus, it has paved the way for realistic representation of the protagonist who suffers from mild autism. The film also suggests how to handle the disease, not the problematic aspects. The grammar of dialogue in the film is good and narration of the story is up to the mark. The dialogues like 'Hum Honge Kaamyab' is fostering positive attitude. In the film, even though he is a disabled person and previously tagged as 'terrorist', he saves hurricane hit Georgia people and has proved to be a Samaritan. Finally, he meets the US President and says 'My name is Khan, and ... I'm not a terrorist'.

Despite several positive aspects of the film, it has some shortcomings in approach and representation of disability. First, the film may not have clicked, if Shah Rukh Khan and Karan Johar were not associated with this film. First half of the movie seems real. The second half seems little superficial in which he meets the President. The question often rises how a common person could meet the President. All the time, Rizwan is guided by Mandira or his sister-in-law Hashina. However, after the interval, he has become efficient in all respects. Practically it is not possible. Thanks to the director's fancy approach and sympathetic attitude like all others.

Generally in India religion, caste-based films run well. So in this movie, religion has taken the driving seat, leaving disability in the backseat. Religion has dominated the disability theme. The word 'Khan' is pronounced more frequently than 'Asperger'. Songs sound pleasant and sequential. However, it may not be feasible for a person who suffers from many problems, not autism alone. The romance between Rizwan and Mandira is found to be designed and mawkish. Asperger, a form of disability, is recognised late in India. In order to create the sense of surprise, sympathy and panicking among the cine viewers, the protagonist is found with such kind of disability.

A Comparative Analysis

The current study reveals that disability representation in entertainment media is somewhat better than news media. The perception and representation in the serials and movies have made transition from superficial to natural. However, the movies still suffer from misrepresentation of disability. On the contrary, news media is callous in representing disability. Major pitfall with the news media is that their coverage on the issue is very scant and in the state of exaggeration. Needless to say again, media's least contribution towards disability concerns has reduced its role from the 'watchdog' to the 'lapdog'.

Suggestions

The fight and advocacy to ensure disability citizenship will not be a distant dream if media plays a justifying role in this connection. Media's role should not just be to pass on the information on disability issues. Media, being an agenda setter for the future discussion, should keep certain priorities based on the emerging issues such as inclusive development, accessibility, issues with ICT and social security. the Press Council of India, in consultation with organisations working for disability, should chalk out a uniform editorial policy. The editorial policy should speak of the modus operandi to determine what kind of reports are to be published and what should be their form, tone and language. Media should show people with disabilities as active participants and connect to various lives of mainstream society by bridging the gap between disabled and non-disabled society. However, these representations should not turn into celebratory stories of will power and determination. In a similar fashion, the Central Board of Film Certification should properly review, rate and censor motion pictures, television shows, television ads and promotional materials pertaining to the issues of disability.

References

Bakshi, K. (2010, June 23). 'Disability and Census of 2011'. *The Hindu*. Mumbai.

Bhas, D. (2006). 'National Policy for the Disabled: No Clear Roadmap for Action'. Retrieved from http://infochangeindia.org/disabilities/features/national-policy-for-the-disabled-no-clear-roadmap-for-actio n.html

Briant, E., Watson, N., and Philo, G. (2011). *Bad News for Disabled People: How the Newspapers Are Reporting Disability*. London: Strathclyde Centre for Disability Research and Glasgow Media Unit. University of Glasgow.

Chauhan, K.S. (2011, November 30). 'Dimensions of Disability in India'. Retrieved from http://indiancivilmovement.blogspot.com/2011/04/dimensions-of-disability-in-india.html

Corporate India Gives the Cold Shoulder to Disabled People (2000). Retrieved from http://www.rediff.com/business/2000/apr/25disabl.htm

Elwan, A. (1999). 'Poverty and Disability: A Survey of the Literature'. *The World Bank*. Retrieved from http://siteresources.worldbank.org/INTPOVERTY/Resources/WDR/Background/elwan.pdf

Enabling Access to Education through ICT. (2010). New Delhi. Retrieved from http://edict2010.in/

Francis, M. (2011, April 4). 'Only 3 Disabled-Friendly Parks in Bangalore'. *Daily News & Analysis*, Bangalore.

Guha, A. (2010, February 12). 'Review: *My Name Is Khan* Remains on the Fringes of Great Cinema'. *Daily News and Analysis*, Mumbai.

Hershey, L. (2001, July 17). 'The Nutty Profession'. rabble.ca. Retrieved from http://www.rabble.ca/news/nutty-profession

Jenkins, S.P. and Rigg, J.A. (2003). *Disability and Disadvantage: Selection, Onset and Duration Effects*. London: London School of Economics. Centre for Analysis of Social Exclusion.

Joseph, A. (2005, December 18). 'Able but Unwilling?'. *India Together*. Retrieved from www.indiatogether.org

Karna, G.N. (2000). 'Disability Rights Movement: Conceptual Framework and Its Implications for India'. *Disabilities and Impairments*.

Katju, M. (2011, November 16). 'I Am a Votary of Liberty; My Criticism of the Media Is Aimed at Making Them Better. *The Hindu*. Chennai.

Klasing, I. (2007). *Disability and Social Exclusion in Rural India*. Jaipur: Rawat Publications.

Lorimer, R. and Scannell, P. (1994). *Mass Communications: A Comparative Introduction*. New Delhi: Manchester University Press.

McQuail, D. (1987). *Mass Communication Theory: An Introduction*. United States: Sage Publications.

Media Representation of Disabled People (2006). Retrieved from http://www.disabilityplanet.co.uk/critical-analysis.html

Menon, A. (2007, June 8). 'Forum Assists Disabled in Employment'. *The Hindu*, Chennai.

Mickey, Z. (2005, January 23). 'Piss on Pity: Clint Eastwood's 'Million Dollar' Snuff Film'. *Press Action*. Retrieved from www.pressaction.com

National Human Rights Commission (2005). 'Disability Manual'. Retrieved on 27 July 2018 from www.nhrc.nic.in/documents/publications/nhrc-book-disability.pdf.

Pinto, P.E. and Sahur N. (2001, May 13). 'Working with People with Disabilities: An Indian Perspective'. *Center for International Rehabilitation Research Information and Exchange*. Retrieved from http://cirrie.buffalo.edu/culture/monographs/india/

PWD Aac (1995). 'The Persons with Disabilities: Equal Opportunities, Protection of Rights and Full Participation Act'. Retrieved from http://nhrc.nic.in/publications/Disability/Annexure-1.html

Raha, S. (2010, June 18). 'India Needs New Legislation on Disability Rights'. infochangeindia.org. Retrieved from http://infochangeindia.org/disabilities/analysis/india-needs-new-legislation-on-disability-rights.html

Sengupta, S. (2008). 'No Rights for the Mentally Disabled'. infochangeindia.org. Retrieved from http://infochangeindia.org/disabilities/analysis/no-rights-for-the-mentally-disabled.html

Siebert, F.S., Petersion, T. and Schramm, W. (1956). *Four Theories of the Press: The Authoritarian, Libertarian, Social Responsibility and Soviet Communist Concepts of What the Press Should Be and Do*. Urbana: University of Illinois.

Sinha, M. (2011, May 11). 'Disability Limits Marriage Choices: Online Survey'. *The Times of India*, New Delhi.

Starkey, J. and Lay, J. (2006, March 15). 'Postie Can't Read Numbers'. *The Sun*, South Carolina. Retrieved from http://www.thesun.co.uk/sol/homepage/news/article41202.ece

Sundar, R. (2005, June 26). 'Women, Disability and Films in India'. *The Hoot*. Retrieved from http://www.thehoot.org/web/home/searchdetail.php?sid=1641&bg=1

Webb, J.A. (2008). *The Voice of Newfoundland: A Social History of the Broadcasting Corporation of Newfoundland*. Canada: University of Toronto Press.

World Report on Disability, World Health Organization (2011). Retrieved from http://whqlibdoc.who.int/publications/2011/9789240685215_eng.pdf

Yeo, R. (2005). 'Disabilities, Poverty and the New Development Agenda', Disabilities Knowledge and Research Programme.

Index